Zen-Brain Horizons

The MIT Press
Cambridge, Massachusetts
London, England

Zen-Brain Horizons

Toward a Living Zen

James H. Austin, M.D.

Also by James H. Austin

Meditating Selflessly (2011)
Selfless Insight (2009)
Zen-Brain Reflections (2006)
Chase, Chance, and Creativity (2003)
Zen and the Brain (1998)

MIT Press books may be purchased at special quantity discounts for business or sales promotional use. For information, please email special_sales@mitpress.mit.edu.

This book was set in Palatino Linotype 10/13 pt by Toppan Best-set Premedia Limited. Printed and bound in the United States of America.

Library of Congress Cataloging-in-Publication Data
Austin, James H., 1925 author.
Zen-brain horizons : toward a living zen / James H. Austin, M.D.
pages cm
Includes bibliographical references and index.
ISBN 978-0-262-02756-4 (hardcover : alk. paper) 1. Zen Buddhism. 2. Brain—Religious aspects. 3. Cognitive neuroscience. I. Title.
BQ9288.A966 2014
294.3'927019—dc23
2013046636

10 9 8 7 6 5 4 3 2 1

To my early teachers Nanrei Kobori-Roshi, Myokyo-ni, and Robert Aitken-Roshi for their inspiration; and to all those whose countless contributions to Zen, to Buddhism, and to the brain sciences are reviewed in these pages.

Where the brain is abnormally moist, of necessity it moves.

And when it moves neither sight nor hearing are still. Instead, first we hear one thing and now another, and the tongue speaks incessantly in accord with the things seen and heard.

But when the brain is still, one can think properly.

Hippocrates (ca. 460–377 B.C.E.)

Contents

List of Illustrations

Preface

> It ought not to be inferred that living by Zen has something unique
> or extraordinary about it, for it is, on the contrary, a most ordinary
> thing, not at all differentiated from the rest of the world.
>
> Daisetz T. Suzuki (1870–1966)[1]

> The skyline is a promise, not a bound.
>
> John Masefield (1878–1967)[2]

Living by Zen includes an awareness coextensive with all the rest of the ordinary, incredible world. So coextensive and so ordinary is Zen that it often regards itself as "nothing special." Indeed, wherever we gaze in Zen we find that its unbounded horizon becomes universal in scope. Turning to look far back at meditation's historical roots, we glimpse an approach that began millennia ago in ancient Yogic practices, then became increasingly institutionalized as it emerged through the cultures of East Asia. When the old Sanskrit term for meditation (*dhyana*) entered China, it changed there to Ch'an. When this Ch'an practice of meditation came to Japan, the word was pronounced Zen.

When we in the West now look back at this rich historical legacy, we discover contributions made by countless worthy ancestors. Why do these pages include so many of their words of wisdom? Because these pioneers seem almost to have anticipated research out on the near horizon of the neurosciences. In this sense, they were already pointing toward a living, neural Zen.

Two worlds meet along this horizon line. Below is firm ground, the earth on which we stand. It beckons us to explore tangible objects just out of reach, waiting to be touched and used. Extending far above the skyline is the infinite vault of the sky. Themes in this book often encourage us to raise our sights in this direction. These skyward dimensions invite us to glimpse loftier aspirations, to explore intangible frontiers where elevated potentials are not yet clearly defined.

Suppose we happen to rise very early, then go outdoors and gaze up above the horizon. Only by looking off to the east will we glimpse the first colors of the approaching dawn. Up there, when we see the bright planet Venus, what will be going on in our brain? Before a single thought enters, two attentive systems will already have taken the lead, blending into one unified image the distance functions of the right and left halves of our visual fields.[3] We need to remind ourselves that this attentiveness plays an automatic *vanguard* role in all of our brain's subsequent mental processing. Why do these pages emphasize the *involuntary* nature of such attentive processing? Because these covert functions, acting silently, make crucial contributions to all implicit learning, to intuition, and to creative insights of various kinds.

To D. T. Suzuki, who brought Zen to the West, living by Zen was a highly practical matter. To *live* Zen meant to be intimately attuned to the ordinary events in one's everyday world. Living Zen wasn't just sitting quietly indoors on a cushion. In keeping with Suzuki's often expressed views about the Japanese love of Nature, and how this deep appreciation entered into the Zen cultural aesthetic,[4] some chapters in this book emphasize outdoor topics. The themes of Avian Zen[5] and Buddhist Botany invite readers to celebrate Earth Day *every* day, not only once a year.

Other chapters begin by looking far back into the remote past for an historical perspective on research that might appear out on some future horizon. The word *horizon* has an interesting history.[6] The French have an expression, *"reculer pour mieux sauter."* It refers to those first deliberate backward steps that help one gather momentum for the next leap forward.[7]

So, part I begins by looking far back into ancient historical narratives in preparation for the next leaps we'll then take into the neural perspectives of this twenty-first century.

Part II reviews themes that evolved during subsequent centuries when Zen and psychology each developed after having been exposed to different cultures.

Part III considers more recent information about how our brain changes when attitudes expand in the background of an increasingly clear, calm awareness.

Part IV explores the fresh perspectives inherent in those dimensions of visual space above our usual eye-level, limited horizon. We have yet to realize the full promise of these dimensions.

In part V we peer further out into the future. Among the topics considered, four themes are of universal human importance. They are creativity, happiness, openness, and selflessness.

Consider this book an invitation to discover in this new millennium the extraordinary promise inherent in seemingly ordinary things.[8]

To sharpen the discussion, short statements or questions are inserted throughout, marked by bullets (•). For the reader's convenience, bracketed references in the text [ ] indicate pages in four earlier books that provide background information on the topics being discussed. For example, [ZB] refers to *Zen and the Brain*, [ZBR] refers to *Zen-Brain Reflections*, [SI] to *Selfless Insight*, and [MS] to *Meditating Selflessly*.

Acknowledgments

I am indebted to Philip Laughlin at MIT Press for appreciating the need to bring this slender volume to the attention of the wider meditating and neuroscience communities. Again, my sincere thanks go to Katherine Arnoldi Almeida for her skilled editorial assistance and to Yasuyo Iguchi for her artistic skill in designing the cover and icons.

I am especially grateful to Barbara Klund for her ongoing patience in deciphering my handwriting throughout multiple drafts of her excellent typing, and for helping to keep this manuscript organized as it expands. Many thanks go also to James W. Austin for converting the color plates' initial colors into a soft-edged digital version and for his valued assistance, together with Scott W. Austin and Seido Ray Ronci, in reviewing and commenting on the manuscript.

I am also grateful to John Hegarty for the functional MRI data, and to Scott W. Austin for the Latin conjugation of *meditatorum*.

In recent years, I have been privileged to share in the inestimable bounties of regular Zen practice with our sangha at Hokoku-an, led by Seido Ray Ronci; with the Dancing Crane Zen Center, led by Meredith Garmon; with the Vipassana/Theravada activities of the local Show-Me Dharma sangha; and in the stimulus afforded by the annual Mind and Life Summer Research Institute. Gassho to all!

While this book was underway for MIT Press, articles were also submitted to academic journals. Accordingly, grateful credit is acknowledged for permission to include portions of: the book review, "The Heart of William James," in *Perspectives on Psychological Science* 2013; 8: 314–315, and the article, "Avian Zen," *The Eastern Buddhist*, vol. 44, no. 1, in press 2014.

By Way of a Personal Introduction

I should not talk so much about myself if there were anybody else whom I knew as well.

Henry Thoreau (1817–1862)[1]

It is a secret which every intellectual man quickly learns, that beyond the energy of his possessed and conscious intellect, he is capable of a new energy (as of an intellect doubled on itself), by abandonment to the nature of things.

Ralph Waldo Emerson (1803–1882)[2]

This is the fifth book of words by a neurologist who has been on a decades-long quest to understand Zen at first hand. Direct personal experiences influence this account. The first occurred at Daitoku-ji in Kyoto in 1974. Following several weeks of meditation, I was astonished to discover how clear my awareness became after my intrusive word-thoughts stopped. Another experience happened months later, again while I was meditating. As I dropped into a state of deep internal absorption, my *physical* sense of Self completely vanished into a vast black, silent space. The major event happened seven and a half years later. My entire *psychic* sense of Self suddenly dissolved while I was traveling to the second day of a retreat in London. In Zen the technical term for this state is *kensho*. [ZB: 519–624; ZBR: 407–410]

Notice what happened just before each of these last two states. On each occasion I had first *abandoned myself* to circumstances, then *glanced up* briefly. Before the absorption I had looked up at a single electric lightbulb that dangled from the ceiling of the unfamiliar zendo where we happened to be meditating that evening. [ZB: 470; ZBR: 322] Years later, just before the awakening into kensho, I also happened to look up. This time I gazed up into the distant open sky, far out beyond that platform of the unfamiliar train station where I was standing. [ZB: 537]

Neither interval of surrender was deliberate. Nor was looking up intentional. Each glance was casual, automatic, free from any willful thought or anticipation. Everything that unfolded next in those fresh, unfamiliar settings was unexpected. Researchers would later discover that a novel context can prompt the ventral attention system to react. [SI: 29–34]

The first book in this series devoted six chapters to attention, a theme long emphasized in Zen. A ringing endorsement of attention by William James opened the first of those chapters: "The faculty of voluntarily bringing back a wandering attention, over and over again, is the very root of judgment, character, and will." [ZB: 69–71] My indebtedness to William James was evident on so many other pages in that volume that friends jokingly accused me (rightly) of citing James more often than the Buddha.

Any homage overdue to the man who was first called Siddhartha or to William James is now expressed in chapters 1, 4, 6, and 7 of the present volume. In fact, the *involuntary* bottom-up functions of covert attention and awareness were known to James and to Emerson. This involuntary faculty of attentiveness is implicit in long-term Zen meditative training. We rely on these *subconscious* attentive functions to automatically detect and redirect our wandering attention. Their hidden, context-sensitive intelligence is crucial. It seems likely to prove at least as essential to our long-term survival and well-being as whatever we try so hard to achieve each time we make a conscious attempt to deliberately focus our attention.

Investigators are just beginning to study some normal skill sets in our brain's automatic pilot that help accomplish such covert Self-correcting tasks. In view of my lifelong orientation toward hobbies that lead me into the natural world outdoors, I've been encouraged to see that researchers are now discovering that our brain responds differently when it is immersed in the green-space sanctuary of a forest atmosphere. These issues are reviewed in appendix A.

Meditative practices continue to evolve as they pass through different cultures. Whether the next chapters find us looking far back into the distant past to be reminded how much wisdom unfolded two millennia ago, or peering out toward each new horizon that promises to rise up ahead of us in the future, one thing seems clear: Human beings are on a long quest to clarify how the training of our attentional skills will help unburden us of our maladaptive sense of Self. Appendix D is a reminder that most of the key topics considered here remain to be clarified by rigorous future research.

Part I

Looking Far Back into the Distant Past

There is commonly sufficient space about us. Our horizon is
never quite at our elbows.

Henry Thoreau (1817–1862)

1

Two Old Men Consult the Buddha

> When there is no self, you have absolute freedom. Because you have a silly idea of self, you have a lot of problems.
> Shunryu Suzuki-Roshi (1904–1971)[1]

People often asked the Buddha, "What is the best way for me to proceed on the spiritual Path?" On separate occasions, he gave similar advice to each of two elderly men. Each man was driven by a sense of urgency. Each understood that his sands of time were fast running out.

After sizing the men up, the Buddha chose to give them a brief strategic answer. Two simple words stand out in his reply. They remain relevant today not only for Buddhist practitioners of any age but also for readers in general and for contemplative neuroscientists as well.

The Venerable Malunkya

One sutra informs us that Malunkya is already an ardent and resolute person.[2] Why does he ask the Buddha to give him a condensed "Dharma in brief"? He wants it so he can remain more mindful when he goes into his next solitary meditative retreat. The Buddha does not give him a quick answer. Instead, he asks a sequence of six probing questions: "Are you still passionately attached to the things that you see . . . that you hear . . . smell . . . taste . . . touch . . . or think about?"

"No," says Malunkya, to each question.

But the Buddha does not accept at face value Malunkya's claim that he has given up all desires that cling to his sensations and attach to his thoughts. For he then says, "You should train yourself to give up such attachments. Because when no attachment remains, then *no you* is in there. When absolutely *no* [agency of] *you* is in there, all sense of personalized space and time disappears. This, just this, ends all suffering." Just this.

Malunkya replies, "I fully understand that the condition you just briefly described is completely dispassionate in its nature." But do his actions then confirm that he fully understands the selfless basis of nonattachment? No. Instead, he goes on to verbalize a very long series of wordy verses. This behavior informs us that he has not yet deeply realized how "just this" distills the Buddha's message, how it points to the selfless state which ends all suffering. [ZBR: 33–37; SI: 11–13, 199; MS: 8, 66–69, 98, 119, 132, 183–184]

The two men meet on another occasion.[3, 4] Although Malunkya had since been meditating elsewhere in seclusion, his overactive mind, which had initially raised our doubts, is still unsettled. Now his thoughts are driven by the big unanswered questions about Self, and he is preoccupied with metaphysical concepts about soul, immortality, and eternity. His ruminations include this question: "Why hasn't the Buddha declared, for certain, that He and the cosmos are infinite or finite?" And his thoughts stray so far that he concludes "if the Buddha doesn't clarify these grievous oversights, I'll renounce my training as a monk." Indeed, at their next meeting, he pressures the Buddha finally to declare, once and for all, where he stands on these deep existential questions.

The Buddha again begins his reply with a question: "Did I ever promise you that if you follow me I will declare that the cosmos, the soul, the body, or the Awakened One are either finite or deathless?"

"No," says Malunkya.

Then, says the Buddha, "your attitude resembles that of a man just wounded by an arrow smeared with poison," a man who insists that "I won't let any surgeon remove this arrow until I first know for certain every last personal detail about which man shot me, learn what kind of bow and bowstring he used, learn which kind of feather was on the arrow, etc., etc.! This wounded man would die before he verified all these minor details. And so would anybody else die if they too insisted on waiting until the Buddha had clarified every last detail about whether the cosmos or existence in general is finite or infinite."

The Buddha continues, "You can live the holy life without needing to have all these conceptual questions resolved. Whether such issues are valid or not—this is not fundamental to our practice of the spiritual Path. Right now, what really matters is that each one of us still continues to be subject to birth and death, to aging, pain, and sorrow. In fact, I have already given you the prescription you need to relieve these urgent causes of your everyday suffering." Here, he knows that Malunkya is already familiar with the four fundamental truths that are the basic prescription for everyone on the spiritual Path: (1) Life is full of dissatisfactions. (2) Our passions and delusions cause these sorrows. (3) The way out of this suffering is to extinguish Self-centered desires and aversions. (4) A practical, eightfold Path exists for doing this.

The Buddha then closes by saying, "When you follow this prescription it will lead to dispassion, to direct knowledge, to insight-wisdom and Nirvana. So, remember what I have specified. And also note something else: I choose not to dwell on other issues that are only of minor practical importance."

Malunkya was gratified to hear these words. The sutras inform us that he ultimately went on to realize a more advanced ongoing stage on the enlightened Way of life. Yet he still had to continue to practice in seclusion in order to drop his clinging attachments to all five of the fetters.[5]

Aspects of Interest in This Story about Malunkya

Malunkya may be older, ardent, and resolute. But he's a talker. Given his earlier need to verbalize a long series of verses, we are not surprised to hear that his discursive mind did not settle down. Not only does he pester the Buddha with questions about the cosmos and afterlife, he even considers renouncing his training if he cannot get straight answers! The Buddha seeks no frothy eloquent words from his trainees. He is alert for simple, convincing evidence that they have deconditioned their old unwholesome ways of thinking and acting. He is waiting to see them transfigured by graceful behaviors that rise instantly and flow freely. He wants to be *shown*. [SI: 217–218]

In the earlier part of this narrative, we observe how the Buddha responded to this elderly man's request for a "Dharma in brief." He replied by pointing briefly to the root of all human problems: our overconditioned Self and its resulting emotional attachments to every *I-Me-Mine* subjectivity.

Bahiya, the Elderly Sage

The Pali word *Udana* can be translated as the "inspired utterances" of the Buddha. One collection of these is called the Udana sutras. The style and content of many pithy utterances suggest that these sutras are of great antiquity.[6] One of the early discourses in Udana 1.10 is a tale about an elderly man, called Bahiya, who wore simple clothes made out of bark cloth.[7] He was venerated in his small seashore community, given alms for his food and lodging, and cared for when he was sick.

Wiser than others his age, Bahiya finally started to wonder, "Have I already entered on the path of wisdom? Is it possible that I've even become somewhat enlightened?" One of his relatives, knowing that the Buddha was then teaching up north in a city called Savatthi,[8] suggested that Bahiya resolve his question by consulting such an authentically enlightened person.

When Bahiya arrived there, he found the Buddha out walking for alms. In the Buddha, he saw a man poised in the ultimate sense, his mind thoroughly at peace, and obviously a fully enlightened person. Bahiya threw himself at the Buddha's feet, imploring him, saying, "Teach me the Dharma, for my own welfare and bliss."

But the Buddha said, "This isn't the time, Bahiya. We are now on our way to gather alms." When Bahiya then repeated his earnest request to the Buddha for the second time, he added that time was of the essence, saying "Given all the dangers, who knows for sure how long either you or I will still be alive?" Again the Buddha explained why this was not an appropriate time.

Bahiya repeated the same concerns about death in his third request. And now the Buddha yielded, having observed something unusual in this old man's three entreaties. He stopped and said, "Well, Bahiya, you should train yourself in the following manner."

We note, at this point, that his advice distills into the very same words as those recorded in the Buddha's separate discourse to Malunkya. In English, their translation from the Pali unfolds into two short sentences: "When for you there will be only the seen in reference to the seen, only the heard in reference to the heard, only the sensed in reference to the sensed, and only the cognized in reference to what is cognized, then, Bahiya, there will be *no you* therein. When *no you* remains therein, then this, just this, will be the end of your suffering."

What happened to Bahiya the moment he heard these words? We are told that this brief distillation of the Dharma immediately released his mind from every last clinging concern. This was indeed fortunate because soon afterward

Bahiya was killed in an accident, a possibility he had just foreseen. When monks asked the Buddha what would be Bahiya's state after he died, he replied, saying, "Bahiya was a very wise person. He had actually been practicing the Dharma for a long time. He did not pester me with minor issues.[9] In this degree of sage wisdom, Bahiya has since become liberated, free both from bliss and from all pain."

Salient Points in This Story about Bahiya

Bahiya had not pursued a formal spiritual Path in an organized manner. Even so, his sage wisdom was greatly appreciated by his community. It was also of a kind discernible by the Buddha's keen "Dharma-eye." [ZB: 123] Even then, we observe how Bahiya's sincere requests for help are deferred three times before they are responded to. These delays are reminiscent of an ancient custom—that of declining a beginner's request for Dharma instruction at least three times. Each delay is a test. It helps to establish that the beginner is sufficiently motivated to at least begin the long process of training. [ZB: 65]

Yet in Bahiya's demeanor the Buddha discerned no rank beginner. This was an old man already tested by long experience, someone who understood that he might not have much longer to live. Because the Buddha had been interrupted while he was out walking for alms, his brief words to this man could not describe the whole long training procedure.[10] Instead, how did he distill its essence? He began by describing how the results of the training process could manifest themselves. This state of consciousness would be shorn of every *excessive* passionate attachment to the egocentric Self. Only at this point—only when "*no you* remains in there"—will the liberated brain awaken into the deep insight-wisdom that directly perceives the intimate reality of "just this" present moment. [ZBR: 545–572]

The Buddha then added that all Bahiya's suffering would stop when his mental processing dropped off its Self-centered overemotionalized intrusions: "This, just this, is the end of suffering." We are next informed that this is what actually happened. Indeed, the sutra says that "Right then and there" Bahiya's mind was suddenly released from every last clinging attachment.[11]

Psychological Implications

The Buddha's words are straightforward: "When no you remains therein"—when the world is experienced directly, in a matter-of-fact manner—"this, just this, is the end of your suffering." Once neural processing lets go of its subjective distortions and wordy complexities, it starts opening up into its more objective, intuitive dimensions. Further refinements unfold during such an awakening: all perceptions enter experience in the form of existential insight-wisdom. "*Just this*" appears to unveil the *Real Reality*. All things are experienced as "just so"—directly, succinctly, and obviously.

Of course, nothing about the brain itself is this simple. When we start to meditate, everyone faces the immediate problem: our discursive monkey-mind. Unfruitful mind wandering warps the sharp clarity of our perceptions. Sticky cobwebs clutter our mental space, impede the scope and efficiency of our cognitive efforts at problem solving. When we try to understand how meditative practices might transform the brain and reverse these attachments, a series of questions helps focus the discussion.

• *What does it mean when there is absolutely "no you," when no remnants of the clinging Self remain in cognition?*

It does not mean that you have lost all consciousness. You are not in coma. You have not lost all mental competence. Instead, it means that the usual automatic pilot in your cognition has abandoned its standard, inturned frame of reference. It has shifted beyond all prior maladaptive references to *I-Me-Mine*. Now consciousness is left free to drop into its other-referential dimension—a refined category of pure, advanced *insight*.

Can you recall having experienced lesser moments of insight in the past? Weren't they often accompanied by some absence of your Self? If you do not recall such a subjective vacancy, perhaps these moments were too brief, or the insights were of a more ordinary kind. Yet some may have prompted you to wonder, "Why didn't *I* think of that before?" (And as soon as you insert *I* and think, this question provides its own answer.) However, during the extraordinary advanced states of kensho and satori, selflessness lasts much longer. Now insights can penetrate to deep existential levels. [SI: 123–146]

• *What happens after these more ordinary forms of lesser mini-insight?*

Some will be further refined, ripened, and actualized during each of your live-and-learn confrontations with reality in ordinary daily life. [SI: 154–155] Careful introspection of your emotional resistance to each real-world lesson helps you appreciate how valuable it can be to gradually *let go* of your unfruitful, clinging attachments. The Buddha's closing remarks in the sutra remind us that letting go is a *twofold* liberation. Indeed, the gradual ripening of equanimity means being liberated from *both* kinds of impassioned excesses: those that cause you to cling to your bliss, not only your major resistances to unpleasant events that cause unwarranted suffering.

Fast forward into the next millennium, when the Sino-Japanese Zen traditions began to employ the word *mushin* to describe various levels of no clinging. *Mu* translates as "no";

shin refers to both heart and mind. Therefore, the term suggests that during the state of "no you," no word-thoughts or emotionalized concepts cling to one's perceptions and contaminate them. Unfettered clarity is the salient impression when the lightning strike of kensho awakens insight-wisdom in the depths of the brain. [ZB: 542-544]

Shodo Harada-Roshi is the highly regarded abbot of Shogen-ji in Okayama, Japan. He condenses the empty-full qualities of kensho's selfless emptiness in one sentence: "This emptiness is not something you can conceptualize; it is a state empty of ego, full of what can come through when that ego has been let go of."[12] Such an emptiness-fullness is incomprehensible to ordinary consciousness. Only deep, direct experience will resolve its paradoxes. [ZB: 570–572; ZBR: 384–386]

How did D. T. Suzuki convey the fact that meditators also undergo a long-term *gradual* ripening of wisdom? He chose a special picture for the frontispiece of the book he entitled *Zen and Sino-Japanese Culture*.[13] The artist of this classic thirteenth century painting shows six persimmons, each in various stages of ripening. Spiritual ripening takes decades, not months.

This first chapter began by looking back many centuries at the Buddha's early discourses. In the ancient Pali sutras, the phrase, "just this" points toward an ineffable state, a blend of selfless, wordless fullness. We will now turn to look forward. Subsequent chapters will take a brief leap toward research in this twenty-first century. We will be asking: What newer implications of "just this" will be arising out there, *above* the horizon?

2

Neuropsychological Aspects of the Attentive Self

Anatomy is destiny.

Sigmund Freud (1856–1939)[1]

Keep your mind clear like space, but let it function like the tip of a needle.

Zen Master Seung Sahn (1927–2004)[2]

Only after Zen-brain relationships are oversimplified do they become easier to understand. So, we begin by weaving the threads of five simpler themes into the contents of this book: Self, attention, emotion, language, and insight. This chapter continues to address a major topic: the Self and the ways it attends to the space that surrounds it. This Self is more than an abstraction. Note the tall capital *S*. It is there to remind us that we have all been conditioned to protect our precious Self. Expect turbulence when any part of your cherished investment feels threatened.

The Greeks had two useful words to describe the Self's dual aspects. *Soma* refers to its tangible physical representation, the body. *Psyche* refers to the Self's mental or spiritual functions. We represent these somewhere in our intangible mind. We will discover that the functional anatomy of the brain also reflects this important distinction between attributes that are physical (tangible) and those that are mental (intangible): we can easily reach down to touch our knee (*soma*) but we cannot touch any intangible thoughts that keep popping in and out of our mind (*psyche*).

The Soma

The distinctions begin anatomically: touch sensation relays up from our knee into the primary somatosensory cortex. This cortex lies behind the central fissure, in the front part of the opposite parietal lobe (please see figure 2.1). Up here, we also develop higher-order proprioceptive discriminations. These tell us where our knee is located in space. This information is further refined in the somatosensory *association* cortex. It is located above and just behind the primary sensory cortex. In this region of the *superior parietal lobule* we start to articulate all the separate sensory messages that are arriving from our hands, feet, head, and other body parts. The result is a total three-dimensional personalized construct. This unified *head-and-body 3-D schema* becomes the basis for our using higher-order forms of integrated behavior to engage the outside world.

There's more. Figure 2.2 represents the two systems of *attention* that arise over the outer cortex of the right hemisphere.

We can begin by asking this question about our Self's dual systems for representing the functions of our body/mind.

• Which of these two major attention systems, because it overlaps the regions that represent the primary and secondary sensory associations of our soma, will have the most ready access to these somatic regions?

The *dorsal* attention system. Its two lateral frontal and parietal modules combine their capacities for directing our focal attention. One module is located back in the posterior intraparietal sulcus (pIPSUL). The other is in the frontal eye field (FEF). Their interactive functions help us focus our top-down attention efficiently, for example, when we look

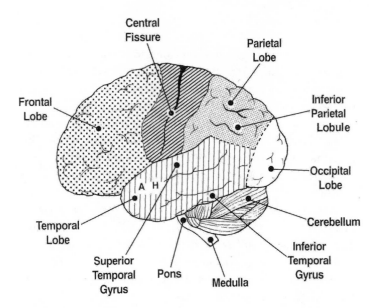

Figure 2.1 A simplified version of major anatomical landmarks on the left side of the brain

At the viewer's left is the convex surface of the *frontal* lobe. Just behind it is the primary motor cortex, then the central fissure, followed by the primary somatosensory cortex. Farther back within the *parietal* lobe, where the black dot rests, is the superior parietal *lobule*. This is our somatosensory *association* cortex. The intraparietal sulcus is the valley separating it from the cortex of the larger inferior parietal lobule beneath. The *occipital* lobe is at the far right. The long *temporal* lobe extends forward from it. The letters A and H refer to the much deeper locations of the amygdala and hippocampus. Both nuclei are hidden from sight, in the innermost (medial) portions of the temporal lobe. Below the cerebral hemisphere are the *cerebellum* and the *brain stem*. The midbrain lies above the pons, also hidden from view. Both structures contain a vital central core of gray matter, the periaqueductal gray. The spinal cord (not shown) descends from the medulla.

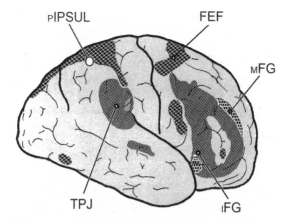

Figure 2.2 A lateral view of the right hemisphere depicting the dorsal and ventral attention systems

In this figure, we're looking at the outside of the right hemisphere. Now, the right frontal lobe is positioned at the viewer's right. The ventral (bottom-up) subdivision of the attention system is shown as gray areas composed of diagonal lines. Its chief modules are the TPJ (temporoparietal junction) and the inferior frontal gyrus (iFG).

The dorsal (top-down) attention system is shown in black checks. Its chief modules are the pIPSUL (posterior intraparietal sulcus) and the FEF (frontal eye field). The two pale dotted zones in the right inferior frontal gyrus (iFG) and middle frontal gyrus (mFG) represent regions of executive overlap. They help integrate the functions of the two subdivisions in practical ways. The results serve our global needs for attention to suddenly shift its focus to some event that might arise from anywhere in the environment—high or low, right or left, near or far.

The figure is freely adapted from figure 5 of a landmark article by M. Fox, M. Corbetta, A. Snyder, et al., Spontaneous Neuronal Activity Distinguishes Human Dorsal and Ventral Attention Systems. *Proceedings of the National Academy of Sciences*, 2006; 103: 10046–10051.

down to use our fingers to manipulate the touch screen of a cell phone.

Some normal people are more competent than others at sharpening the kinds of attentional skills cited in the chapter's epigraph by Master Seung Sahn. These better performing individuals already show distinctive *baseline* patterns of their resting functional MRI activities.[3] Their slow spontaneous patterns of fMRI connectivity predict how capable they can become when their visual attention undergoes further training.

A stringent task was used in this training experiment by Martin et al.: the subjects had to *detect* the symbol ⊥ when it appeared briefly down among many other distractions in the left lower quadrant of their visual field.[4] [MS: 101–102, 214–215] The subjects who could detect this low target best turned out to be those who achieved a fluid blend of two sets of skills. Their versatile connectivities seemed to enable them (1) to focus on one local spot (while suppressing adjacent distracting stimuli), and (2) to *detach* from this excessive *top-down* attentional control, at least during their earliest learning trials. Our physical and mental competence depends on a similar blend of *flexible, implicit* skills. They tap subconscious resources. These skills enable subjects to improve their accuracy during tasks that are currently being used to train the elementary skills of perceptual learning (see chapter 14).[5]

Suppose we are not subjects being tested in a lab. Suppose we are out in the real world where our task is to eat spaghetti with a fork or to sew on a small button. In what part of space do we accomplish these careful manipulations? Down within easy reach of our soma. This is *our* near space. It lies close in. In this domain of peripersonal 3-D space our innate *parietal* lobe skills of proprioception and touch operate at a premium. Each time we need to focus attention on some tangible object we hold in our hands, we are using our dorsal attention system.

But suppose we are outdoors. We are trying to identify which birds are issuing those calls we hear far off in the distance, 100 yards away. Now we require keen *distant* sensory skills, discriminations based on vision and hearing. To distinguish among options this far beyond reach of our hands, we must draw on *temporal* lobe interpretive capacities. By Freud's era, most medical students were learning that these two lobes—the parietal (upper) and the temporal (lower)—expressed very different neurophysiological functions. Medical students still learn that the *lower* parts of one occipital lobe are responsible for seeing into the *upper* parts of space on the opposite side. Everyone needs to be reminded that these basic anatomical differences carry important implications.

The Psyche

The omni-Self of our psyche emerges from a larger matrix of networks. These are represented among many anatomical levels. That said, two major cortical regions serve the essential higher processing functions consistent with much of our personal psyche. [ZBR: 200] Notice that many of these autobiographical functions of the Self begin in networks represented along the *inside* surface of the brain, not on the outside regions that represent our physical body and modes of attention.

Chapter 3 discusses these regions of the psyche in greater detail. There, figure 3.1 will identify the *medial* prefrontal cortex (mPFC), in front. Farther back is a very large part of the *medial* posterior parietal cortex. It will serve to represent other related higher processing functions. A small personalized contribution to psychic functions is also represented in the angular gyrus out on the lateral cortex of the inferior parietal lobule.[6] [SI: 53–83]

- How can this preamble of basic functional anatomy help us relate to the selfless perceptions of a sage like Bahiya?

The neural evidence indicates that we first register these bare sensory perceptions (e.g., touch, proprioception, vision, hearing) in the *back* half of the brain. As these impulses relay forward in the brain *they become much more entangled with myriads of other associations.*[7] Elaborate linkages occur, both with language and with other sticky attachments. Many attachments are sponsored by the emotionalized limbic subjectivities and *I-Me-Mine* concepts of our Self. Without knowing it, we become conditioned. [ZB: 327–334]

In the early milliseconds, as these first sensory signals register in the back of the brain, they might seem to represent a version reasonably close to reality, or at least convey some almost mirror-like sense of objectivity. Indeed, long ago, Zen Master Dogen (1200–1253) emphasized this instantaneity, noting how immediately the moon image happens when one sees the moon reflected on the calm surface of a pond.[8] [ZBR: 441–443] The longer a clear, undistracted, stable awareness attends just to these initial sensory networks that automatically register just this moon image, the more likely this first image could continue to reflect sensory reality. Yet, complications lurk in every emotional overreactivity programmed into our limbic system. Each subjective veil *attached* to our sensory and cognitive associations obscures and distorts this reality. We become overconditioned by habit energies that infuse our emotional history into every percept and bias every action.

This qualifying preamble of functional anatomy can help us understand something important about Bahiya.

Seasoned by his many decades of mature introspection into lived experience, Bahiya's early maladaptive emotions could gradually have ceased to reverberate at their youthful, high amplitude levels. [SI: 237–244] A sage whose emotional drives have become gentled is less easily hijacked by unwholesome urgencies of the moment.

> • But can such overemotionalized attachments gradually drop off? Can our former liabilities become so deconditioned that they are much less disturbing to our field of consciousness?

Later chapters continue this important discussion. We begin to answer it here by referring to certain other slowly-developing skills. These are referable to the transformed perspectives of "a mind clear like space," that more optimal mind to which Master Seung Sahn also pointed. What other qualities besides those identified earlier as *calmness, *clarity, and *spaciousness could also ripen over time into the mature attitudes of a sage? [ZB: 660–663] The range of qualities includes

*openness,
*receptivity,
*no-thought wordlessness,
*instant, effortless discernment.

Ripening

The asterisks identify seven important attributes that emerge in the human brain during a slow developmental process akin to the ways persimmons ripen. Humans also learn by encountering life, day by day, decade after decade. This ripening is a glacially slow process of erosion. [MS: 128–129] Only gradually do we round off our edgy maladaptive subjectivities. Only slowly do more objective percepts arrive within a calm, clear, sensitive level of enhanced awareness.

Such an ongoing awareness seems gradually to have become transformed. The impression conveyed is that the scope of clarity of our *mental space* appears to have expanded (see chapters 9, 10). It seems increasingly to be managed by the simplicity and stability of an increasingly competent autopilot. The result is not a spaced-out diffuseness. Instead, more practical options seem to be sponsored within a much larger volume. In addition, an easier access develops to deep instinctual levels of kindness and compassion. This allows new behavioral options to rise up spontaneously and flourish creatively (see chapters 14, 15).

In this new millennium, we sense, as did Emerson, that the ingredients of such a long-term maturing process seem almost to express the reprogrammings of a subconscious intellect. It is much more intelligent than we could ever imagine. [ZB: 622] The silent operations of this faculty are now referred to as *implicit learning*. [MS: 136, 148–149, 155, 171] Similar relearning components are also the fruits of mechanisms now summed up under the term *neuroplasticity*. Chapters in parts IV and V suggest that open, undistracted settings—the kinds that facilitate flexible creative responses in general—may also be accompanied by calmness, clarity, and the other attributes just identified with asterisks.

Maturation

Maturity implies the capacity to make wiser decisions with greater objectivity. Maturing opens up options to behave toward others in ways that express authentic selfless compassion (Sanskrit/Pali: *karuna*). Can such a lower-profile self ease us into more genuine relationships with other persons? It can, because it has let go of many earlier clinging attachments to its former sense of sovereignty. One prerequisite for this transformed behavior is a heightened and deepened level of global awareness. How can such an awareness look out with greater clarity into the world? Its larger perspective rests on a firm foundation: a simplified, uncluttered, unfearful attitude of mind [ZB: 641–645] (see chapter 15).

Global awareness ripens into the capacity to discern potential events as options that take place inside the larger volume of mental space. This vast space is not the ordinary impractical projection of our fervid imagination. Instead, our brain represents this mature space as a special kind of empty stage on which the play of potential events becomes instantly interpretable. Why? Because, as Seung Sahn taught, events take place in mental dimensions. Clear space and focused attention allow events to appear more meaningful as well as more discrete. [ZB: 487–492]

Maturation has a long horizon. No fixed boundary limits it to any single decade. We have every reason to think that 35-year-old Siddhartha continued to mature in wisdom on his travels during the next 44 years after that major awakening at Bodh Gaya. And at some points on his long Path, a few chosen words would guide two elderly men toward "just this." This core insight would later become a teaching available to assist persons of any age to mature further in wisdom.

The ancient sutra phrase "just this" defines a distinctive moment of insight-wisdom. It is synonymous with other words, including "thusness," that try to distill the essence of what enters direct experience once the maladaptive Self drops out and allocentric processing fully awakens. To D. T. Suzuki, this word was "suchness." He viewed it as "the basis of all religious experience." [ZB: 549–553; ZBR: 361–363, 368–369, 416–417]

Chapter 3 considers how these states of deep insight-wisdom alluded to in ancient Pali sutras and old Zen lore necessarily express a remarkable mental atmosphere. In this fresh perspective, a clear consciousness looks out into the ordinary world. Out there it discovers how *extra*ordinary and inclusive this world *really* is when emptied of all maladaptive subjectivities.

3

Neural Correlations of Meditating Selflessly

How can you even hope to approach the truth through words? You will awaken to the truth of Zen in the blink of an eye during a deeply mysterious wordless understanding. This sudden comprehension arrives when your mind finally drops off all cluttered concepts and discriminatory thoughts.

Ch'an Master Huang-po (d. 850)[1]

What Zen communicates is an awareness that is potentially already there but is not conscious of itself.

Thomas Merton (1915–1968)[2]

We do not see things as they are. We see things as *we* are.

Anonymous

• What else does the phrase "no you" imply in the old Pali sutras?

We observed how "no you" begins. It assigns, as a target for daily practice, every overemotionalized function that had served to reinforce our dominant sense of a personal Self. That's the hard part. Next, the good news. It predicts that we will stop suffering when we drop these maladaptive limbic attachments from our usual repertoire.

- What is the simplest way to conceptualize this personal sense of Self?

The previous chapter identified its dual aspects. Starting with our tangible physical body, we observed that this somatic Self was represented chiefly among the upper parietal and frontal regions over the brain's *outside* surface (see figures 2.1 and 2.2). We then noticed the overlappings that could help link the *somatic* aspects of our Self with the dorsal system of our attentiveness.

This chapter turns toward distinctly different regions. These regions sponsor the intangible Self of our *psyche*. Indeed, many key regions contributing to the psychic omni-Self are represented next to the midline. Here, they lie deep inside the *medial* prefrontal and posterior parietal cortex. Some of these regions confer our private sense of identity with that familiar person who is definable using the noun *I* and the pronoun *Me*. This same person owns possessions. If any possession falls within the clutching grasp of the adjective *Mine*, it must be defended.[3] [ZB: 43–51] *My* political and religious opinions are especially sensitive.

But let's start by exposing those problem layers of the *I-Me-Mine* that have even deeper roots. This means introducing four points about the neural levels of the Self. They often go unacknowledged.

1. Our soma and psyche are deeply rooted. They are not just represented up in the cortex. Each of these two big systems of high-level Self-generating functions is *co*-activated. This means that they share rapid oscillations with deep *subcortical* regions. These shared oscillations unite our cortical functions with those co-arising from (and usually anticipated millisec-

onds before by) corresponding sets of subcortical nuclei. Nuclei are large aggregates of many nerve cells.

2.   Three subcortical nuclei play a crucial *excitatory* role in this regard. [SI: 85–121] These limbic nuclei are located down in the dorsal layer of the thalamus.

• Why are they called the limbic nuclei?

Because they serve to relay various emotionalized messages up from the limbic system. These messages then ascend through the limbic thalamus to activate our cortex. The resulting reverberations of the Self can cause big problems.

3. Fortunately, an inhibitory gate also surrounds the thalamus: the *reticular nucleus*. Its inhibitory transmitter is gamma-aminobutyric acid (GABA). When GABA is released and closes this gate, it shifts *out of phase* the usually well-synchronized timing of these fast, bi-directional thalamo ↔ cortical oscillations. This shift serves to interrupt and shut off those excessive contributions from the limbic system that would otherwise keep reverberating up and down from the cortex. [ZBR: 167–179] The resulting silence is selective. It has some analogies with what you hear, and what drops out, when you put on a set of noise-canceling headphones. [MS: 34–37].

4.   Buddhist practices apply a comprehensive approach to long-term meditative training.[4] In a variety of ways, many practices help diminish the upsetting impact that unwholesome cortico ↔ limbic emotional reverberations can have on the normal operational integrity of our psychic and somatic Self. [ZB: 141–145]

• How can a meditative practice help us let go of these maladaptive aspects of our Self?

Two important ways are by the training of (1) a fine-grained focal attentiveness, and (2) a clear, generalized global awareness. However, this dual approach, like all meditative training, must be *lived* daily. To be effective, it must be integrated in a balanced manner and actualized in how we behave in everyday life. In this regard, chapter 2 specified a basic normal function of our *dorsal* attention system: it serves to help us *focus efficiently* on tangible targets relatively close to our body. A standard term for this is *concentrating*. To concentrate means to be exclusive, to choose only one point on which to focus. The word has a Self-referential implication that is often lost sight of: *we are* the active agency. *Our* motivation has chosen, consciously or subconsciously, to devote our own attentive energy to focus on this single site.

For example, when we first sit down to meditate, we usually begin by using two techniques of *concentrative* meditation. First, we usually focus our gaze down in this one-pointed manner (because that is how we were taught to begin). Having chosen one spot, our two eyes converge on it, at an angle down some 30–45 degrees below the horizontal. [MS: 42–52] Second, we also focus attention on following our breath in and out. Again, *we* make a choice. We choose to follow either (1) the actual sensation of air flowing in and out, or (2) the proprioceptive messages that arise from the corresponding in and out movements far down in the lower abdomen. Clearly, this concentrative form of meditation is a voluntary, top-down, executive act, one that we refer to actual motor and sensory portions of our somatic (physical) Self. Concentration techniques can evolve into the absorptions when they are intensified (voluntarily or involuntarily). [ZB: 467–518]

Receptive meditation techniques are introduced during the next stage. [ZBR: 29–32; MS: 42–52, 203–204] They exemplify a more effortless, choice*less* approach. Chapter 2 identified the attributes of openness and receptivity as among the key qualities infusing this kind of global awareness. Now the eyes are free to diverge slightly from their former inturned focus on one spot. Vision and hearing can open up, expanding into a bare spatial *awareness* that can become more universal in scope. This receptive approach to meditation evolves gradually. It becomes increasingly *in*clusive, involuntary, bottom-up, and other-referential. In the distant future, these several attributes may facilitate the shift into intuitive, insightful modes of consciousness. [ZB: 519–624]

- What does "other-referential" mean?

It helps now to become familiar with another useful pair of Greek words. The first, *ego*, is in common use when we refer back to the axis of our Self. The second word, *allo*, points in the other direction. Indeed, it means "other." Within this vast frame of allo-reference is everything in the outside environment beyond the surface of our skin. Our skin surface serves as both a tangible and a conceptual division. Beyond it, the rest of the whole other world expands into the endless space out *there*. [ZB: 34–47] Thomas Merton's sentence in the chapter epigraph turns out to be a highly accurate description. The allo-perspective is already there. Because it operates subconsciously we don't know it exists.

Now for a contrast. First we observed that the course of our egocentric processing stream overlaps the functions of our *dorsal* attention system as it rises upward on its *parietal* trajectory. We have just been informed that a second stream exists. Its specialty is the *anonymous* processing of visual and auditory information. It follows a *lower*, ventral pathway among the allocentric networks. This "other" frame of reference is more global in nature. Its visual course begins down in the *lower* occipital region. It runs forward through the temporal lobe, then flows on into the lower frontal lobe (see figure 3.1).

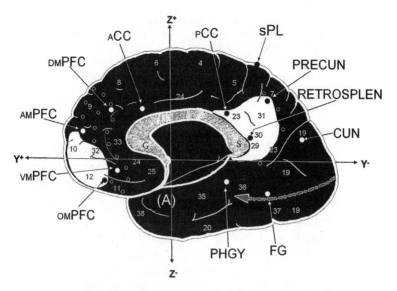

Figure 3.1 The inside surface of the right side of the brain, depicting the medial origins of the psychic Self as remote from the allocentric processing stream

Chapter 3 focuses on the functions of the two large white areas and the long gray, curving, arrowheaded line at the viewer's right. Begin with this long, curving, arrowheaded line. It starts low down, in the lower occipital cortex at the back of the brain. Let this represent the major initial ventral trajectory of our allocentric (*other*-referential) processing stream. As its messages relay forward into the temporal lobe, notice that they will pass through the color sensitive region of the *right fusiform gyrus* (FG).

The two large white areas are located higher up, a substantial distance away. In front is the *medial* prefrontal cortex (mPFC). Its multiple connections normally contribute adaptive autobiographical and allied executive functions to our omnipresent *psychic* sense of Self. The larger white area is farther back in the *medial* posterior parietal cortex. Its connections serve to bring its topographical memories of events into useful links with the more executive agencies of our autobiographical Self. The resulting coalitions enable us to remember how to navigate within our environment. This figure cannot show (aside from its hint of the location of the amygdala (A) all the other origins of our overconditioned emotional longings and loathings. After these limbic messages

Figure 3.1 (Continued) have ascended through the deep limbic nuclei of the thalamus, their oscillations rise up to engage these two white medial regions. The small white numbers refer to the numbering system devised by Korbinian Brodmann to identify different cortical areas. [ZBR: 146–148] For example, area 19 identifies one part of the occipital association cortex as Brodmann area 19, abbreviated BA 19.

Some patients can suffer discrete damage to this lower network. Their resulting allocentric deficit of global visual processing involves objects in both the right *and* left halves of the visual field. Why is this called object-centered neglect?[5] Because the patients neglect that particular half of any discrete *object* anywhere in outside space—to the *left or right*. And the neglected half of that object is on the side opposite their brain dysfunction.[6] [SI: 64–70]

The parallel distributed pathways of allocentric visual processing are reasonably close to, and accessible by, the *ventral* attention system. They remain relatively distant from the regions representing the physical Self of our soma and the mental functions of our psyche. The primary modules of this lower attention system are chiefly within the *right* temporo-parietal junction (TPJ) and the *right* inferior frontal gyrus (iFG) (see figure 2.1). This right TPJ serves a circuit-breaker function. Its connections enable attention to disengage from its previous topic. Once detached, attention can then shift automatically to point toward the reprocessing of the next newly salient stimulus.

Notice that this right ventral system for our normal online alerting and reorienting functions *is bilaterally aware*. Within its basic level of global awareness, this system stands poised to serve a reflexive role. This means that it can react quickly when a relevant stimulus event arises on *either* side of our environment. This characteristic *automatic* reaction to such an unexpected stimulus occurs long before there is time to think any long discursive thoughts. [SI: 29–34] These facts help explain why centuries of Zen literature cite instances when a person's brain, suddenly surprised by a bird call, is instantly triggered into a state of kensho (see chapter 6).

• How could such an abrupt, involuntary shift in attention coincide with the dropping out of the person's sense of Self?

Now for another contrast. Neuroimaging research in this century has shown that an *inverse* relationship normally exists between the regions that represent our attention and those that participate in our Self-centeredness. [SI: 109–121] Especially when external attention networks suddenly turn *on*, many Self-referential regions will turn *off*. These simultaneous, *reciprocal* capacities are noteworthy. They enable each substantial, brisk activation of our attention systems to coincide with the *deactivation* of our innermost frontal and posterior parietal regions. Remember: some parts of these same medial regions could otherwise be contributing maladaptive degrees of the Self-centeredness that complicates our access to more useful psychic resources. This normal seesaw, negatively correlated relationship can be oversimplified visually as follows:

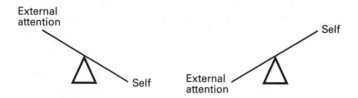

• But states of awakening are not just selfless. Why are they also infused by an impression of reality? Why is this impression so meaningful and perfect that it transfigures the appearance of what had seemed, only an instant earlier, to be the ordinary outside world?

Meaning does not materialize out of thin air. Meaningful impressions coalesce in association networks, especially in associations within the temporal lobe and their connections. Meanings spring from configurations that can also access our normal allocentric spatial processing pathways. [ZBR: 357–371; SI: 189–207] Allocentric spatial representations often link with activations of the right hippocampus in human subjects.[7] Moreover, inherent coalitions of allocentric functions could become further enhanced, clarified, and sustained as the result of deep subcortical shifts at a thalamic level. These pivotal changes could serve to liberate this "other" frame of reference, freeing it from its prior domination by our weighty egocentric frame of reference.[8] Now all things as *they* really are could seem especially *real*. Some of kensho's direct sense of authenticity could also arrive when highly efficient degrees of fast processing accompany such an uncluttering of entanglements from our usual elaborate Self. [SI: 145–146]

- What could explain the way that a person's usual discriminating word-thoughts and concepts vanish during a major state of awakening?

Eleven centuries ago, Master Huang-po was aware of this silence. His description for such powerful quieting translates as "the Stillness beyond all activity." [ZB: 633–638] Meditators soon discover how much valuable, quiet, productive time they waste while generating useless trains of noisy word-thoughts. Why do we produce so many discursive thoughts? Mostly because our habitual Self-preoccupations are activating impulses in deeper striatal and limbic regions. These can keep rising up to agitate the language networks in our frontotemporal cortex (L>R).[9]

- Why is so much language referable to this left side of our brain?

It's not clear why so many language functions evolved on the brain's left side, (or why the liver is over on the right side of our abdomen). Huang-po's prescience as an early observer of silence is apparent, given how little was then known about brain physiology. Not until 1861 were we in the West enlightened about the fact that our normal language functions were dominant on the left side. Then, Pierre Paul Broca (1824–1880) reported that damage to the left inferior frontal region caused verbal silence. A lesion here blocked the (motor) articulation of his patient's speech. And we waited until 1874 for Carl Wernicke (1848–1905) to show, again on the left side, that the superior temporal gyrus was our dominant region for decoding the meaning in receptive (sensory) speech (see figure 2.1).[10]

Let's now review four key contrasts in chapters 2 and 3, with the aid of figures 2.1, 2.2, and 3.1:

1. The *left* upper temporal and lower frontal regions are dominant for these normal sensory and motor language functions. In contrast, corresponding temporal and frontal regions over on the *right* side are dominant for the *ventral* attention system's capacities for spatial attentiveness. These ventral regions enable the brain to be aware of, and to react to, stimuli anywhere on either side of our environment (see figures 2.1 and 2.2)

2. The *egocentric* processing stream is overlapped by the *dorsal* attention system. This overlapping occurs over the upper and outer parts of the cortex. Up here, in the superior parietal lobule, our somatic Self's sensory-motor association functions start to become integrated into the schema of our whole body. These parietal associations representing our physical Self are further refined in the inferior parietal lobule.

In contrast to these attentive regions over the outside of the brain, most autobiographical and topographical correlates of our *psychic* Self are represented elsewhere. These networking functions arise chiefly on the brain's *inside* surface between the two hemispheres. Here, they are distributed among the medial prefrontal and posterior parietal regions (see figure 3.1).

> 3. The *allocentric* processing stream begins anonymously much farther down (see figure 3.1). This other-relational frame of reference pursues a lower trajectory. This permits it to be accessed relatively easily by the lower modules of the *ventral* attention system rather than by those distant, Self-entangled modules higher up in the dorsal attention system. Moreover, whereas the right side of this ventral system is dominant (R>>L), each side of our *dorsal* attention system directs its vanguard functions—to an *equal* degree (R=L)—toward the opposite side of the environment.
>
> 4. When attention is activated, deactivation occurs in the (mostly medial) frontoparietal regions representing the psychic Self, and vice versa.
>
> • Do other important differences exist between the left and right sides of the brain?

Yes. For example, our left temporal lobe contributes especially to fine-grained *semantic* understanding of language. *Semantic* is another word for "meaning." The temporal lobe's tightly organized templates are coded to instantly identify, interpret, and infuse meaning into what we perceive. These basic categorizing functions enable us to understand and to express spoken, silent, and written forms of language in an orderly, accurate manner.

Skill sets of this kind are an essential prelude to comprehension in general. In this regard, the right temporal lobe helps instantly integrate more subtle kinds of *non*verbal information in the form of ideas. Such an ideational approach to decoding enables us to formulate and interpret atmospheres of aesthetic appreciation in art and music. These are examples of the kinds of nuanced functions that could coalesce when intuitive forms of comprehension unfold into *wordless* insights of all sizes and depths.

It sometimes helps to remember a further qualification. Yes, the primary functions of our right and left hemispheres are complementary. Yes, in this respect, they do interact chiefly as allies. However, each side quietly maintains a subversive system of its own. These autopilots on one side serve silently to restrain and *inhibit* regions on the opposite side.[11] [ZB: 358–367]

These significant differences in the ways our lobes and two hemispheres function are a preamble for the themes to unfold in subsequent chapters. Once again we return to events that happened millennia ago.

4

Buddhist Botany 101

Until we can see a big Buddha in a small leaf, we need to make much more effort . . . When you see a large Buddha in a blade of grass, your joy will be something special.

Shunryu Suzuki-Roshi (1904–1971)[1]

The Tree of Understanding, dazzling straight and simple, sprouts by the spring called Now I Get It.

Wistawa Szymborska (1923–2012)[2]

Religions thrive when they find expression in metaphors and iconographic symbols. Sudden comprehensions arise in outdoor settings. Early Buddhist teachings shared a rich, earthy relationship with native trees, plants, and flowers.

A Memorable Event in the Spring

People everywhere appreciate that all life hinges on Earth's fertility. Just as April finds us celebrating the bounty of Mother Earth on Earth Day, so was it customary long ago for people living in southern Nepal to honor their vital affinities with the Earth. How did they emphasize the ennobling virtue of hard farm work out in the field? In that era, ca. 550 B.C.E., they reserved a special day, calling on royalty for the distinction of plowing the first ceremonial furrow in the soil.[3]

On this memorable day, young Prince Siddhartha is attending that spring planting festival, and his own father's hands are performing this royal plowing ritual. Left to himself, Siddhartha sits off to one side. There he chooses the cool shade afforded by a rose-apple tree to shelter himself from the heat. Mindfully attentive to each breath in and out, secluded from sensual pleasures and unwholesome states, he enters spontaneously into the first (*jhana*) state of meditation. After emerging from this memorable state of rapture and bliss, he then goes on to carefully examine his thoughts in solitude.

Fast forward to India, decades later. Here we find him 35 years old, exhausted and emaciated by the severe austerities involved in his six-year spiritual quest. What resources remain to him? What can he possibly do that he hasn't already undergone? Fortunately, his long-term memory recalls that event under the rose-apple tree long ago. This was the day when he dropped into the initial state of meditative absorption. He scans subconscious levels of meta-awareness and integrates them into a key insight: *This* is indeed the Path to enlightenment. This *remindful* recollection proves crucial. At long last, he realizes how he needs to proceed.

As each narrative story unfolds in the next pages, we will often find him choosing again to sit in meditation *beneath a tree.* He advises his followers to do the same. Furthermore, he will follow a "Middle Way" on this later meditative Path. This approach steers clear of the two extremes, austerity and overindulgence.

Let us begin by examining the first botanical reference. It was only under a particular tree that this pivotal initiating event became so memorable in young Siddhartha's consciousness.

The Rose-Apple Tree

This branching, broad-crowned tree (*Syzygium jambos*) is native to Asia.[4, 5] Other than its ample shade, what else might draw a person's attention to it in the springtime? First, its greenish-white flowers have multiple stamens. Each stamen is three inches long, so they all stick out like a bunch of spikes. Second, the tree's narrow leaves are already a glossy red color when they begin to issue from their buds. Only after its maturing leaves make chlorophyll do they turn dark green. Later still, once the greenish-yellow fruit fully ripens, its size will finally attain two inches. Although this mature fruit now yields a fragrant bouquet, it becomes edible in preserves only after much more culinary processing. In Hawaii this rose-apple tree is called Ohia-ai. Sheltered in groves, in that climate, it grows 50 feet high and casts a long shadow.

Given the many dubious legends that have grown up around the Buddha, why can a sutra that specifies a rose-apple tree[6] convey a useful message for contemporary Buddhists? We live in an era when the phrase "post-traumatic stress disorder" too often reinforces the notion that memories cause damage. That's not the message here. This story about the rose-apple tree affirms that pivotal *positive* resources reside in long-term memory. *Remindfulness* is practical. Effortlessly scanning our whole past, it sponsors vital and affirmative insights. These insights illuminate moments all along the meditative Path. Remindfulness, operating silently, improved Siddhartha's life, and it has the capacity to improve our lives. [MS: 94–100, 180–181]

Under a Pipal Tree

Next we take up the more familiar events in Siddhartha's story. Now he is in northeast India, ca. 528 B.C.E. His long-term memory circuits have just reminded him of this singular link to a tree in his youthful past. Informed silently by this insight, he now understands what he must do. Which tree does he select this time? He chooses a tall pipal tree. When he sits under it, he intends to remain there in meditation until he finally becomes enlightened.

The details of what happens next may vary, yet accounts over the centuries agree that this is a person whose consciousness then underwent a total transformation.[7] Having dropped off all former overconditioned layers of Self-centeredness, he awakened under this "tree of understanding." He finally saw with deepest insight-wisdom into the non-dual nature of existential reality. The site where this epic transformation happened was thereafter called Bodh Gaya.

Ch'an master Yun-men (864–949) helped to perpetuate one potentially informative version of the story.[8] This was the intriguing legend that Siddhartha, after having meditated through the night, *looked up above the horizon* into the *eastern* sky before dawn. There what captured his attention was the bright morning star, the planet Venus.[9] Such a striking visual event could help trigger an awakening. Independently, in the Pali canon, the Buddha confirms the remarkable brilliance of the morning star.[10] In fact, he hints that the morning star's potent illuminating capacity is only surpassed by the way that the practice of loving-kindness itself "shines forth, bright and brilliant" to liberate one's mind.

Some early legends suggest that he also may have reached down and "touched the earth" shortly after he became enlightened. This *mudra* (symbolic gesture) has become part of Buddhist iconography. It is often interpreted as though the Buddha were calling upon the Earth itself to confirm that he had "achieved" this great, liberating, awakening.[11] A more humble interpretation suggests itself: the touch of one's fingers representing a simple contact with the soil. Such a universal gesture could reflect the deep realization of someone who had become so open at that moment as to feel intimately unified within the oneness of the whole universe. In such an all-inclusive context, the ground at one's feet could serve as the closest tangible point of direct Nepali reference. We observed that a similar down-to-earth theme was part of the Nepali custom on that earlier spring day when young Siddhartha first meditated under the rose-apple tree. Every gardener whose fingers reach into the soil in the springtime shares in the primal sense of grace conferred by this touching renewal with the elemental fertility of the earth itself.

The Buddha remained under this pipal tree for several days, integrating the profound implications of this fresh understanding into his newly transformed consciousness. As he reflected on how such a remarkable state of awakening had liberated him instantly from all prior suffering he realized what his next role in life would be: he would become a teacher, helping others learn how to relieve their suffering. This would be the Path he followed for 45 years.

The Bodhi Tree

Bodhi means "awakened" in Sanskrit and Pali. Soon the names of the tree, this man, and this place were all transformed. Originally, the pipal tree was just another member of the fig family. Thereafter, it was honored by Linnaeus with the special name *Ficus religiosa* ("sacred fig"). Its wide, heart-shaped leaves, reaching some 6 inches in length, narrow into a remarkably long-tailed tip. This unique tip can extend for another 2 to 3 inches. It serves as a metaphor for the heartfelt extensions of loving-kindness and compassion that reach outward toward others from the core of Buddhist practice (see figure 4.1).

The Bodhi leaf evolved into a symbol closely associated with Buddhism. (In Christianity the palm serves as a reference for the events linked with Palm Sunday.) Bodhi leaves serving this symbolic purpose illustrate the cover of an art book entitled *Leaves from the Bodhi Tree*.[12] The presence of Bodhi leaves in this scene identifies the Buddha as the subject of this otherwise ambiguous stone sculpture carved in the eleventh century. The clues are the heart-shaped leaves with the long drip tails, covering the branch over his head.

A reasonably close relative of that original tree still exists. Its shade welcomes pilgrims who journey today to Bodh Gaya in the Indian state of Bihar. We are informed that *this* Bodhi tree grew from a sprout that had been transplanted from a much older tree that had been growing for centuries in Sri Lanka.[13] That aged tree, in turn, is said to have been grown from a branch taken from the original, ancient Bodhi tree up north at Bodh Gaya. In the third century B.C.E., this cutting from that original tree was said to have first been rooted in a golden container, then shipped south to Sri Lanka as a gift from Ashoka, who was then the Buddhist Emperor of India. There, it flourished in a special garden in the ancient capital of Anuradhapura.[14]

In recent years, Bodhi tree leaves have served to illustrate the first page of the newsletter of the Honolulu

Figure 4.1 Leaf from a Bodhi tree (*Ficus religiosa*)

Notice the distinctive tail issuing from the bottom of this broad leaf. (This tail is 3 inches long in the original leaf). The flexibility of the long stem, which is of equal length at the top, is another feature. It distinguishes the heart-shaped Bodhi leaves from the rose-apple tree's short stem and narrow, lance-shaped leaves.

Diamond Sangha, a Zen community founded by Robert Aitken-Roshi (1917–2010). The cover of Thich Nhat Hanh's recent book *Your True Home* is graced by three distinctive Bodhi leaves.[15]

The Lotus Plant Enters Buddhism

For millennia, the perennial lotus blossom symbolized the purity inherent in the authentic spiritual Path. It was widely understood among Hindus and then Buddhists that the special beauty of the lotus flower in full bloom remained unsullied, free from clinging attachments that originated in the muddy ooze down at the bottom of the pond. Accordingly, for aesthetic reasons, it became traditional for the early artists to portray their deities on a throne of open lotus blossoms. Beyond this ancient role in iconography, the bloom of the sacred lotus (*Nelumbo nucifera*) was later adopted as the National Flower of India.

The large Asian lotus flowers are colored various shades of pink in their natural aquatic setting. An intrinsic metabolic cycle prompts them to become warmer and to disperse their scent as the blossoms open up between 5 a.m. and 6 a.m. This is another reminder that Siddhartha's awakening was said to have occurred just at the first hint of dawn. [ZB: 621]

The lotus enters Buddhist narratives in several other ways. A later sutra, called the Lotus Sutra, became emphasized in the Mahayana Buddhist tradition as it moved north to evolve in China, Korea and Japan. Most verses in the sutra are not directly attributable to sayings of the historical Buddha. They express metaphysical themes through parables that originated in India during the first century and were translated into Chinese by the year 255.[16] This Lotus Sutra remains relevant for our purposes. Its name symbolizes the warmth inherent in the lotus bud as it goes into bloom and that open-hearted warmth exemplified by the key principle of authentic compassion (Sanskrit: *karuna*).

This ideal quality of compassion was initially embodied in the Indian bodhisattva named Avalokiteshvara. It was later venerated as Guanyin in China, and finally as Kannon or Kanzeon in Japan. This universal symbol of Buddhist compassion becomes most effective when it is closely associated with a refined degree of wisdom. How is this refinement to be expressed? In the art of detecting, discerning, and skillfully responding to each *sound* of the suffering that arises from the anguished world.

Meditators have a practical reason to be aware that their keen sense of hearing (audition) can play a potential role in the physiology of their own awakening. When a meditator's hearing channels become sensitized, a sudden auditory stimulus—such as the "clack" of a pebble striking a stalk of bamboo [SI: 112–113], the "boom" of the temple drum signaling lunch time,[17] or the unexpected "caw" of a crow (see chapter 6)—sometimes becomes the trigger that helps open this receptive brain into an awakened state of kensho-satori.

A Flower Is Used in the Later Teachings

D. T. Suzuki once mentioned a story that entered into Zen Buddhist teachings in later centuries.[18] The Buddhist sangha on this occasion is said to have been gathered on Vulture Peak. There, the Buddha is invited to lecture at length. He says not a word. Instead, he simply holds up to the audience a single flower. It is only one of many flowers that had just been given him. His senior disciple, Kashyapa, nods and smiles softly. He alone comprehends the significance of the silent message: he will be entrusted to lead the sangha later, after the Buddha dies.

Several resonances came to be associated with this story about a single flower. The first is that the essence of the Way remains inexpressible in ordinary language. The message is that a special, subtle relationship will emerge between master and student. Only after years of working together would this wordless intuitive communication so ripen that it served to bridge their mutual understanding. The Japanese term *nenge-misho* refers to this wordless gesture. It is the implicit acknowledgment of merit equivalent to the transmission of the authority to teach others.[19]

A Handful of Simsapa Leaves

The Buddha's effectiveness as a teacher often hinged on the way he chose other simple tangible nearby objects to illustrate his message. For example, we find the sangha dwelling on another occasion in a grove of simsapa trees.[20] Picking up a mere handful of these fallen leaves, the Buddha asks the gathering, "Are there more leaves in my hand, or in the simsapa trees overhead?" They reply that the trees overhead obviously contain many more simsapa leaves. The Buddha uses this sharp contrast in numbers to make his point: he had chosen only a few teachings previously to emphasize to his followers. Why had he concentrated on these few? Because countless other teachings were not essential to the spiritual Path, nor were they "the kinds of direct knowledge which might lead to enlightenment." Which fundamental truths *did* he emphasize? The Four Noble Truths: "Suffering, the origin of suffering, the cessation of suffering, and the Way leading to the cessation of suffering" (see chapter 1).

The Simsapa Tree

The simsapa tree is *Dalbergia sisu*. If some today still call it the Ashoka tree, they perpetuate the name of the Buddhist emperor who reigned ca. 272–ca. 236 B.C.E. and whose presence lingers in several stories herein. In India, the Dalbergia tree can grow to a height of 80 feet. Its clusters of yellowish-white flowers resemble those of pea plants and later develop into a flat pod.[21]

A Basket of Understanding Lined with Lotus Leaves

Elsewhere in the early Pali sutras, the Buddha reemphasizes that his disciples need to understand *deeply* the four ennobling truths of suffering.[22] Thus, he says, "You might think it's possible to hold on to your [intellectual] understanding of these truths *before* you arrive at the deeper levels of insight. However, this is like trying to hold water in a leaky basket when you've only constructed it out of pine needles. But later, *after* you've made this deep breakthrough, you can finally retain your comprehension of the truths of suffering. Now your basket of understanding resembles one made out of broad, sturdy, lotus leaves that will finally hold water."

The Lotus Leaf

Lotus leaves have an unusually waxy, microtextured surface.[23] The leaves' extraordinary ability to shed water is now described by a special term, the lotus effect. In a pond outdoors, drops of water keep rolling off lotus leaves. This useful hydrophobic property helps explain why the Buddha would have selected lotus leaves to line the inside of a water-retaining vessel. This self-cleaning action helps the plant wash off harmful insects, spores, and toxic substances that might cling to an ordinary leaf. The lotus leaf metaphor becomes of further interest to Buddhist meditators in every era who hope to shed their own pejorative clinging attachments.

It is a cold February morning. The Buddha and his disciples have been staying in yet another forest of deciduous simsapa trees. The Buddha is sitting at rest on a thin layer of simsapa leaves that had fallen to the ground.[24] Young Hatthaka is walking by. Seeing the Buddha, he stops, comments on how hard the ground is and expresses the hope that the Buddha had slept at ease even though his thin garment would not have protected him from the cold winter wind.

"Yes," says the Buddha, "I am one of those who does sleep in ease. And now in return, let me ask you, young man: Suppose a well-off homeowner—or his son—were each to own well-insulated homes, have a warm bed, and have wives to attend to them. Will these men necessarily sleep in ease?" "Yes," says the youth. But the Buddha continues: "Suppose each of them were also burning with the emotions of longing, or those of loathing, or their minds were consumed by the fires of delusions. Under *these* conditions, would they then sleep miserably?" "Yes," is the reply. "Well," says the Buddha, "to be enlightened is to be spared from each of these three afflictions. The person who has abandoned these unwholesome passions and delusions can sleep in ease."

The Buddha acknowledged that he was only the most recent of countless other enlightened teachers who had preceded him. In this context, he is reminded of an earlier religious teacher by the name of Araka.[25] How had Araka introduced the important principle of impermanence to his hundreds of disciples? By continuing to remind them: "Human life is short, limited, brief, full of suffering and tribulation. One should understand this thoroughly, lead a pure life, do good things. Just as a dew drop vanishes from a blade of grass as soon as the sun rises, so too is each human life like this dew drop—short, limited, full of suffering and tribulation."

Later, in Japan, Zen Master Dogen (1200–1253) elaborated on the image of a drop of dew on a blade of grass. In the first chapter of his major work, he observed that one single drop of dew on this leaf of grass still suffices to reflect the full moon and the entire sky.[26]

The Buddha Meditating Under the Banyan Tree

On another occasion after he became enlightened, we discover the Buddha again meditating at the base of a tree. This time, he has chosen a banyan tree.[27] Sitting erect, in the full lotus position and in deep meditation, he is an imposing presence. Dona, a Brahmin passerby, is struck by the nobility of his appearance. Somehow, having just glanced at this meditator's footprints in the dust, he is under the impression that these imprints display rare characteristics of the kind that he associates with divinity. So, in his next probing questions, he seeks to place the Buddha at one particular level in either the holy or the human pantheon.

To each such question the Buddha responds, "No." Instead, he uses a botanical reference that may now have a more familiar ring. These words describe the nature of his present state as resembling that of a mature person who now lives unsullied by the world. This state is "like a lotus bloom that rises up out of the water, unstained." He concludes by saying simply, "Think of me as 'awakened.'" In any era, a salient characteristic of being awakened to the world is being liberated from the bondage of one's Self-centeredness.

The Banyan Tree

The banyan tree, *Ficus benghalensis*, has many remarkable characteristics. These led to its being recognized as the

National Tree of India. One of the longest-lived and largest trees, the banyan has numerous aerial roots that reach down into the soil from its low-spreading branches. These roots not only supply nourishment. They also form secondary trunks that help anchor the tree into the earth. In these respects, a big old banyan tree is reminiscent of the ways that Buddhism's different branches are still extending themselves, century after century, to become grounded in the cultural soil of many lands.

The Buddha's Explicit Advice about Places to Meditate

The Buddha was a monk who lived in the forests and served as an exemplar for his followers. He not only meditated at the base of a pipal tree or banyan tree, he gathered his community in groves of simsapa trees. In still another forest, how did he advise his disciples to avoid the hazards of sensuality? He suggested that they go into a solitary retreat in the wilderness and practice meditation either at the base of a tree or in an empty dwelling.[28]

Induced Visions Including Ashoka Trees

The Lankavatara Sutra is another sutra that originated in later centuries.[29] Its words invite readers to visualize an imaginary setting: a Buddhist audience said to have gathered on the peaks of Sri Lanka. Up here, when a man called Mahamati requests a teaching, the Buddha allegedly conjures up many beautiful scenes. These images become visible and are shared by everyone in the assembly. In this scenery, groves of Ashoka trees and other forest trees now glisten in the sunlight. Then, having created this imaginary setting, the Buddha suddenly causes everyone's visionary scenes to vanish! Why? The Buddha then explains the basis of this teaching: *all of our perceptions—like these transitory visions—are only projections of our own mind.* Don't cling to them. They don't last. The message is, Don't stay attached to what your imagination happens to perceive (nor cling to doctrinaire interpretations of the Dharma). Instead, realize that the essence of the spiritual Path resides neither in abstract words nor in metaphysical visions. Where, instead, is truth to be realized and authenticated? Within the depths of your own direct, insightful daily experiences.[30]

The Buddha's Final Teaching

Knowing that he was dying, the Buddha selected his final place of rest. It was in the space between two sal trees, in a forest near Kusinara.[31] There, the essence of his final words to his followers was simple: "All things are impermanent. Make diligent efforts to become liberated."[32] The sal tree is *Shorea robusta*. It is a tree native to East India, noted for its yield of close-grained, hardwood timber and large, broad leaves.

In Summary

These landmarks in early Buddhist history are reminders that we are part of Nature. The early teaching stories were often grounded in the simplest botanical references to particular trees, leaves, flowers, or a single blade of grass. These living plants also have DNA. They co-arise from the stardust in the universe, just as we humans do. They too undergo cycles of birth and death.

Consider how many fundamental topics have just been reviewed:

* the pivotal affirmative role of *remindfulness*,

* our intimate changing, seasonal relationship with the generative powers of the Earth,

* awakenings that arise like the lotus in full bloom, unsullied by any attachment to their earlier muddy origins,

* the refinements of insight-wisdom that ultimately help generate the warmth of authentic compassion,

* the vital role of states of deep insight that enable one to retain one's comprehension of the Four Noble Truths of Suffering,

* a subtle allusion to shedding superficial clinging attachments,

* the total release from a life of suffering that arrives *after* one has finally extinguished the three lingering fires of greed, hatred, and delusion,

* the base of a tree as a place to meditate in solitude,

* the transient nature of the Self and its mental projections,

* the key roles of direct authentic experience and diligent practice.

Botanical resonances serve to remind generations of Buddhist seekers how they, too, can grow: by staying in touch with their own deep affinities with trees and plants that are rooted in the earth. This earth is the place where each fallen leaf serves finally to replenish the soil, where each dewdrop that evaporates from a blade of grass rises up to rejoin the clouds.

Part II

Looking Back into Earlier Centuries of the Common Era

> Words and speech are only thinking, and thinking means suffering. You must throw them all into the garbage!
>
> Zen Master Seung Sahn (1927–2004)

A Glimpse of "Just This" in Tang Dynasty China (618–907)

As the two men part, his young disciple says, When someone asks me to describe my master's truth, how shall I answer?

Master Yunyan pauses, then finally says, "Just this is it."[1]

This disciple is Dongshan Liangjie (807–869). He is important because he later co-founded a major school of Ch'an called Caodong in China and Soto in Japan. However, young Dongshan remained perplexed for a long time after he and his master parted. What had Master Yunyan meant when he said, "Just this is it"? The monk could never understand.

But then one day Dongshan happened to be crossing a stream. Suddenly, he glimpsed his own reflection in the water. Triggered into an enlightened state, he finally realized what his master's "just this" had implied. Following the convention of that era, he then composed his enlightenment poem. [ZBR: 434–435] Its last line tried to condense the inexpressible essence of this sudden awakening. This poetic realization of reality translates as the phrase "to merge with thusness."

The commentary to this dialogue[2] adds some clarification to what is implied by "just this" and "thusness." For example, it mentions the Huayan school of Buddhism that had emerged earlier during the Sui Dynasty (581–618). One of its sayings was, "Inner reality is already complete in itself; when words are born, inner reality is lost."

The early Ch'an school associated with Bodhidharma also asserted that one could never understand the actual flash of insight-wisdom by using words or letters found in the ancient scriptures. [SI: 202] That is why this brief chapter, like chapters 1 and 4, simply leaves hints that point to the need for direct experience.[3] Chapter 6 draws on other Zen lore from the Tang Dynasty that points to the same conclusion.

6

Avian Zen

> I once had a sparrow alight upon my shoulder . . . I felt that I was more distinguished by that circumstance than I should have been by any epaulette I could have worn.
>
> Henry Thoreau (1817–1862)[1]

> I don't know anything about consciousness. I just try to teach my students how to hear the birds sing.
>
> Shunryu Suzuki-Roshi (1905–1971)[2]

> Seeing begins when you forget the name of the thing you see.
>
> Paul Valery (1871–1945)[3]

Birds capture our attention. Pivotal avian moments are embedded in the world of literature and in the lore of Zen Buddhism. What happens to us when we hear *deeply* and resonate with the call of a bird? The next pages sample centuries of evidence that a bird call can trigger openings into awakened states of consciousness. They present a plausible physiological explanation for this phenomenon. They also suggest why our hearing and seeing attentively in the outdoors is such an excellent meditative practice.

In his later years, Ikkyu Sojun (1394–1481) would become a legendary Rinzai master in Kyoto. While he was still a young monk of 26, Ikkyu went out one night alone in a rowboat on Lake Biwa. Out there in the dark, he wasn't expecting a crow to fly overhead. Its "*caw*" suddenly triggered his deep awakening.[4]

So Sahn (1520–1604) was a Korean master who unified the Zen and sutra schools of Buddhism. When he was in his 20s, he was enlightened by the sound of a rooster calling.[5]

Unexpected events that catalyze a peak experience are not unique to Zen. [ZB: 452–457] Nor is their association with birds limited to earlier centuries in distant lands. The spiritual teacher Steve Gray (a.k.a. Adyashanti) recounted a contemporary experience of kensho-satori.[6] It happened when he was 31, after he had practiced Zen for the previous 12 years. While he was preparing to meditate, a bird called outside his window. Immediately, "from my gut, I felt a question arise that I had never heard before: 'Who hears this sound?'" Arising next was an extraordinary emotionless state, during which his former Self/other boundary dissolved. Now, "I was the bird and the sound and hearing of the sound, the cushion, the room, everything." This was followed by a comprehensive insight: an original "emptiness, prior to the oneness, forever awake to itself."

I recently had occasion to interview Adyashanti privately. Without disclosing the particular question I was interested in, I invite him to sit down and to simply return to the way it was that morning. He is composed as his words describe how this episode began.

He has just taken his seat, but has not yet begun to meditate. Indeed, he adds that he was not actually intending to meditate at that point. Suddenly, a bird calls outside the window. I ask him *where* this sound is coming from. His right arm reaches *up and out* into the air at an angle of 60 degrees, at the same time that he gazes up to the right toward his right hand.

I invite him to identify what *kind* of bird. At that instant, he did not recognize which species of bird it was. No word label was ever attached to this bird, neither then nor subsequently. He still does not know. However, that morning, this bird sound and the rest of his consciousness became instantly fused into *one field* somewhere in the space directly in front of him.

The Japanese Zen master Bassui (1327–1387) had posed a similar hearing question: "Who hears this sound?" It became the classic koan, "Who is hearing this sound?"[7] When the late Robert Aitken-Roshi (1917–2010) recommended Bassui's koan to me as a practice, he cautioned that *hearing* was the point, not mere *listening*.[8] When one hears a sound, perception is an actual fact of experience; listening for something is only a preliminary step. Why would a distinction that emphasized actual hearing rather than listening become increasingly cogent? Because when researchers improved their neuroimaging studies during the next decade, they began to regard a subject's effortful trying to "listen harder" as an example of the top-down approach to paying attention. Chapters 2 and 3 introduced this top-down concept. It is the kind of focused attentiveness that meditators engage in when they choose to activate their *dorsal* system of attention. Anatomically, top-down refers to this more voluntary executive system. Its functions are represented in the *upper* parietofrontal region of our cerebral cortex. We have seen that this system arises close to the somatic representations of our physical Self. [MS: 13–20] (see figure 2.2)

More about the Functional Anatomical Aspects of Hearing (Audition)

In contrast to this more deliberately influenced "northern" route, most other hearing functions happen *choicelessly, effortlessly, automatically*. These early steps in hearing (like those in vision) begin much lower down in the brain. They occur along the more "southern" pathways during the first milliseconds of perception. These kinds of essentially *reflexive*, habitual functions are now increasingly regarded as examples of bottom-up attentive processing. A brief survey of both the voluntary and involuntary networks of audition can help us understand why Aitken-Roshi himself practiced and recommended Bassui's old koan.

What can we see? Only what lies in front of us. In contrast, we hear what happens *all around* us. This global auditory field encompasses 360 degrees. The deep roots of our hearing pathways evolved early, down in the primitive brain stem, eons before those later refinements that now serve us so well for vision.

The more primitive parts of our hearing system still process coarse subcortical, survival-type messages. They race up in a hotline from the colliculi, through the back of the thalamus and into the orbital part of the frontal cortex. [ZBR: 159–160] What about the course of our usual, more sophisticated, fine-grained auditory information? Once through the thalamus, it travels quickly on up to our *primary* auditory cortex in the temporal lobe (Brodmann area 41). Up here, these auditory impulses are first transformed into the neural codes for language. This occurs especially on the *left* side, in the nearby auditory *association* cortex (BA 42), chapter 3 reminded us that as these impulses begin to relay forward, their further processing enables them to be expressed in the form of word-thoughts.

In Aitken-Roshi's experience, auditory stimuli were more effective sensory triggers than were visual stimuli. Various lines of evidence support this suggestion. Notice, for example, where our primary auditory cortex and our auditory association cortex are located (see figure 2.1). They lie very close to the specialized *bottom-up attentive functions* of the temporoparietal junction (TPJ) *and* to the multiple association functions of the adjacent superior temporal gyrus. This TPJ region engages in circuit breaker functions. They help us to disengage attention so that it can then be redirected to its next target. The next interactions become crucial because they then link our frontal lobe and temporal lobe functions. Each time an unexpected bird call startles us into reflexive attentive processing, these ramified networking alliances, led by the *ventral* attention system, serve many of our usual cortical needs for more refined decoding and pattern recognition functions.

What else happens the instant we hear an unexpected bird call or glimpse some relevant avian stimulus that captures our *visual* attention? First to react will be the even earlier, deeper receptivities. These are the signals that convey messages from the colliculi in our midbrain up to our thalamus. [ZB: 240–244] So, how can we further cultivate the sensitive awareness that has instant, effortless access to our deep, global processing functions? We can regularly practice both concentrative and openly *receptive* styles of meditation, doing so in ways that minimize our Self-centeredness. [MS: 20–30]

Sky-watching, cloud-watching, and bird-watching are excellent outdoor practices. They help train us instantly to detect, recognize, and shift toward *any* unexpected auditory or visual event. [MS: 54–60] Notice how often these receptive practices shift one's attention primarily *up and out*. Here, *up* means toward events that might arise in elevations of space above one's usual eye level and ordinary mental horizon. *Out* means "out there," in the distance, toward distant events arising *farther away* from one's physical body. Events in the history of Zen become more interpretable when viewed from this spatial perspective of functional anatomy.

Attentive readers may notice that ordinary language often links the upper domain of space to particular refinements of our psyche or our soma. With regard to cultivating wisdom, we're encouraged to "wise-up." When we wish to get into good physical condition, we'll work hard in order to "shape-up."

Early Zen Lore

Exacting teaching practices developed in the Tang Dynasty (618–907). Chinese Ch'an masters were not only wary of troublesome words. They also expected their more awakened trainees to respond in certain ways. Some of their requirements might seem almost to have anticipated the neuroscientific distinctions sketched in earlier chapters. The patriarchs sought behavioral presentations, actions that were expressed in brisk *body language*. [ZB: 668–677] Why did they insist that their pupils *manifest* immediate *physical* responses? They wanted to observe the *earliest* clinical evidence of (what we today regard as) reflexive pathways. The masters were emphatically *not* interested in hearing discursive speech. Wordy conceptual explanations imply that multiple synaptic delays have occurred. Linguistic constructs, like other algorithms, keep branching out in the course of being further refined. Our language networks have widespread extensions. These reach down from the cortex to interact with subcortical regions bilaterally (see chapter 3, note 8, and chapter 8, note 7).

Indeed, the records indicate that the early Tang master Damei Fachang (752–839) once gave his monks the following explicit *non*branching advice: "Reverse your mind, and arrive at its root. Don't pursue its branches!"[9] Even on his deathbed, Master Damei still exemplified this deeply *root-oriented* Ch'an style of teaching students through direct experience. Just as he was about to draw his final breath, a squirrel suddenly chattered. Capitalizing on this last opportunity to instruct his monks, Damei exclaimed: "It's just this thing! Not something else!" Was his parting advice some abstruse celestial concept? No. He simply pointed his monks' attention to just this one ordinary sound. This natural stimulus had just entered the neural root of their auditory system. *Just this.* Direct experience.

A later Tang master incorporated avian examples into his auditory teaching methods. Jingqing Daofu (868–937) routinely posed simple hearing questions to test his monks.[10] For example, he would ask, "*What* is that sound outside the gate?" An unenlightened monk once answered, "The sound of a quail." Master Jingqing was not deaf. He had heard and recognized that bird call many times before. He was not probing for any such *species* label based on mere words. Indeed, he had previously warned his monks that their deluded thinking was turned "upside-down" if they voiced such discriminating language.

The bird outside the temple gate emits only bare sound energies. When such sound energies first reach the ear drum their earliest neural roots are still very far removed from branching out into word labels. The term *quail* can arise in networks only during the later milliseconds. Discriminating word labels are like an artificial band that ornithologists clamp around a bird's leg. No aluminum band ever replaces the living reality of that actual bird. Nor can a finger capture the real moon by pointing at it.

Why does master Jingqing seem so refractory, so uninterested in an answer that would seem only reasonable to us? Though he probes his monks with simple direct questions, he still remains highly alert to every nuance of their next responses. His attitude is *"Show* me. Don't *tell* me."* [SI: 217–218] He is capable of waiting years to be shown this *behavioral* evidence confirming that his monks had dissolved their old Self/other boundary. He knows that when they actually do become enlightened, their overt *body* language will manifest their awakening. Meanwhile, no spoken language satisfies him.

Passages in the Mahayana Surangama Sutra suggest that the Buddha also emphasized *turning* one's stream of awareness successively farther back.[11] One wonders: Which vital functions shift when such a turning occurs way back down toward the deep *root origins* of one's consciousness? [ZBR: 39–40] What happens when the lightning strike of *prajna* dissolves every *psychic* root of one's Self into emptiness and—simultaneously—the brain awakens into that paradoxical fullness, the ineffable insight-wisdom of kensho-satori? [ZBR: 357–387] In this state of "suchness," no Self-identity remains. Such a moment of oneness is not owned by any imperial Self. In this "thusness," no agency of an ego exists that must thrust its own personal top-down modes of discriminating discourse into complex, branching networks.

Bassui was still a young monk when his consciousness was overturned by such a profound awakening. The auditory trigger for his first deep realization was the turbulent flow of a distant mountain stream. At dawn, after Bassui had meditated through the night, this simple natural sound suddenly penetrated his whole being. [ZBR: 39] At such an instant, when hearing *turns far back toward its precognitive roots*, all body-mind boundaries of one's former Self vacate the scene. Every primal fear drops out of this non-dual state of perfection. All sense of time dissolves into an awesome impression of eternity (*achronia*). [ZBR: 380–381; SI: 183–196]

Avian Links to Achronia: The Writings of Stevenson and James

Before William James published his classic *The Varieties of Religious Experience*, he was familiar with a European legend. In this story, the call of a bird suddenly prompts a monk to drop into this state of zero time.[12] In 1898, when James recounted this fable—about the call of a nightingale—he included many comments about it that Robert Louis Stevenson had already made in an earlier essay.[13] Stevenson, a Scot who suffered from tuberculosis during his short life (1850–1894), had realized that this legend held deep existential implications. He understood that only an extraordinary state of consciousness could cause a monk to lose *all* sense of time for a very long period. Indeed, said Stevenson, the deep resonances of meaning within such a remarkable state would be so special that they would touch "very near the quick of life."

As Stevenson begins this tale, we find the young monk walking in the woods far outside his monastery gate. Suddenly, he "hears a bird break into song. He hearkens for a trill or two . . ." Abruptly, he loses all sense of the passage of time. Later, his awareness of time returns. At this point, the monk finds himself standing back at that same familiar gate of his compound where his walk had begun. Yet now, none of the monks inside look familiar, nor do they recognize him. The sole exception is one brother monk, who now appears many decades older. When the weight of all this evidence finally sinks in, our monk then realizes what has happened: after he heard this bird call, he had lost all sense of conscious time for the past *50 years*!

Of course, this is a very tall tale. We today will not be misled (nor were Stevenson and James) by a fable that grossly exaggerates the brief duration of a remarkable physiological phenomenon. To Stevenson, long familiar with metaphor, it seemed reasonable to stretch the yarn about this "time-devouring nightingale." He did so simply to dramatize how such very special moments have qualities that quicken and lend spice to our private lives. Facing an early death, Stevenson had come to realize that the universal fabric of each human life could be woven out of two main strands: Always would we keep "seeking that bird"; rarely would we be graced by the reality of actually "hearing it."

Indeed, this prolific author of *A Child's Garden of Verses* and *Treasure Island* ventured to observe that it was poetry's unique contribution to point us toward such moments of "true realism." Is this an exaggeration? Or could it be close to the attributes that make some poetry so special? For example, in Japan, the old saying is, "Poetry and Zen are one" (*shizen ichimi*). Poetry, as Stevenson explains, can penetrate that secret place in our "warm phantasmagoric chamber of a brain where joy resides." There, he said, poetic resonances might become amplified into "a voice far beyond singing." In such recesses of memory reside capacities to remind us of "those fortunate hours in which the bird has sung to *us*."

One can only speculate about the degree to which Stevenson may have become absorbed in the enchantment of some nightingale's song. Later, William James so valued this same nightingale metaphor that he returned to it in his essay "What Makes a Life Significant?"[14] He hinted, as had Stevenson earlier, at the way the deep levels of this story alluded to life's eternal meaning, wherein all apparent conflicts might finally be peacefully reconciled.

Earlier avian tall tales from Asia can serve to remind meditators how to sit quietly during a long silent retreat. One legend about Ch'an Master Yongming Yanshou (904–975) is that he remained so immobile during a three-month retreat that a bird built its nest in the folds of his clothing![15]

Other Literary References to a Bird Call's Penetrating Impact

Poetic license was the province of another European author, Rainer Maria Rilke (1875–1926), a sometime contemporary of Paul Valéry. Rilke's notebook described how a bird call once resonated in his own consciousness.[16]

> [A] bird-call was there, both in the outside and in his inner being . . . [It did not break at the boundary of his body, but] formed of the two together an uninterrupted space in which, mysteriously protected, only one single spot of purest, deepest consciousness remained."

When such an auditory stimulus does penetrate deeply and resonate within a person's poetic sensibilities at an especially receptive moment, one can understand how it might travel pathways innocent of any word label for one particular species. In this regard, the Zen teacher Joko Beck once received the following report from a practitioner: "In sitting this morning, it was quiet and suddenly there was just the sound of a dove. [Yet] there wasn't any dove, there wasn't any me, there was just this."[17] Some of the uses of "just this" back in Tang Dynasty era are explored elsewhere.[18] [SI: 11, 13, 199] Chapter 1 describes how this phrase was introduced into early Indian Buddhism.

The Benefits of Practice in the Outdoors

What counsel can be given to meditators who wish to practice more selflessly? One approach is to incorporate outdoor experiences seamlessly into your whole program of daily life practice. [MS: 54–60, 130–131] (See appendix A.) Random events arise unexpectedly in Nature. They can often capture your *focal and global* attention. [ZB: 644–667] You do not need to be a Thoreau, alighted upon by a sparrow, to feel anointed during the direct experience with a wild bird. Many birders bring an innate, elementary enthusiasm to the entire world of Nature. In 2007, Sam Keen, a literary birder, teamed up with a gifted watercolorist, Mary Woodin, to create a slender book, a gem of reflections entitled *Sightings*. Its pages describe and portray extraordinary unpredictable encounters with ordinary wild birds.[19]

What causes Keen's perceptions to sharpen in the outdoors? In this fertile silence, he discovers the sights and sounds of the sacred. Some reverent events arise visually, in the radiant sunburst of a goldfinch. Other insights enter at twilight in the haunting flute-like song of the native American wood thrush. What makes this bird call so special? The wood thrush call "belongs to a family of experiences that usher us into a threshold where sound trails off into silence, time disappears into timelessness, and the known world is engulfed by the great mystery." These ethereal qualities resemble those of the European thrush, its cousin, the nightingale in Stevenson's story.

The writings by James, Stevenson, and Rilke suggest that their thoughts could resonate within this avian domain. Only after multiple visits to Japan would the present writer's quest finally be rewarded by an actual glimpse of its furtive bush warbler. In the interim, although I had been repeatedly charmed by the liquid warble of this unseen *uguisu*, the mere sight of it had eluded me. This symbolized how Zen's covert levels of existential meaning were unfolding just beyond the reach of this beginner.

In the outdoors, it was the flight of swallows that intrigued Master Hakuin Ekaku (1685–1769). Their effortless acrobatics served not only to elevate Hakuin's gaze into the sky but also deepened his appreciation for being alive. The evidence is in his calligraphy.[20] The brush-play in one of his many ink paintings carries this universal message: "For everyone crossing the ocean of life and death, how enviable is the swallow's flight."

What other contemporary advice can be offered to meditators whose active monkey-minds keep leaping from one branching thought to the next? Robert Aitken-Roshi offers a practical suggestion in the following verse:[21]

> When thoughts form an endless procession
> I vow . . . to notice the spaces between them
> And give the thrushes a chance [to be heard.]

Notice how these verses *turn one's attention* back into those silent spaces wherein awareness resides with no-thoughts (*mu-shin*). A bird call sometimes actualizes its triggering potential when it penetrates such wordless depths.

In field and forest, where might such a fresh stimulus come from? from above? behind? either side? from afar? perhaps from underfoot? Surprises can arrive from anywhere when one is outdoors. Therefore, *all* perceptual systems become more alert, not only hearing and vision, when one bathes in the open atmosphere outdoors (see appendix A.)

In Summary

Wild birds symbolize the essence of natural, primal energy. Birds freely wing it in the open sky, seeming to burst the bonds of gravity that limit other earthlings. In their songs and instinctual behavior, birds help us to celebrate, in ways remote from words, the mysterious reality of the incomprehensible natural universe that we all inhabit. Thus, when Nanrei Kobori-Roshi once said to me, "Zen is closest to poetry," he was voicing much the same truth about poetic reality to which Stevenson had referred.

Homage to William James

> The more unconscious one keeps in the matter, the more likely
> one is to succeed.
>
> William James (1842–1910)[1]

William James was quoted in the introduction in relation to attention. Chapter 6 mentioned him twice in the context of the nightingale metaphor. This chapter reviews some of his ideas on the competence of our subconscious mechanisms. In the century since he died, no one has surpassed him in the prescience with which he anticipated themes now within the larger scope of neuropsychology. James's words live on in a centenary edition, *The Heart of William James*. It suggests countless ways that his far-sighted perspectives have illuminated our contemporary discourse.

This centenary edition collects 17 of his essays from the definitive 19-volume set of *The Works of William James*, published between 1975 and 1988 by Harvard University Press. The essays begin with the topic of emotion (1884). Unfolding in chronological order, they close with his prescription for a moral equivalent of war (1910). In the intervening 26 years, James's many-faceted mind explored diverse topics. They include his crucial contributions on habit (1892), will (1899) and pragmatism (1899).

Front and center is the essay, "What Is an Emotion?" James points out that how we *act* toward another person will transform our own emotional state of mind. Indeed, we may feel some of our former cold-heartedness starting to melt as we continue to practice some age-old elementary practices that Buddhism refers to as loving-kindness (Pali: *metta*).

Is it really this easy? Can we actually thaw our own attitudes just by learning how to "Smooth the brow, brighten the eye, contract the dorsal rather the ventral aspect of the frame, speak in a major key, and pass the genial compliment?" In "The Gospel of Relaxation," James explains some psychological roots underlying this calm and erect postural approach to everyday behavior. He suggests that each of our actions generates "ceaseless inpouring currents of sensation." In return, this neural feedback reshapes "from moment to moment what our own inner states shall be." A recent review provides psychological evidence in support of James's behave-as-if principle.[2] In the essay, "The Hidden Self," James predicts which persons "will be in the best possible position" to study such subtle phenomena. They will be the investigators (like James himself) who "pay attention to facts of the sort dear to mystics, while reflecting upon them in academic-scientific ways."

We discover his prediction amply confirmed not only in his classic book *The Varieties of Religious Experience* (first published in 1902)[3] but also in the way that research into the psychology and neuroscience of meditation has exploded during the past three decades. In 2008, when David Brooks coined the term "neural Buddhism" in his *New York Times* article, he foresaw how our whole culture would be influenced by this recent brain research.[4] Comprehensive reviews of this topic have recently been published by Hölzel and colleagues and by Malinowski.[5] They summarize many of the neural mechanisms currently believed to operate in this important field in which James was a major pioneer.

Of course, researchers in laboratories are not the only ones who can benefit from carefully examining contemplative/spiritual phenomena. Indeed, in the essay "Habit," having provided useful maxims for how to behave, James advises educators at *every* level "to *make our nervous system our ally, instead of our enemy*." Following his private interview with Swami Vivekananda at Harvard in 1892, James lamented the lack of comparable meditative practices throughout education in the United States. In his talks to teachers and students, he pointed out that education had caused much harm by sponsoring excessive tension. As these words are written in 2013, meditation has finally been introduced into education at every level from grade school through graduate school.[6] It is also flourishing in corporate enterprises,[7] and is being tested for effectiveness in a group of U.S. Marines undergoing training at Camp Pendleton.[8]

James advocates a more relaxed lifestyle. He does so in ways that could help advance the cause of those who are now introducing secular meditative practices into societies worldwide. In "The Gospel of Relaxation," he contends that "we must change ourselves from a race that admires jerk and snap for their own sakes." Instead, what does he believe our communities of the future should provide? This future setting should be a place where citizens no longer "look down upon low voices and quiet ways as dull" but rather cultivate "harmony, dignity, and ease" for their own sake.

Anticipating research into the kinds of creative freedom that flow selflessly, James states this basic psychological principle: "Strong feeling about one's self tends to arrest the free association of one's objective ideas and motor processes." He asks, Do we truly "wish our trains of ideation and volition to be copious, varied, and effective?" Then he says, "we must form the habit of freeing them from our inhibiting influence of reflection upon them, of egoistic preoccupation about their results." In short, stop ruminating and wasting precious time. *Just do it!*

James was restored by the hours he spent engaged in the outdoors. Reserved for his letters is one account of an episode when he spontaneously experienced profound "spiritual alertness" and "intense significance." This "boulder of impression" overcame him one moonlight night. It followed his day hike up Mount Marcy in the Adirondacks. [ZB: 523–524] To preserve one's "full youthful elasticity," he counsels simple hygienic measures: getting ample sleep and exposing oneself daily to "the morning sun and air and dew." Because Nature's bounties were themselves "sufficiently powerful intoxicants," no other stimulants and narcotics were deemed necessary. [ZB: 424–426; ZBR: 291–302; SI: 267–268]

The title of the next essay poses this hard question: "What Makes a Life Significant?" James offers no easy answer. For him, no *ordinary* levels of our usual ideals and aspirations will suffice. First we have to stick our necks out, accept substantial new risks and fresh challenges. Only then would emerge our deeper, sterner, traits of character and *novel uplifting ideals*. These alone can enable us to prevail. Few of these requisite skill sets were fully developed in our earlier repertoire.

This essay did not suggest that his readers seek the *actual* challenge of an outward-bound experience. Nor did it prescribe a rigorous meditative retreat. However, in a context in which he refers explicitly to the Buddha, he specifies which three "underground virtues" are the deep traits of character that emerge under duress. This triad is "courage, patience, and kindness." These pivotal qualities, hard-tempered during adversity, would seem to have been criteria high on the list of the Nobel committee when it chose an exiled Tibetan-born candidate, the 14th Dalai Lama, to receive the Nobel Peace Prize in 1989.

James was a practical philosopher. He advanced the elementary principle of pragmatism from an earthy perspective. While staying grounded in the present moment, he could still reach up to pluck low-hanging fruits from a situation, accepting that those now within reach were more immediately useful than some of the deeper roots. Notwithstanding, he still held that our most deeply rooted authentic beliefs were "really rules for action" in the world at large.

What about the slippery issue of truth? James believed that our various theological belief systems had developed only as "secondary accretions" in the course of a long cultural history. Of primary importance to him were the vast numbers of direct, "concrete religious experiences," not doctrinal concepts. By providing fresh intuitions for renewal, these intimate experiences enabled "humble private men" to transform their lives.

The "Energies of Men" was his presidential address to the American Philosophical Association in 1906. In it, James observed that the ways we actually behave in the world are far from optimal. Even so, we still possess private, deep, reservoirs of untapped potential energy to draw upon. When such surges of excitation infuse our consciousness, they "carry us over the dam," stimulate us to make renewed efforts that are driven by fresh ideas and novel insights. However, James's pragmatism also included *don't* as well as *do*. He emphasized that restraint (Sanskrit: *shila*) still has a powerful role to play in our behaviors. Why did he advocate the regular application of common sense—urge our "saying 'no' to some habitual temptation?" Because he had found that these small "single successful efforts of moral volition" had a weighty influence that could endure for many days.

How can we train ourselves to develop this greater willpower? In *The Principles of Psychology* (1890), James prescribes first applying our "faculty of effort" in small incremental steps. This means doing the "little heroic things" we really do *not* like to do. Instead, *do them anyway*. Later, when it takes major reserves of willpower to accomplish the real heavy lifting, we will then be well-equipped and not unnerved by the challenge. [ZBR: 31]

The essay entitled "The Will" came from his book *Talks to Teachers* (1899). Here, he clarifies why we benefit by deliberately choosing to say *yes* to the *positive* aspects of our everyday life. It is because a negative idea "quickly vanishes from the field" of consciousness whenever we affirm our positive options. He found that this simple strategy of affirmation was much more effective than trying to submerge unwholesome ideas "by repression or by negation."

The final essay in this collection was published only a few months before he died in 1910. In it, he concedes that war can create group cohesiveness by its appeal to our sense of patriotism. However, he expresses the hope that war will become only "a transitory phenomenon in human evolution." Let every angry emotion that war stirs up be replaced by those peaceful behaviors that have become, in his memorable phrase, "the moral equivalent of war."

The 17 essays in *The Heart of William James* still pulse with systolic prescience. They exemplify a distinctive sensibility for today's readers who seek authentic psychological insights and spiritual nourishment. More than a century ago, James foresaw that "a wave of religious activity is passing over our American world." He predicted that this larger movement, driven by its native optimism, would have the potential to release "a firmer, more elastic moral tone." Readers struggling to survive in this century's unrelenting turmoil now have this fresh opportunity on their horizon. They can share in James's optimism that their innate sense of pragmatism will someday "come to its rights" and help us all "in our struggle toward the light."

Part III
Sampling Recent Reports

Use words to explain thoughts, but silence once thoughts have been absorbed.

Master Tao-sheng (360–434 C.E.)

Recent Clinical Information

Zen practice requires detachment from thoughts.
Ch'an Master Foyan Quingyuan (1067–1120)[1]

A neurologist's job is to stop brain damage. Why did the case reports cited in an article and book by Kapur present so counterintuitive a view?[2] Because under certain circumstances, damage to the nervous system can actually *improve* behavioral functions. [SI: 180–186] This result, called paradoxical facilitation, is uncommon. However, in some instances a patient's brain functions can be enhanced to levels *above* normal.

In this regard, a common theme links several chapters in this book: we are all patients, suffering from Self-inflicted wounds to the psyche. Sooner or later, most of us start to realize that it is counterproductive to keep overloading our brain with inappropriate and emotionally charged trivia. We discover that trivial distractions stir up troop after troop of monkey-mind word-thoughts that distort the clarity of our awareness. A millennia-tested remedy exists for this constant low-priority chattering in our frontotemporal networks. It is to learn to meditate in relaxed, attentive silence. This does not necessarily mean Buddhist meditation. Some forms of Christian apophatic centering prayer also bypass the usual mental clutter caused by our cognitive and emotional dissonances.[3]

Consider the implications of the report by Etcoff and colleagues.[4] These authors found paradoxical facilitation in patients who had a chronic receptive aphasia caused by a particular kind of left posterior brain damage. These ten patients could not understand spoken language. However, the researchers were more interested in certain brain functions other than this chronic loss of word comprehension. Accordingly, they designed their study to test these patients' capacities to analyze the subtle *emotional* clues that are hidden in facial expressions. When the patients were shown videotapes of normal human faces their task was to discern, just from these dynamic expressions, which of these persons were lying. It turned out that aphasic patients who had left posterior brain damage made significantly *better* judgments about which persons were lying than did their 20 matched controls. Half of these controls had normal brains; the other half were patients who had chronic brain damage on their right side.

In 2008, Taylor reported a personal odyssey that began with an acute, major left-sided hemorrhagic stroke.[5] A noteworthy aspect of that report was that the damage appeared to dissolve both (1) her receptive *and* expressive speech functions, and (2) her left central areas involved in somatosensory functions. In the *inner silence* caused by this severe left hemispheric brain damage, she then became a selfless witness to some of that sense of unification and inner peace that certain normal persons might experience during a so-called peak experience.[6, 7] [SI: 152, 294]

These case reports indicate that *gross* lesions to cortex, white matter tracts, and subcortical regions, however interesting in themselves, seem more often to give rise to further questions rather than final answers that are of authentic spiritual significance. [MS: 193–195, 227]

When we look back at the comments made by the early masters Tao-sheng and Foyan; when we consider the discussions in chapters 5 and 6, examine the reservations based on gross anatomical and clinical grounds, as well as those in the lengthy notes,[8] what is the take-home message? This range of evidence seems to be an open invitation to keep asking, How do words get in our way? Could rigid entanglements that arise, directly or indirectly, among language networks in our left hemisphere compromise our awareness of the world, hinder our access to intuitive functions that might otherwise help us express innate degrees of insight?[9] If so, then what role might meditation play in reversing this situation?

9

Mindfulness Starts as Present-Moment Awareness

> Over time, you will begin to catch glimpses of your mind's basic state of awareness . . . What begins as a glimpse can gradually be extended, and you can start to understand that the mind is like a mirror . . . images appear and disappear without affecting the medium in which they appear.
>
> The 14th Dalai Lama[1]

> Just resting in choiceless awareness, in open presence, moment by moment by moment . . . and reestablishing awareness if you get lost and carried away, which of course is bound to happen, over and over and over again—nothing wrong with that.
>
> Jon Kabat-Zinn[2]

Caroline Rhys Davids (1857–1922) was a pioneer scholar in the Pali language. When she came to translate the old Pali word *sati*, "mindfulness" seemed to be its nearest single-word equivalent in English. However, the original meaning of the Pali term *sati* was much more elastic. Why couldn't all of its aspects be described as just being aware of the *present* moment? Because the original meaning of *sati* also included its broad overview function: to "facilitate and enable one's *memory*." [MS: 92–97] Memory recalls past moments.

How does our memory operate normally? At the near end of each stimulus event—right *now* in *this* present moment—bare awareness of a stimulus takes less than one-third of a second. Our working memory can easily address simple tasks within such a short processing window. [SI: 14–21] However, the rose-apple tree incident illustrates Siddhartha's *remote* memory. Remote memory can store a crucial event from childhood, but not recall it in a useful context until decades later (see chapter 4).

Ideally, as our memory unfolds on a long sliding scale of time, it needs to be serviced by: (1) a keenly focused tactical attention that incorporates current events into short term working memory, and (2) levels and degrees of discriminating awareness that can reach back into longer-term memory. Other resources then act, consciously or subconsciously, to pick out only the most useful item from a whole lifetime of strategic and policy options.

These several components of *sati* seem to have been encoded within the separate accounts of a large and very flexible memory bank. Its ample capacity has separate vaults in which we can store short-term recent deposits. Moreover, withdrawals can be made—without our willful, top-down signature—whether we had earlier registered such deposits subconsciously or only consciously.[3]

This is a remarkable continuum. So, let us acknowledge the full scope of these surveillance operations and the way they extend into our memory functions. The reason a new word, *remindfulness*, is introduced in the next section is to emphasize the practical implications of retaining the original broad overview meaning of *sati*. When and where would the huge topic of awakening called Buddhism have arisen had Siddhartha not recalled what happened under that rose-apple tree?

Remindfulness

Webster's International Dictionary contains mindfulness but not this word. Let *remindfulness* refer to our normal, autonomous, affirmative memory skills. These are the kinds that stay poised on silent standby alert. They accomplish useful Self-correcting overview functions. Emerson considered that this involuntary faculty served as our natural source of "guidance." How could such silent messages guide us? Not because we used high-brow logic to deliberately access abstract thoughts. This guidance arrived, he said, through a subtle kind of "lowly listening." [MS: 145–150]

This complex system relies on the confluence of intuitive skills that arise *subconsciously*. Wordlessly, they

* *detect* the fact that our attention is not usefully focused on what now might be more appropriate,

* *disengage* this currently misguided attentive processing,

* *identify* and select the potentially more useful information held in our memory storage,

* *retrieve* this relevant information from its storage in memory.

With attention now reattached on the sharp tip of this latest topic, attentive processing functions can redirect this topic toward its more appropriate goal.

• *How can we cultivate such an intelligent continuum of discerning remindful capacities?*

By engaging in ongoing concentrative *and* receptive meditative practices, *both on and off the cushion*. As these broad overview skills co-evolve incrementally within every-day awareness, their priorities develop along lines that are *increasingly intuitive*. [ZB: 125–129, 295–298] Moreover, these newer dimensions of remindfulness orient themselves spontaneously toward larger Big Picture issues. Some of them might resemble that old-fashioned word *conscience*. The more competent our basic physical and psychic sense of Self becomes, by virtue of having dropped off its earlier maladaptive attachments, the more such novel insights seem likely to spring up effortlessly. On rare occasions, deep insights can be life-changing.

Research Pointing Toward New Horizons of Remindfulness

Thoreau understood that "all memorable events transpire in morning time and in a morning atmosphere." Indeed, he cited the ancient Veda saying that "all intelligences awake with the morning." [ZB: 621] His comments are in accord with some fMRI investigations from Washington University.[4] This research shows that greater normal connectivities normally develop in the morning hours among those medial temporal regions (including the hippocampus) that are significantly involved in our memory. [ZB: 180–189] Not until the evening hours will more connections develop that increase the links between our higher neocortex, striatum, and brain stem.

An important fMRI study of meditation was reported by Hasenkamp et al. in 2012.[5] The subjects were 14 adult meditators. Their assigned task was to focus their attention on following their breath while their eyes were closed. The five meditators who had practiced for 3,000 hours represented a high-practice group. The nine meditators in the low-practice group had averaged only 450 hours or so.

This fMRI study was designed to distinguish between four adjacent events during meditation. Ordinary mind wandering occurred during the first of these intervals. The second interval was of greatest interest in the present context of remindfulness. Why? Because at this moment, the subjects first became *aware* that they *were* mind wandering. Suddenly, they realized — they *detected* — that they were no longer focused on their earlier goal of following the breath. A light bulb of remindful awareness now seemed to have turned on. This mismatch signal detected a conflict: what they were actually doing was not what they had intended to do. This remindful event had a particular neuroimaging signature. Its mismatch coincided with bilateral activation of the anterior/middle insula and the dorsal part of the anterior cingulate cortex. The authors used the term "salience network" when referring to this interesting circuitry.

Parenthetically, it becomes useful at this point to define *salience*. Why? Because we need to distinguish between its initial and later origins. *Salience* refers to a special meaningful quality, one that instantly infuses significant import into an event. Much prior evidence indicates that the immediate varieties of perceptual salience begin silently, *subconsciously*, deep in our brain. [ZBR: 175–176] Let's refer to this immediacy as salience I. Most of this early significance is assigned to a stimulus by the pulvinar, the largest association nucleus in the thalamus. In recent years, our higher-level assignments of salience came to be associated with activity coordinated among regions of the cortex. [SI: 138, 238] These networks of salience II include the insula, its overlying opercular region, and their links with the dorsal anterior cingulate gyrus. [ZBR: 82–85]

Back now to the fMRI monitoring of those two groups of meditators who had just detected that their minds were wandering. The subjects who had more meditative practice showed more activity in their left *inferior* temporal region. This finding is interesting in view of the possibility that longer-term meditative practice could tend to be associated with some bottom-up forms of attentive processing along the "southern" pathways (see chapter 12).

This instant of remindful realization within awareness resembles a mini-insight. [ZBR: 271–275, 337] After it, the meditators could go on first to disengage and then to shift their focus of attention. At this point in the third phase (when attention had just been disengaged and was now detached), the *right* dorsolateral prefrontal cortex showed increased activity. Other active cortical sites now included the superior, middle, and inferior frontal gyrus (see figure 2.2).

The evidence suggested that the cingulo-opercular networks were part of the subtle system that could bring higher-level salience II functions into the interval of discernment and detection. In contrast, the usual lateral frontoparietal executive networks were participating during this next interval of disengaged detachment. These findings are supported by other research into the general nature of problem solving skills that evolve slowly in the course of normal human development. [SI: 238]

Lutz and colleagues conducted an important multi-disciplinary study of how changes in the cortical salience network and amygdala were related to the pain responsivities of 14 long term, advanced practitioners.[6] These adepts, averaging 46 years of age, had meditated for over 10,000 hours in two established Tibetan traditions. They were also experts in performing the style called "open presence meditation" during fMRI monitoring. [MS: 89–90] They performed this practice for a brief, 45-second interval prior to their receiving the warm (32°C) or hot (49°C) thermal stimuli.

This hot stimulus felt *less* unpleasant to the adepts than to their matched controls. The adepts showed *lesser* degrees of anxiety-related baseline fMRI signal activity in three regions while they waited on the brink of being exposed to pain: their left anterior insula, anterior mid cingulate cortex, and amygdala. However, they also showed *more* fMRI activity in these insula and cingulate sites *during* the pain. Importantly, as the hot stimulus continued, the fMRI signals from these same regions then habituated *more* rapidly. The lesser degree of anticipatory reactivity found in the experts' amygdala just *before* the pain was also associated with this faster neural habituation that occurred in their anterior mid cingulate cortex *during* the actual pain.

The findings appear consistent with the possibility that these advanced meditators had already arrived at subtle *attitudes* of openness and acceptance. Attitudes referable to our limbic and paralimbic regions underlie our awareness and covertly influence it. In expert meditators, these attitudes could still enable pain to be experienced but not to go on to develop its usual unpleasant subjective resonances. It is of interest that some advanced Tibetan practitioners can also include intervals of thought-free vastness during their openly receptive state of "open presence." [ZBR: 397] (see chapter 11).

To review every important new advance in meditation research is far beyond the scope of this slender book. However, contemporary meditation research is beginning to meet appropriate basic standards [ZBR: 214–215], and comments on a sample of recent relevant reports are included in the Notes section.[7, 8]

Serial fMRI Changes as Awareness Becomes Thought-Free

Erb and Sitaram's study of meditation specifies the particular kind of awareness that becomes free of thoughts.[9] [ZB: 96–99, 141]. They monitored Thich Thong Triet, a meditation expert of decades-long experience, and eight experienced members of this master's sangha. Their approach to Sunyata (emptiness) meditation is especially relevant to the thesis outlined in chapters 1, 6, and 13. Their practice centers on the "just this" kind of selfless advice that was condensed for Bahiya and Malunkya millennia earlier.

How do Erb and Sitaram summarize the way this technique guides its practitioners? They choose capital letters to characterize it with the explicit phrase "Not Naming the Object." In short, these experienced practitioners have learned to settle into bare, open-eyed forms of *wordless* neural processing when they meditate. This natural approach enables them increasingly to see, hear, feel, and "know" the objects within their experience, yet to steer clear of any impulse to attach word-thoughts or allied concepts to what they are experiencing. Zen is on familiar ground with the "just this" approach (see chapters 3, 5 and 6).

In this respect, the condensed results of six separate study sessions with Master Thong Triet are noteworthy. They summarize how his thoughts drop out during four successively deeper levels of his meditative awareness. These successive levels are on the path of the meditative absorptions. [ZBR: 313–322] The words used by this Sunyata School describe these levels as

1. verbal awareness (the usual inner silent verbal dialogue that tags the in-breath with one word and the out-breath with another);

2. tacit awareness (the ordinary kinds of awareness that attend, in fewer words, to one's usual daily activities);

3. awakening awareness (the states of increasingly clear enhanced awareness that can exist during walking, standing, sitting or lying down, after these acts have become relatively free from subjective wordy intrusions);

4. cognition awareness (the deepest stage of meditation, during which all thought stops and breathing can stop occasionally (e.g., for 15 seconds, in the case of this master).

In brief, as meditation deepens successively, certain initial fMRI activations fall. Especially reduced are those signals that had been so prominent in both superior temporal gyri during the person's usual nonvocalized internal dialogue. Moreover, activation increases elsewhere at about the same time: in the right inferior frontal gyrus, right insula, right cerebellum, and visual association cortex (BA 18/19 L>R). (See figure 3.1, together with figure 11.1 and its color counterpart, plate 1.)

In the group analysis of all meditators, two *de*activations coincided with the gradual disappearance of discursive thoughts. These deactivations occurred in their prefrontal polar cortex (BA 10) and in their posterior cingulate region (see figure 3.1). As meditation deepened, the semantic language regions of their superior temporal gyrus also became *less* activated at the same time as their visual association cortex became *more* activated (BA 18, 19). These several examples of reciprocal change will become of special interest with regard to a working hypothesis: occipital lobe *disinhibition* provides a potential explanation for the release of some visual phenomena during meditation (see chapter 12).

First-Person Reports of Long-Term Transformations of Awareness

The subtitle of this book refers to Living Zen. To live Zen is to be grounded in directly experiencing, and responding to, the fresh living reality of each present moment. [ZB: 76–77; SI: 13, 203–205; MS: 137–138] The title of this chapter specifies that these mindful qualities *begin* as awareness of the present moment. [ZB: 125–129] Chapter 2 indicated that as meditation evolves, an interesting tendency develops: the *scope and clarity* of one's mental space seems to expand. To these two impressions, we have just now added *sati's* original overview attributes of remindfulness. Some practitioners notice other refinements of their awareness. One variety can be described as "ever-present awareness." [ZBR: 184–187] Transcendental meditation practitioners report that this sense of an ongoing awareness extends itself even into their sleep. This particular quality is then described as "witnessing sleep."

Robert Forman is a professor of comparative religion at City University of New York. He has practiced transcendental meditation for the past 43 years. He once described this extra quality of awareness as being "ready for things, even in the depths of sleep." [ZBR: 237] Forman's introspective accounts can serve here as a useful springboard for further discussion. They are summarized in a long article in the *Network Review*.[10] He describes how his consciousness changed as the result of a significant shift that occurred in January 1972. Four sentences condense the nature of this change: "Behind everything I am and do now came to be a sense of silence, a bottomless emptiness, so open as to be without end. This silence bears a sense of spaciousness or vastness, which extends in every direction. This silent expanse is not something I have to remember to be; it takes absolutely no effort to maintain it. It is as effortless to be this as it is to have a right hand."

Forman's vast new silence had four main features:

1. Background thoughts disappeared. Yet an element of promise was implicit in this seeming absence. By this, he means that a gratuitous *subconscious* process of *incubation* was still going on. The example he gives is what happens when a student asks him a question. Although he is aware that his conscious mind is "completely silent," yet the correct answer still pops up to the surface of his mind out of the background of this "richly pregnant silence." (Chapters 12, 13, and 14 in the present volume provide other examples of the creative, problem-solving potentials that are inherent in this less cluttered

mental space. It is suggested that one's intuitions become free to bob up to the surface of consciousness once the chattering distractions drop off that had previously entangled the whole mental field.)

2.   A shift occurred in who or what I am. Forman's earlier tight subjective sense of "who I am" became more like an "it."

3.   A further shift occurred into "witness consciousness." While this involved both "seeing and at the same time being *aware* of the seeing," these intervals did not seem dual. Instead, each moment was witnessed in a "quite natural and integrated manner." Each moment was "utterly effortless" and "astonishingly fresh!"

4.   A similar natural and unobtrusive witnessing awareness occurred during sleep (as referred to above).

As a long-term meditation practitioner, Professor Forman's apt descriptions are in keeping with the first-person reports of many others who describe a persistent, ongoing shift in the relationships that had previously existed in their perceptual awareness and in their underlying sense of Self.[11] He is familiar with the religious literature that describes enlightenment as "glorious gloriousness" and "absolute perfection." However, none of his personal experiences presented themselves in this exalted manner. Instead, to him, "Enlightenment is the unmingling of a commingled reality."

•   What does this last sentence mean?

Let's begin with what seems to constitute our everyday ordinary sense of reality. We have observed that it actually contains a blend of *two* components: the *Self* frame of reference (dominant, overt) and the *other* frame of reference (subordinate, covert). Therefore, when Forman refers to a commingled reality, his words would seem to be describing the components of this everyday duality, this complex merger of these *two* versions of reality: egocentric and allocentric (see chapter 3).

- How do we blend these two functional compartments into one impression?

Our brain registers stimuli as signals from the outside environment. In the early milliseconds, it reorganizes these messages into patterns. We use our own powerful Self-centeredness to squeeze these patterns into our own personal frame of reference and co-opt them as our percepts.

The last three sentences help us understand the concise "unmingling" to which Forman referred. In neural terms, unmingling corresponds with a deep shift. This shift allows the existing, yet hidden allocentric frame of reference to assume a novel overt prominence throughout the whole foreground field of consciousness. No longer must this other-centered perspective play its former subordinate role to our Self-centeredness. Now out in the open, so to speak, it infuses consciousness with an astonishing, fresh perspective.

Forman had commented decades before that most of the "pure consciousness events" that occur during meditation tend to be "rudimentary." [ZBR: 391–392] Some of these simpler forms of conscious awareness would seem to represent only minor changes within meditators' ventral and dorsal attention systems, those co-sponsored by the more ordinary shifts that can occur in thalamic and subthalamic regions. [ZB: 402–404] During such rudimentary events, some trivial word thoughts and other dispensable mental processing could be bypassed and briefly drop out of the field of consciousness.

- What about those other key qualities of our mental space—the complete silence, effortlessness and spaciousness—that Forman also mentioned?

To the degree that they permeated and transformed his own awareness, they could appear consistent with what he currently conceptualizes as "the first state of enlightenment." Such an ongoing development would represent an *entry stage* on the very long Path toward the culmination that words might try to describe as "the great unmingling."

Forman's account describes the fact that he suffered from acute anxiety when he was an adolescent and a young adult. In candor, he then explains that neither his many years of meditation nor these qualities of silence that had entered his ongoing awareness served to reverse his severe anxiety problems. Therefore, he still sought psychotherapy for these symptoms,[12] a reminder to all readers that meditation is no panacea.[13]

One of his current goals is intriguing. He says this goal is "to live jazz in the soul, and under any circumstance, on the subtle ground of spiritual spaciousness." Qualities of spaciousness were among those included in that mature ripening of awareness that can develop during long-term meditation (see chapter 2).

- But where does living jazz fit into a book about living Zen?

Its spontaneity is part of the competence that can arise and be manifested in intuitive behavioral responses. [ZB: 119–125; 668–677] (Soon it will be hinted at by Louis Armstrong's remark in the epigraph that opens part IV). Jazz also entered into a report about meditators by Brown and Engler.[14] [ZB: 132–134] These authors used the Rorschach test to study trainees who were at different stages along the Path of Theravada Buddhist meditation. Four of the subjects in the more advanced group had previously experienced states of insight. Given that these prior insights had struck an impersonal note, would their responses to inkblots also be more impersonal? No. Instead, these meditators' Rorschach responses proved to be "deeply human and fraught with the richness of the living process." The advanced meditators were responding in ways that were not only creative but that also made abundant metaphoric use of color. [ZBR: 229–232] Their behaviors demonstrated "a very unusual quality and richness of life experience." Indeed, it was described as like "the extemporaneous music of a jazz musician."

In 2008, Limb and Braun reported an excellent fMRI study of professional jazz pianists.[15] [SI: 149] Notably, *during* their spontaneous jazz improvisations, the pianists were activating two high-level association regions. One was their prefrontal cortex at its dorsal medial pole (BA 10; see figure 3.1). The other was their anterior temporal cortex (BA 20–22; see figure 2.1 and chapter 14). Simultaneously, they were *de*activating their dorsolateral frontal cortex, their lateral orbitofrontal cortex, and many sites in their limbic system. [ZBR: 159–160] In contrast, the task for the jazz musicians in a different study was simply to listen to someone *else* playing on the piano. These 22 subjects then had only to decide whether those melodies were being improvised or were merely being imitated.[16] Those melodies judged to have been improvised did strike a responsive chord, in one sense, for they generated more activation in the listener's amygdala. Improvisations also activated the listeners' anterior insula/frontal operculum region.[17] [SI: 253–257]

The creativity we hear expressed in authentic jazz improvisations seems to flow effortlessly, from the bottom up. The fluid creativity expressed in some art forms provides a visual counterpart for this auditory receptivity. Robert Henri

(1865–1929) was an outstanding art teacher most noted for creating realistic oil paintings spontaneously. He said this about his own style of letting go: "The object isn't to make art. It's to be in that wonderful state which makes art inevitable." [SI: 123, 143, 313]

Vago's review illustrates why awareness is more complex than is generally appreciated.[18] This chapter began by considering subtle ways that the normal background processes of awareness evolve in form and content in during years of meditative training. The next chapter continues to discuss the emergent qualities that can permeate the matrix of awareness of long-term meditators.

10

Subconscious Background Qualities That Can Infuse Awareness

Explanations and demonstrations are only expedients to help you realize intuitive understanding.

Ch'an Master Foyan Quingyuan (1067–1120)[1]

Actually true activity is intuitive activity, free from various desires and restrictions.

Shunryu Suzuki-Roshi (1904–1971)[2]

These two statements, eight centuries apart, emphasize that long-term meditative training cultivates *intuitive* skills. This chapter continues to explore how some background attitudes that infuse the form and content of our awareness could evolve in ways that slowly contribute to states of awakening.

To begin with, when we sense that some small insight rings true for us, the connections in our association networks are likely to have joined up in a special way (see appendix B). [ZB: 386–387] Many of these meaningful neural links that lend an impression of certainty will tap into ordinary varieties of our temporal lobe processing functions. These sophisticated networks reflect our covert conditionings, subconscious recollections, long-forgotten expectations, and primal preattentive codes not yet given names. [SI: 141–146]

Let's be clear about what this last sentence implies. For meditators, it means that because most of their normal, ordinary waking awareness and perceptions are functioning at pre-conscious levels, they are probably developing new capacities—silent skills they are not *aware* of—to retrieve potentially useful portions of this subconscious information. [MS: 145–163]

Strick and colleagues conducted two experiments on Zen meditators that lend support to this statement.[3] The 63 meditators in the first experiment had completed six months to five years of prior Zen practice. Between 6 p.m. and 9 p.m., one Zen group was led by a Zen master and meditated for 20 minutes. The second Zen group served as controls. They relaxed, without meditating, also for 20 minutes. Both groups then went to individual cubicles. There they performed three sets of five Remote Associates Tests using a computer screen. (For example, given three words, search your remote associations for that single fourth word that they all share in common.) The subjects who had just meditated solved more test items (7.00) than did those subjects who had merely relaxed (5.94). The results were statistically significant, $p = .02$.

In the second experiment, the response times of 32 Zen meditators were measured during similar word association tests. Again, the subjects who had just meditated solved more Remote Associates Test items than did the controls (6.82 vs. 4.87), $p < .01$. They also solved them faster (in only 13.22 seconds vs. 16.37 seconds), $p < .05$. In addition, the groups were then asked to free-associate to a new collection of 20 questions. However, in this instance, each question might have not one but three or four possible answers (e.g., "Can you name one of the four seasons?"). This time—*before* each question—a priming-word answer was supplied *subliminally* on the screen (e.g., "summer"). No subject could see this priming word consciously because it lasted only 16 milliseconds.

The question was: Could meditation unveil any *subconscious* receptivities for this subliminal priming? If so, would this hidden awareness enable the subliminal priming word to reshape the answer? The meditators' answers did match the hidden priming words at the p = .06 level, just short of statistical significance. In contrast, the relaxed control group showed no priming effect.

The Remote Associates Test is often interpreted as a test for verbal creativity, a task that combines an initial divergent search with convergence functions. Therefore, the experiments suggest that these particular Zen meditators (who had been tested while meditating in the *evening*) showed evidence consistent with enhanced creative processing. [SI: 125–130, 154–188] Chapter 14 continues this discussion.

Maturing over the Decades

Functional MRI research confirms that adults develop more hierarchical depth in the ways they process awareness than do juveniles.[4] [SI: 237–244] Decades ago, it might have sufficed to say that one's brain simply learns by being exposed to life's experiences. Now a more technical term for such learning is *neuroplasticity*. Both terms involve multitudes of implicit mechanisms and prompt us to ask how decades of practicing a living Zen might influence one's development as a mature person. [ZBR: 137–141, 347, 399–401]

Carl Jung (1875–1961) drew attention to the fact that our moral capacities and attitudes evolve during the later decades. He used the word individuation to refer to this maturation. Individuation did not mean the selfish behavior of a Self-centered individual. Rather, it identified a normal developmental process, one that helps to *unify* each individual person's modes of cognition and behavior *at both conscious and subconscious* levels. The results enable our full range of adult options to be actualized fruitfully in intelligent, affirmative, adaptive behavior.

Keil and Freund recently tested the responses of 217 subjects from rural Germany to a wide range of visual and verbal stimuli.[5] This population ranged in age from 18 to 81 years. The subjects who were younger responded more to the emotional content of pleasant pictures and words. In contrast, the older subjects tended to respond with *dis*pleasure when they encountered topics that they perceived as arousing.

Multiple aspects of maturity can be nurtured in meditators who persist on the mindful, introspective Path of long-term training. [ZB: 125–129] The earliest steps along this continuum move us beyond our childish *I-Me-Mine* attitudes and selfish behaviors. The next steps transform these pejorative qualities in directions that represent the *You-Us-Ours* kinds of allocentric and *eco*centric identification. In later stages, these ideal mature reprogrammings tap further into the native resources of our potential virtues. Ultimately, the gradual transformations of character can evolve toward unbounded kindliness (Sanskrit: *maitri*). Meditators who happen to drop into major awakenings along this Path can accelerate this slow process of subconscious ripening. [ZBR: 394–396; SI: 239]

Vaillant provides a useful analysis of the way this normal process of adaptive coping evolves longitudinally in a college population that was followed carefully for 75 years.[6]

The state of kensho is infused by a direct, authoritative impression: these experiential perceptions *are* real Reality. [ZB: 543, 573–578; ZBR: 335–342, 366–371, 422–424] This novel comprehension of all things as *THEY REALLY* are strikes instantly. Its amplified interpretation of reality seems perfectly obvious. It penetrates internally with the same direct, unshakable certainty one feels when one swallows cold cider on a hot day. This immediacy of direct experience enters long before any notion might arise that words could burden the event with the label "cold cider." [ZB: 599]

Geologists provided us with the term, "plate tectonics." For meditators on the long Path, major awakenings seem to accomplish an abrupt shift in *trait tectonics*. The depths revealed during such deepenings leave a strong, residual impression: consciousness has undergone a shift at its *core*, not at its surface. In contrast, meditators' other "continental drifts" of character change evolve so slowly as to be almost unnoticeable. On the other hand, old friends can appreciate the cumulative results of these incremental shifts in retrospect if they witness them after a long interval.

During ordinary events when we experience scenes in three-dimensions, the right hippocampus and amygdala co-activate early while we register the gross incidental details. In later milliseconds, the temporal lobe cortex helps us recognize finer, discrete patterns, aided by its right perirhinal region and the cortex at the temporal pole.[7] During the state of kensho, it is plausible to consider that a brain could be registering several levels of somewhat similar comprehensions. Simultaneously, it could be accessing other pathways represented among value systems relatively near the allocentric pathways. These deeper levels that confer a sense of coherent perfection had not been tapped into before to this degree. [SI: 141–152] Once these rare semantic functions are engaged, they could be amplified by disinhibition at the same instant that one's overintrusive egocentric networks had dropped out their prior sense of Self. [ZB: 605–607; SI: 180]

Non-Duality

Some traditions reserve the term *non-dual*, to describe major states of awakened insight that are impregnated with existential meaning. *Non-dual* implies that only *one* view of reality replaces our conventional commingled, (egocentric >> allocentric) versions of everyday reality. At whatever level such states of oneness are experienced, their perspective is novel. It seems to lie beyond every conceptual belief system that the person had used previously to divide the whole world into only two separate categories, Self versus other.

A visual attempt was made to illustrate that such a model state of insight-wisdom lacks this split into two divisions, (that it is in fact *non*-dual). [ZBR: 339–341] Those two parallel compartments, which had previously represented the Self/other split, were depicted as transformed into oneness. The concepts of non-duality and intersubjectivity are currently being applied to psychotherapy and meditation.[8] Two recent books based on personal interviews are available for readers interested in the diversity of interpretation within this general topic of awakening and non-duality.[9, 10]

Reality

Meanwhile, it is clear that the extraordinary states of awakening differ from those other kinds of conventional "realness" that researchers are trying to measure under artificial conditions. For example, some laboratory experiments describe tests for the usual sense of "realness" that infuses ordinary reality. The investigators create events that are actually experienced, then contrast them with make-believe events that the subjects had only imagined.[11] Under such experimental conditions, "real" events are still associated with increased fMRI signals in such appropriate limbic sites as the left posterior cingulate cortex and ventral anterior cingulate cortex (other sites include the right precuneus and presupplementary motor area).[12]

The insular cortex has extensive functional connections with limbic and paralimbic regions. [ZBR: 95–99; SI: 253–256; MS: 20, 102] These make it difficult to untangle an authoritative impression of certainty and attribute it solely to some defect of prediction caused by a dysfunction of the insula per se.[13] [ZB: 542–544]

- Given that an authentic state of deep awakening is more intimately experienced than ordinary reality, what else might infuse this state with the impression that it is manifesting an ultimate degree of significance?

Some of its intrinsic sense of novelty could be explained by the fact that this moment —for the very *first* time— is now dominated exclusively by allocentric processing. Some of its special quality of direct salience could come by virtue of an accelerated rate of preattentive processing, one sustained at *sub*cortical levels for longer than usual. [ZB: 529; SI: 35–36,139–141]

- What is the implication of the fact that each of this author's two different alternate states of consciousness occurred in a novel environmental setting, a place where he had never been before?

I've always been a curious-minded person. Novelty stimulates me to ask adverbial questions.[14] [ZB: 285–286;

ZBR: 159, 165] Gallagher estimates that some 15 percent of normal people become highly stimulated when they are in fresh surroundings.[15] They also tend to exhibit more approach behaviors when the environmental settings are unfamiliar. She uses the term, *neophiliacs*, to describe people who are especially drawn toward novelty.

In contrast, *neophobes* tend to show avoidance behaviors. This category of risk-averse people makes up another 15 percent of the population. Thus, the remaining term, *neophiles*, applies to the majority of people (some 70%). When they encounter the unfamiliar, neophiles respond with intermediate degrees of mild curiosity and interested awareness.

The next chapter provides examples of how remaining open and curious can lead to unexpected benefits.

Part IV

Looking Out into the Distance above the Horizon

Questioner: Why do you always look *up* while you're playing the horn?

Louis (Satchmo) Armstrong: I don't know what I'm looking for, but I always find it.

Reprocessing Emotionally Traumatic Imagery While Elevating the Gaze

> I will lift up mine eyes unto the hills, from whence cometh my help.
>
> Old Testament, Psalm 121 (King James Version)

The treble clef signifies the upper registers of a musical score. This chapter also involves looking *up*, this time into our superior visual fields. It begins with a story about two adult women. At a young age, each had undergone a major episode of emotional trauma. Later, as a mature adult, each woman in her own unique way stumbled into an empirical approach, one that would dissolve the emotional distress attached to her earlier traumatic event. First she revisualized this old disturbing memory. Then she projected the scene *up* toward her *superior visual fields and out into the distance*.

This pair of observations suggests a novel, testable working hypothesis: by elevating the line of sight and *revisualizing the event above the horizon*, networks representing these *upper* visual fields *out there* are enabled to access other reprocessing mechanisms that have the potential to relieve early, major psychic trauma.

This narrative has a fourfold purpose: (1) to specify how each subject proceeds to revisualize and reprocess in her upper visual fields, (2) to review recent research suggesting mechanisms that could help relieve various degrees of emotional trauma, (3) to stimulate investigators to critically evaluate this empirical approach in a larger, diverse patient population, and (4) to place elevations of gaze in a larger context that includes meditative practice, intuition, and creativity.

Background

This chapter began unexpectedly in 2010. It evolved during a training conference for chaplains at the Upaya Zen Center in Santa Fe, New Mexico. As one of the lecturers, I was describing the two ways that meditation techniques train our attention (see chapter 3). To illustrate how these differ physiologically, I projected and discussed the slide version of color plate 1 (see also figure 11.1). The caption explains how our *top-down* attention proceeds in an executive manner, an approach that is often deliberately focused and requires

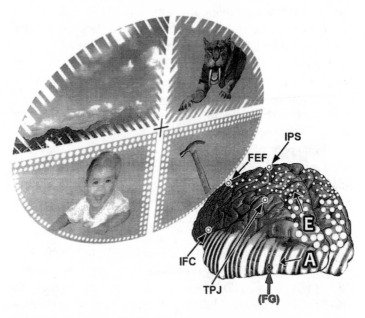

Figure 11.1 Egocentric and allocentric attentive processing; major differences in their efficiencies. (See also color plate 1).

This view contrasts our dorsal *egocentric*, top-down networks with those other networks representing our ventral *allocentric*, bottom-up pathways. Your vantage point is from a position behind the *left* hemisphere, looking at the lower end of the occipital lobes.

Figure 11.1 (Continued) This person's brain is shown gazing up and off to the left into quadrants of scenery. The items here are imaginary. The baby and the hammer are in the space down close to the person. The scenery above and the tiger are off at a distance.

Starting at the top of the brain are the two cortical modules of the top-down attention system: the intraparietal sulcus (IPS) and the frontal eye field (FEF). They serve as the attentive vanguards for our subsequent sensory processing and goal-oriented executive behavior. Notice how they are overlapped by the upward trajectory of the *upper* parietal → frontal egocentric (**E**) system. It is shown as an arc composed of white circles. Notice that rows of similar white circles also surround the *lower* visual quadrants containing the baby (at left) and the hammer (at right). Why? To indicate that this dorsal, "northern" attention system could attend more efficiently—on a shorter path with a lesser wiring cost—to these *lower* visual quadrants. This enables our parietal lobe senses of *touch* and *proprioception* to handle easily such important items down close to our own body.

In contrast, our two other modules for cortical attention reside lower down, also over the outside of the brain. They are the temporoparietal junction (TPJ) and the regions of the inferior frontal cortex (IFC). During bottom-up attention, we activate these modules of the ventral attention system, chiefly on the *right* side of the brain. They can engage relatively easily the networks of allocentric processing nearby (**A**). The diagonal white lines that represent these *lower* temporal → frontal networks is also seen to surround the *upper* visual fields. Why?

This is to suggest the ways this lower ("southern") pathway is poised globally to use its specialized pattern recognition systems. These are based on our senses of vision and audition. Each serves to identify items off *at a distance* away from our body and to infuse them with meaningful interpretations. The FG in parenthesis points to this pathway's inclusion of the left fusiform gyrus. This region, hidden on the undersurface of the temporal lobe, contributes to complex visual associations, including our sense of colors.

effort. In contrast, the *bottom-up* approach engages awareness effortlessly in a more reflexive, global manner. The neural basis of these distinctions is well established.[1, 2]

This same color slide also illustrated two important practical outcomes:

* We express an inherently Self-centered bias when we use our *upper* occipital → parietal → frontal pathways. These help us focus on things close to our own bodies—the baby and the hammer. Messages that flow along this so-called "Where?" pathway pursue a dorsal trajectory. This pathway has links with our superior parietal lobule. We represent our body *schema* here. The overlappings between this *somatosensory association cortex* and our dorsal attention system are very important. They enable us to reach out efficiently to grasp things in *nearby* space. Therefore, the programs coded among these upper, "northern" networks are poised to do much more than simply ask "*Where*?" In fact, their circuits help us solve a most urgent spatial question: "*Where is this thing in relation to Me and My body*?" Notice how much our physical sense of *Self-centeredness* is implicit along this upper frame of reference.

* A second, very different category of cognitive functions exists. Notice that it begins *anonymously* along the *lower* pathways of attentive processing. This is the so-called "*What* is it?" route. It starts farther down in the *ventral* occipital → temporal region. Thereafter, the trajectory of this "southern" stream extends forward through the temporal lobe and into the *inferior* frontal cortex. Along this lower pathway, many interactive functions express an outward-looking, *allocentric* frame of reference. These are coded for "other" efficiencies. They begin with an early orientation toward recognizing objects that might present themselves (1) in the *superior* visual fields, and (2) *out there, farther from our body.* The distant scenery and the ancient predator are the examples shown in figure 11.1. Noteworthy in this regard are special *semantic* skills. These

arise nearby among the temporal lobe's networks of associations. These adjacent skill sets do more than help this lower processing stream identify objects. They also help this pathway imbue with *meaning* what it sees and hears. This semantic pathway not only asks, "*What* is it?" It also asks, urgently, "*What does it mean?*"

At this conference the next day, an experienced clinical psychologist lectured on ways to reduce the stressful impact of psychic trauma. During the discussion period that followed her presentation, she added a personal story. Why? Because it illustrated how suddenly and completely she herself had once been relieved—while in a classroom *seven years earlier*—of her major fear. This fear had haunted her since her teenage years.

Her vignette (in the next section) prompted further questions and comments from me, especially in view of the points that were illustrated with the slide and discussed the day before. What was special about the particular spatial context in which her emotional relief had occurred? Why was she suddenly relieved while she was reprocessing this old traumatic scene *above* her usual eye level and in the domain of her *upper visual fields*?

An audience member had witnessed each of our presentations and each of the open discussions that followed. She became intrigued. On her own initiative, she came to this decision: she would project—into *her* upper visual fields— her most emotionally traumatic event. This episode of intense fear had deeply troubled her since she was a child. Encouraged by her empirical results, she then sought me out. This led to her becoming the subject of the second case report.

I interviewed each person separately during this conference. Each subject was contacted by telephone several times subsequently, submitted a typewritten narrative report, reviewed her condensed report, and gave written permission for its publication. (Their initials are changed.)

Case Report 1

K.K. is a 57-year-old Ph.D. clinical psychologist who has an active private practice. Her extensive professional experience has been sought during major national and international disasters. In this role, she has helped patients and caregivers cope with stress following severe physical and mental trauma. This narrative begins by describing what she had experienced during the revisualization in that class seven years earlier.

In 2003 she was taking a training course in a biologically based approach to relieving psychological trauma. She had volunteered to be the subject for an in-class demonstration. She took a seat in front of the class. There she sat, facing the woman who was her teacher. The setting felt comfortable and safe. When the teacher invited her to revisualize one major traumatic episode, she chose the dramatic event that happened when she was 14 years old.

She revisualized her mother standing in front of her.

"My mother and her husband were having a fight. One of them held a knife and it had sliced the other person's hand. I can't remember who cut whom. All I can see in my images of this scene is the bleeding hand.

"The teacher then asked me to broaden my view beyond the bleeding hand. As I gazed into this scene in the kitchen, I saw the window in the background above the kitchen sink."

During this next phase of her revisualized narrative, she gazed *up* and *out* through this 3-foot by 4-foot window. "It was night, and there were stars outside in the sky. I looked out the window and had the sense of being connected to the universe in a way that made all the emotions linked with this scene in the kitchen much less frightening, even insignificant . . . a sense of calm washed over me."

During this unusually calming wave of consciousness, and while feeling "this connection to the vaster world outside the kitchen window," she also remained distantly aware that she was describing the event in front of the class. But something crucial had happened: she was *immediately relieved* from all fear. Before this moment in class, "I could not go to bed at night if a knife was in the dish drainer." After that classroom session seven years ago—after her awareness shifted up beyond the bleeding hand and out through the window—"I no longer had that fear."

Notice a distinction: she did not deliberately intend to look up in class in order to gaze out through that kitchen window. This happened. In the remote past, she had been only vaguely aware that a suggestible subject who made a willfully *strained* effort to substantially elevate the gaze might enter into a trance. However, she excluded deliberate straining as an explanation for any of the events that had unfolded *spontaneously* after her revisualization of the event back in the kitchen became elevated beyond the bleeding hand.

Case Report 2

O.R. is a 57-year-old former school system secretary. She was enrolled in this 2010 Upaya conference. It was her idea to test the process of deliberately gazing up and out. The first major traumatic event she chose to revisualize was an episode of fear. This fear had haunted her since she was 11 years old.

The First Observation

The first revisualization she selected was the dramatic nighttime episode when her stepfather tried to molest her. They were alone in the front seat of his car. He had stopped the car on a bridge. She remembers being "deathly afraid" of falling off the bridge and down into the canal 60 feet below. She was strong enough to wrestle him away from her. Among her traumatic emotions was the feeling that her mother had abandoned her by not protecting her from his advances.

She chose the word *retrieval* to summarize the mental processing steps involved in recalling and revisualizing this traumatic episode. First, she deliberately raised her chin up in order to elevate her line of sight above her usual visual horizon. Next, she imagined herself back inside the car in that scene of intimate conflict. She then "proceeded to look past him, out the driver's side window, and up at the distant trees. The trees appeared soft and shimmery in the moonlight. They were a hundred yards or so away, off to my right and twenty to thirty feet above where I was looking." Though the moon itself was blocked by the car roof, "it was a bright moon, and it lighted the treetops. Looking up at the trees, there was simply a feeling of peace."

"When I looked back then into the car, or do so now, the scene is simply an image. The pain, the fear, the feeling of abandonment is softened. I see that he is just an ignorant man, raised by a child molester himself, and simply a product of his childhood. The fear is gone; I have escaped, now, by way of the trees. I can't be hurt from this point on. My mother, too, is forgiven. She has not abandoned me to this result; she is simply who she is, trying to survive in her own little world. Using this technique, I have since returned to this image many times. It remains soft and inconsequential. I have been growing up. It's over. I can *let it go*. It's not hardwired anymore. It's no longer a lump in my throat, but a warmth and forgiveness."

Subsequent Observations That Day at the Conference

Twenty minutes later, encouraged by the success of this first experiment, she decided to test this new technique on another kind of emotional episode that remained deeply disturbing. Major feelings of green-eyed jealousy, not fear, had led to its deep, intense, ongoing emotional discomfort. This traumatic incident had occurred when she was an adult. It happened during a wedding reception. At this time, her "significant other" (now her husband) was describing to her how he had been flirting with an attractive young unmarried woman wearing a black dress. Once again, she *gazed up* while she retrieved this scene and reimaged it high up at an angle toward the line "where the wall joins the ceiling."

"I took my feelings of shame and embarrassment up to that line, allowed their power to push and disseminate in that area." The next dynamic process of revisualization lifted her man up by his shirt to the level of this ceiling and then projected him out through the French doors at the end of the hall. From there, the retrieval process tossed him up into space and "far out into the sun." At this point, a substantial softening dissolved the intense jealousy attached to the earlier scene. Reviewing this episode subsequently, she found all earlier "shame and embarrassment" had also vanished. It "feels more like the memory of a bad party, but is no longer personal. Looking back on the scene now, I see the young woman as simply who and where she is in her life— single, without a man, when mine looked good and was promoting himself to her."

Later Observations

Back home, after this 2010 conference ended, she applied the technique successfully a week later to relieve a second major instance of jealousy. She had felt this emotion intensely ever since a separate episode in 2006, *after* she and her partner were married. During a dance, her husband was on the sidelines. He was obviously enjoying the dancing movements of a different woman in a black dress, and she was also reciprocating his attention. During this retrieval, she projected both her husband and this new dancing lady out the door of the dance area, down a long hall, out through the lobby area in back, into the parking lot, and then "up into the blue sky of late afternoon." At this point, the revisualization now "veered to the right, toward the light of the sun, and I just let them go."

During this dispersal up into the sky, no hand of hers is the actual lifting agency. Instead, the two persons are somehow "magically retrieved by the front of their shirt and dress," then raised toward the ceiling and out the door up into the sky. "I let them go there. It gives me pleasure and more relief and a deeper fading of the details when I retrieve the image and take it outside and into the sky. Usually, taking it outside and up is *BEST*."

To project her visual imagery *down below* the horizontal "had never been part of my approach—they would hit the pavement." Yet, she did project her imagery to a slightly lower site above the horizon during a fourth experiment. On this occasion, reported six months later in a letter, her objective was to relieve strong negative feelings of resentment toward two persons who had earlier jeopardized her relationship with her husband. In this instance, she first gazed up at an angle of only 5 degrees above the horizon. She then revisualized the couple as standing a *long distance* away from her "in an ice field in Northern Europe (an image new to me, and never seen before). I walked them out on the ice, up an incline to an elevation some 300 yards away, where their feet seemed only about at my chest level . . . Then I simply asked them to go.

At this point, I felt a lifting of the hurt they had caused. I can now sit in the same room with them and not feel pain."

Using this technique of elevating her line of sight while reimaging and reprocessing up and out, O.R. has markedly softened and dissolved the emotional distress linked with each of her years-old episodes of deep-seated fear, jealousy, and resentment. Notice, as in case report 1, that all four emotionally distressing events were retrieved out of very *long-term* memory. Each abrupt release from this range of emotionally traumatic events had occurred after she had first been ruminating over them for *years*.

Current, Less Traumatic Incidents Require an Interval of Cooling

O.R. then identified, by herself, an important temporal limitation in the effectiveness of this technique. Back home, again after the conference, she recounted a less stressful emotional experience. Shortly after the latest heated argument with her 19-year-old daughter, she went off by herself, retrieved the image of this fresh incident, and again looked up toward the ceiling. This time her revisualization "did NOT work. I was still angry and hurt. *Things still felt too hot. The episode had to cool before I could put it into storage.*" Then, after things had time to cool overnight, her *next* morning's revisualization proved effective. Subsequently, this prior, ongoing troubling relationship with her daughter became softened. "Now I can stand outside the fray, a little easier. I'm still a Mom. I still worry and hurt for her, but I know that relief from these arguments is possible." This episode suggests that reprocessing emotionally traumatic imagery while elevating the gaze is not effective until after the acute emotional incident has *cooled*. The duration of such requisite cooling periods remains to be determined.

Reviewing Salient Details of These Revisualizations

- The basic operational mode is *gazing up and out in a gentle manner*. No repetitive eye movements enter into these gently *sustained* revisualizations.

- The reimaged scene begins, as did the original trauma, with visual details inside the space *near the subject*. Events shift during the next phase. Now the revisualized scene is registered at elevations above the usual eye level, *off at a distance* far beyond this earlier envelope of close, threatening, immediate peripersonal space.

- The primary emotional incident is now reprocessed in a new spatial perspective *above* the usual visual horizon. It is accessing events referable chiefly within the space occupied by the subjects' prior *superior* visual fields.

- Older traumatic memories can undergo a substantial emotional release when projected out and reprocessed into the distant sky. This can be a nighttime sky or a daytime sky, sunny or ice-cold.

- The revisualization experience in case report 1 developed its own momentum *involuntarily*. This occurred *after* K.K. was invited to *broaden* her field of vision. This next phase evolved spontaneously. It swept her awareness upward, out through the window, and into the starry sky beyond.

- Subject O.R. begins her several upward and outward revisualizations more *intentionally*. Her introductory phase involves deliberate top-down attentive processing. This continues in an upward direction toward elevations some 30 to 45 degrees *above* her usual visual horizon. The next reprocessings reflect her freedom to liberate dynamic, creative imagery at long distances.

- In retrospect, O.R. regards her abrupt releases from major degrees of long-sustained emotional distress as resembling the kinds of "growing up" insights involved in natural maturation.

- While an acute, emotionally stressful incident remains hot, it requires a cooling-off interval for the technique to be effective.

Psychophysiological Considerations

The author is a skeptical clinician. Like the reader, my first inclination might easily have been to dismiss such reports as anecdotal and empirical. However, the subjects' substantial verbal, behavioral, and written documentation verifies that each of their most deep-seated fears was relieved suddenly and thoroughly. Moreover, by way of explanation, a review of the literature identifies *seven* relevant lines of research. These converge in support of a novel working hypothesis: Traumatic memories have some potential to be relieved when the sensorimotor act of gaze has access to the mental reprocessing space represented *above and beyond* one's usual visual horizon.

1. Psychological Dimensions of Perception in Superior Space and Distant Space

Our dominant mode of top-down attention is Self-centered. Where do we routinely point most of our visual fixation? We direct it toward one small central spot of concentrated fine-grained focusing. Yet, the whole of ambient space also supplies a wealth of important information. [ZB: 487-495] Space was so important a topic to William James that he devoted 148 pages to the chapter on space in his classic textbook on psychology, more pages than to any other subject.[3] Notice the special feeling we have about this envelope of space close to our own body. It is "*our* turf." We "own" it. We guard it from others. A beneficial anonymity develops when we *let go* of all the maladaptive conditioning that causes us to cling so hard to this peri-personal space that we must protect it as "*Mine.*"

Suppose we gently *gaze upward*. What happens? It helps reorient other *attentional resources*. Where? *Toward an elevated domain of more objective, impersonal processing.* Figure 11.1 illustrates that when the viewer's mental space opens up and becomes elevated into the distance *out there*, it may also access more readily its lower, most objective, *allocentric* (other-centered) resources of attentive processing. It is a short distance between the inferior occipital gyrus and the nearby lower temporal cortex. Evolutionary neurobiologists refer to such shorter paths as involving a lesser wiring cost. Discussions elsewhere amplify the potential benefits that evolve during this gazing *up and out into the distance*.[4] [MS: 20–37, 72–91]

It makes a big difference how and where we access space. Crucial functions of the psyche become enhanced when one's perceptions of space expand superiorly. Myers-Levy and Zhu found that normal subjects could develop positive changes in their subsequent mental processing by becoming *subliminally aware* that a greater vertical expanse of space existed *above* their eye level.[5] Subjects who were in a *high*-ceilinged room generated more thoughts related to freedom and greater degrees of abstract ideation. They could also retrieve, spontaneously from memory, more items seen earlier without needing to be cued. The review of "grounded cognition" by Barsalou explains how changes in the basic ways people represent their sensorimotor information can create similar positive changes. These benefit their ongoing mental attitudes and interpretations.[6]

Normal subjects of all ages respond more creatively when their tasks are portrayed as originating at far distant, *not proximal*, locations. When people imagine that events are occurring at distances that are suggested to be faraway, test results show that their creativity becomes enhanced. This increased creativity has been demonstrated both in university students[7] and in elementary school children.[8]

Suppose that the artificial test stimuli are fine-grained targets. In this instance, researchers assign tasks only in the foveal *center* of the subjects' visual fields, say, at locations a mere 4 degrees up or 4 degrees down from eye level. Then normal subjects perform less well in their upper visual fields than in their lower visual fields.[9] However, these subjects are being challenged to perform a top-down task while they are sitting a mere 57 centimeters (22 inches) away from the TV screen. In contrast, K.K. and O.R. were generating long-distance perspectives in space under field conditions. The degrees of elevation that they projected in their mind's eye extended far beyond their usual horizon, way up into the distant sky.

An important step in studying this elevated visual dimension is the recent report by Bayle et al.[10] They point to an "adaptive advantage" that exists out in the periphery of our visual field, not in the center. This enables the larger nerve cells in our visual systems to react instantly when a threatening event occurs in the environment. In their behavioral study, 20 adults had only 140 milliseconds to glimpse pictures of emotional faces. Notice where these subjects were glimpsing the test faces: at eccentricities up to *40 degrees above the usual visual horizon*. As anticipated, the subjects reacted more efficiently to a face expressing fear than to a face expressing disgust.

Behavioral studies show that fear-producing images influence both how we originally perceive visual word images and how we later recall them into revisualizations.[11] When centrally located items are transmitted only in the form of fine-grained visual details, they can interfere with a variety of later processing steps. On the other hand, the transmission of coarse-grain visual details carries some potential to enhance these later processing steps.

2. The Lability of Memories

Research in forensic psychology reminds us that the accuracy of our memories and of so-called eye-witness reports is unstable at best. Memory-linked associations undergo reconstruction while they are in the process of being retrieved. This inherent lability of episodic and semantic memories opens up important possibilities: memories can not only be modified in their factual content, but they can also drop off some old attached emotions in the act of being recalled.[12] Indeed, it was when subjects K.K. and O.R. had projected their earlier traumatic imagery *up* into the far *distant* sky scape that they abruptly dropped off the major negative emotional *attachments* linked to these older fearful memories. The Buddha specified that a wide variety of emotional attachments could cause us to suffer, not only fear.

3. Recent Event-Related Potential Studies (ERP)

Wu and colleagues conducted an important visual ERP study.[13] They measured the sequences of events that unfolded along the *dorsal* occipito → parietal system. [ZBR: 159, 185, 190–192] They further distinguished those event-related reaction potentials of this "northern" system from the more global reactivities that were arising farther down in the *ventral* occipito → temporal "What?" system. During the first 148 milliseconds of *preattentive* processing, their subjects' bare spatial awareness was still openly dispersed throughout its larger field. Even so, the innate capacities of this global, "southern" system could already *bundle* and discern the essentials (gist) of relatively complex facial features. How sensitive was this ventral system's early ERP peak? It arrived some 80-162 milliseconds *before* the focal attention of its "northern" counterpart's system brought its top-down, feature-binding skills into conscious awareness.

Psychological conflicts can be resolved. They disappear sooner if researchers supply positive external visual or auditory stimuli that can defuse an already anxious situation. Once these resources are introduced, the subjects show appropriate changes in their earlier ERP configurations.[14] This objective evidence confirms a link between positive resources and the relief of emotional stress. The ERP findings could become of interest to investigators seeking to understand what enables the distress of a person like K.K. to vanish as she shifts into deep, intimate feelings of "being connected to the universe" the moment she looks *up* through a kitchen window and *out* at the distant stars.

4. Recent Functional MRI Research

Arcaro et al. tracked the responses of our *lower* visual pathways as they relay forward into the posterior part of the parahippocampal gyrus.[15] Extra-large visual response fields reside in this posterior parahippocampal region. In addition, the visual associations in the *superior* visual fields are coded *preferentially*. They respond strongly to stimuli that register items throughout both the central *and* peripheral zones of whole scenes. These attributes would seem to fill almost all the optical requirements for a system that could deliver sharp visual clarity throughout a globally coherent spatial field. (Such a prescription might serve as a useful preamble for functions that we might later incorporate into what we regard as our mind's eye). [ZB: 482–499]

Three sites in the right hemisphere normally help us process visual tasks in different parts of space (see also figure 11.1). After these sites were first identified by fMRI in individual subjects, their separate functions were disorganized by the effects of localized transcranial *magnetic* stimulation.[16] These disruptions confirmed that tasks in far space engage the *ventral* occipital cortex. In contrast, tasks in near space engage the cortex higher up in the posterior parietal region. This region corresponds with the location of the egocentric **E** in figures 11.1 and color plate 1. However, our frontal eye field (FEF) functions are more flexible. The FEF can contribute its focal attentive, top-down functions either when we search for details in the near frame or in the more distant frame of spatial reference.

Huijbers and colleagues carefully studied the fMRI correlates and reaction times of 21 normal subjects who were engaged in different visual and auditory imagery tasks.[17] Four regions proved crucial. The subjects activated these sites both when they succeeded in developing a mental image *and* when they retrieved this image later from memory. These four regions were the hippocampus, posterior cingulate cortex, medial prefrontal cortex and angular gyrus (see figure 3.1). All four, of course, are part of that larger (mostly medial) constellation of familiar network sites normally involved in the way we represent much of our egocentric psychic Self plus its intimate topographical details in our event memory.[18] The two key regions forming the core of this macronetwork are considered to be the medial prefrontal cortex (mPFC) and the posterior cingulate cortex (pCC).

In a separate report, Huijbers et al point out that when human subjects deliberately work to retrieve their memories, they couple the hippocampus with these same three other regions of the default network.[19] In primates, more than two-thirds (69%) of the place cells in the hippocampus are coded to respond allocentrically; only a minority (10%) express the egocentric frame of reference. [ZBR: 100–101] Could such imbalances in the percentages be different among those human subjects who begin as especially Self-centered individuals? We don't know.

The preceding lines of evidence supplement those from direct personal experiences. They lead to a testable working hypothesis: a meditator's more *allo*centeric *spontaneous* varieties of creative, insightful functioning could coalesce during *casual instances*—those that happen to combine looking up, sel*fless* processing, and a loss of fear. In contrast, other spontaneous retrievals that remain more *Self*-centered may tend to be associated with personalized imagery that happens to be projected into vision at or *below* the center of a meditator's gaze. [SI: 97]

5. Fear in Relation to Pathways through the Amygdala

Fear is a powerful emotion. The amygdala makes pivotal subcortical contributions to our fears.[20] [ZB: 175–189] The useful phrase "weapon-focusing effect" is discussed by Axmacher et al.[21] In this chapter, the words take on special meaning for two reasons: (1) with reference to that sharp kitchen knife lodged deep within subject K.K.'s fears for many decades, and (2) with regard to yet another incident that relieved suffering, described at the end of this chapter.

When a weapon causes fear, it intensifies the sharp focus of our spotlight of attention. Instantly, the impulses coding for fear diverge throughout the many hotline connections of the amygdala. Suffering continues for those unfortunate persons whose habitual ruminations follow only these well-worn, negatively charged fear pathways. What they need to do first is delete or bypass these resonant fear pathways at sites closer to their origin. Next—as William James foresaw—they need to mobilize other positive resources. The goal is not just to reinstate, but to build to its *new* optimum the full competence of their self-image.[22] Research discussed in the next two sections clarifies how the human brain could achieve the first of these objectives.

6. Cortical Processing Pathways That Can Relieve Negative Emotions

The meta-analysis of PET and MRI research by Diekhof et al. examines how we can normally reduce our emotional over-reactions when events are threatening or unpleasant.[23] For example, at the moment when a negative emotional event is being drained of its prior affect, the evidence suggests that an activation within the ventromedial prefrontal cortex could be the cause of (or be co-responsible for) the *de*activation of the left amygdala. Moreover, when a person's positive affect coincides with a *broadening* of their visual field, these two events can be associated with activation of the orbitomedial cortex.[24] Importantly, activations down in this lower, medial orbital prefrontal region are also being correlated with a variety of useful, positive, improvisational modes of problem-solving behavior. [SI: 18, 45]

7. Deep Subcortical Gates in the Thalamus That Can Block Negative Emotions

Signals sent from the cortex, reaching adaptive mechanisms deep in the thalamus, can also shield the brain from an over reactive limbic system (see chapter 3). In this regard, Min has comprehensively reviewed the pivotal inhibitory role played by the reticular nucleus of the thalamus.[25] Acting in its capacity as a bidirectional gate, the reticular nucleus is positioned to shut down aversive sensory, hypothalamic, amygdaloid, and other limbic anxiety signals. These messages could otherwise ascend to the cortex through the three limbic nuclei of the thalamus. In turn, the reticular nucleus can also shield our limbic system from being overinfluenced by stress signals descending from overdriven higher cortical regions.[26] [SI: 87–94; 109–121]

An important practical point relates to GABA, the brain's major inhibitory transmitter. When GABA is released from this reticular nucleus, it can regulate vision *selectively* in either the upper or the lower visual fields.[27] Two lesser nuclei also serve to inhibit the limbic thalamus: the zona incerta and the anterior pretectal nucleus. [ZBR: 178–179] How could the GABA released by these three inhibitory nuclei regulate consciousness selectively? By nudging thalamo ↔ cortical oscillations out-of-phase. A simple analogy may help explain how the release of GABA might interfere with their synchrony. A noise-canceling headphone is currently advertised in many magazines. Its electronic circuits, powered by a tiny AAA battery, operate in a comparable manner. [MS: 35–37; 108–109] Try one out. Hear for yourself.

Zikopoulos and Barbas describe a novel, excitatory amygdalo → reticular pathway.[28] Their findings clarify how some normal messages that speed from the amygdala into the reticular nucleus actually turn out to *reduce* the effects of excessive amygdala activity. This pathway's extra-large nerve terminals directly stimulate the cell bodies of *inhibitory* neurons in the reticular nucleus. Therefore, the resulting extra release of GABA by these reticular nucleus nerve cells could provide a speedy feedback to block overdriven mechanisms in the limbic thalamus that could otherwise relay up to overstimulate the cortex. Another important fact is that two key pathways converge on the reticular nucleus. This dual convergence of information about attention *and* emotion helps clarify a model of kensho. It suggests how, when a triggering stimulus captures attention, the resulting over-reactivity of the anterior reticular nucleus could serve to inhibit those limbic nuclei of the dorsal thalamus that are specialized to subserve emotional functions. [SI: 109–117]

Does the Technique of Gazing Up and Out Involve Eye Movement Desensitization?

This chapter describes reimaging and reprocessing mechanisms linked to *gentle* elevations of the usual line of sight. They differ substantially from the deliberate *repetitive*, to-and-fro, sensorimotor sequences proposed as mechanisms during active eye *movement* desensitization and reprocessing (EMDR).[29] Transient, active, fast eye movements from *side to side* can briefly reduce the vividness and emotional resonances of traumatic images that are revisualized from the past, although such results are not invariably sustained.[30] Notably, the original relief from major traumatic stress has been sustained for at least seven years in case 1 and for more than three years in case 2.

No descriptions in the EMDR studies just cited, or elsewhere to my knowledge, specify the particular angle and distance inside the vast volume of space where the subjects were projecting their imagery. One comment from the early report by Shapiro is of interest: "Vertical movements appear to have a calming effect and are particularly helpful in reducing extreme emotional agitation, dizziness, or nausea."[31]

Caveat

The author's goal in these pages is to stimulate other investigators to rigorously challenge this empirical approach. Many people of all ages have the capacity to infuse emotions and auditory memories into the scenes that they revisualize in their mind's eye.[32] No guarantees can ensure that every person who tries to revisualize while gazing up and out will immediately be relieved of psychic trauma in ways superior to current somatic experiencing or cognitive techniques.[33] Each subject in the two case reports is familiar with her own psyche and with psychological processes in general. Other subjects may lack the requisite neural capacities, as described by Huijbers et al., [34] that could enable them to visualize and reprocess as effectively as these two intelligent women.

Weapon Focusing in Another Case Report

In case report 1, K.K. described how she had been suddenly released from major fears linked to a knife. This happened during a brief, extraordinary, involuntary state of consciousness. A knife is a potent weapon for arousing fear. Wielded by an assailant, its edges slash and draw blood, its point plunges deep. A knife can also be turned inward against oneself.

Suzanne Foxton recently described a remarkable alternate state experience.[35] Why is her account of this state relevant to some aspects of case 1? Because this experience served as a pivotal turning point in her life. Following this, Foxton recovered from her actively suicidal severe depression. Her narrative, like that of K.K., further illustrates how a novel perspective that looks up and out—when associated with a sudden shift into an unusual state of consciousness— evolves into a major release from deep-seated damaging emotions that have lasted a long time.

It began in the kitchen. Foxton was washing up knives at the sink. Abruptly, the "biggest, most dangerous knife became very 'knife-ish' . . . There never was a more perfect knife . . . It was just as it should be, as everything is." At that moment, "I then just saw that everything had always been like that, the whole time." [But] something like the ego "had been [standing] in the way of it. Whatever I was looking for was this knife and whatever else happened to be around."

By this time she had entered into the depths of a profound experience that had opened into "boundlessness." Overcome by this state, she next found herself "crouching on the kitchen floor, saying 'Whoa!'" She then wandered around the kitchen, repeating aloud: "It's so obvious." This repetition of the word *obvious* is intriguing. It has a long history that links it with the extraordinary, fresh living experience of an alternate state of consciousness.[36]

The entry of what she calls a "physiological phenomenon" also makes her narrative noteworthy. Her words describe it as a novel perspective that began in association with the sense that her consciousness was undergoing a kind of awakening. It enabled her to "see things slightly above the usual where the eyes come out." When she illustrates the origin of this elevated point of view, she *looks up into the space to the right of her head.*[37] She also describes it on another occasion as feeling "like I was seeing from just next to the right of my head and a little higher than my eyes." Following this acute, dramatic experience of psychological release in the kitchen, her psychiatric condition gradually improved. Since then, her ongoing awareness has become focused on each event as it arises in the present moment: "nothing is happening that's not happening right now, right now."

Commentary

The two mature women in cases 1 and 2 found it empirically useful to be looking *up and out into the distance* when they revisualized earlier incidents of severe emotional trauma. Their relatively simple technique seems to involve mechanisms other than (1) a soft optical sense of being visually distanced from events at the moments when they are recalling a traumatic scene, and (2) a motion-induced optical blur of this scene while it is being recalled.

During the approach they describe, subcortical and cortical networks appear to tap into deeper physiological levels of attentive processing. This reprocessing seems to develop a powerful momentum. The brain appears to be shifting into an altogether fresh, objective perspective. The results can be

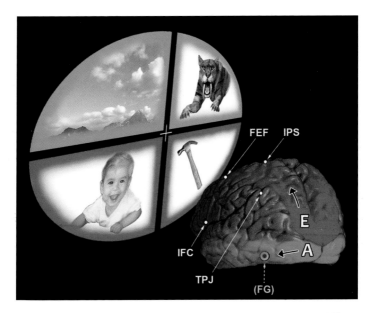

Plate 1 Egocentric and allocentric attentive processing; major differences in their efficiencies

This view contrasts our top-down dorsal *egocentric* networks with those other networks representing our ventral *allocentric*, bottom-up pathways. Your vantage point is from a position behind the *left* hemisphere, looking at the lower end of the occipital lobes.

This person's brain is shown gazing up and off to the left into quadrants of scenery. The items here are imaginary. The baby and the hammer are in the space down close to the person's body. The scenery above and the tiger are off at a distance.

Starting at the top of the brain are the two modules of the *dorsal*, top-down attention system: the intraparietal sulcus (IPS) and the frontal eye field (FEF). They serve as the attentive vanguards linked with our subsequent sensory processing and goal-oriented executive behavior. Notice how they are overlapped by the upward trajectory of the *upper* parietal → frontal egocentric (**E**) system. This Self-referential system is shown as an arching red pathway that begins in the upper occipital region. Notice that a similar red color also surrounds the *lower* visual quadrants containing the baby (at left) and the hammer (at right). Why? To indicate that this dorsal, "northern" attention system could attend more efficiently—on a shorter path with a lesser wiring cost —

Plate 1 (Continued) to these *lower* visual quadrants. This enables our parietal lobe senses of *touch* and *proprioception* to handle easily such important items down close to our own body.

In contrast, our two other modules for cortical attention reside lower down over the outside of the brain. They are the temporo-parietal junction (TPJ) and the regions of the inferior frontal cortex (IFC). During bottom-up attention, we activate these two modules of the ventral attention system chiefly on the *right* side of the brain. There, they can engage relatively easily the networks of allocentric processing nearby (**A**). The green color used to represent these *lower* temporal → frontal networks is also seen to surround the *upper* visual quadrants. Why?

This is to suggest the ways this lower ("southern") pathway is poised *globally* to use its two different specialized systems of pattern recognition. These are based on our senses of *vision* and *audition*. Each serves both to identify items off *at a distance* from our body and to instantly infuse them with meaningful interpretations. The yellow FG in parenthesis points to this lower pathway's inclusion of the left fusiform gyrus. This region, hidden on the undersurface of the temporal lobe, contributes to complex visual associations, including our sense of colors.

Plate 2 Lateralization of the color field to the left

After beginning as a thin haze lower down and centrally, and having then risen to infuse *both* sides of the visual fields symmetrically, this yellow-green hue now becomes more dense as it shifts over into the *left* half of the visual field. The white oval area below depicts the gap between partially closed eyelids through which external light is still entering.

Plate 3   Coalescence of green into the left upper quadrant
   After 15 minutes or so, the left-sided greenish color becomes more saturated. As it tends to coalesce in the left upper quadrant of the visual field, its background luminosity increases.

Plate 4   Midline circular zone of pink-purple
   This figure depicts the color that next tended to arise, since 1974, out of the initial thin grayish red-pink haze. During these early decades, this circular area of color occupied central midline locations as the open-eyed meditator was gazing down. Currently, this midline pink-purple hue usually precedes the phase shown in the next color plate, yet it might also return many minutes later to follow it.

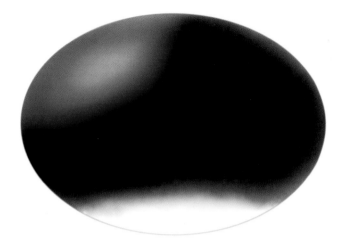

Plate 5   Coalescence of pink-purple into the left upper quadrant

The pink-purple-colored area becomes more saturated and luminous as it coalesces up in the left upper quadrant. The left superior quadrant localizations (depicted here and in plate 3) occur whether the subject's open-eyed gaze is directed down or straight-ahead, or is directed gently up at an angle of 30° into the dark field under partially closed eyelids.

transformative: an abrupt, sustained release from deep fears—fears that for many years had been narrowly focused down on a bleeding hand, cut by a knife, or had been caught up in a desperate struggle at night in the front seat of an automobile.

Thoreau appreciated the space outdoors, and observed that we had plenty of this available space that opened out beyond our own elbows into the distant horizon.[38] The evidence reviewed converges from multiple lines of research. It suggests that fresh, creative potentials can open up when humans access the *global* properties of this mental space, [39] including that which extends *above* their usual visual horizon.

Who else might benefit from the novel dynamic reprocessings that evolve as they visualize and revisualize from an elevated perspective? This review is intended to illustrate that several kinds of rigorous behavioral, neuroimaging, and evoked potential evidence will be required to critically address *each* dimension of this important question.[40]

Evidence presented in this chapter and earlier explains why it can sometimes be an advantage for meditators to elevate their attentiveness and awareness into the upper visual fields.[41] [SI: 113–116; MS: 74–91] These empirical suggestions find independent confirmation in recent recommendations of different techniques that can support a mindful meditative practice. This teaching about adopting an elevated gaze is offered by the well-credentialed Zen teacher and physician Jan Chozen Bays.[42] She aptly entitles her chapter "Look Up!"

Chapter 12 examines other evidence that correlates the lesser wiring cost and early orientation of our lower brain pathways with visual phenomena of a different kind. These phenomena involve colors and emerge spontaneously during meditation. They can also lateralize and become referable to the upper visual fields.

12

Spontaneous Color Imagery during Meditation

> Colors are the deeds of light—at once, light itself, and the results of light.
>
> Johann von Goethe (1749–1832)[1]

Colors were an early interest in my childhood. Not until I was 49 did I begin to practice formal Zen meditation in Kyoto, Japan. Soon, like other novices, I noticed that a soft play of colors could enter my central field of vision. If such "deeds of light" commonly occur in meditators, why consider them now?

- Distinctive color and luminosity phenomena can emerge during meditation. It is time to describe them in greater detail and give them an appropriate name.

- Not until 2009, when I was 84, did I notice that these colors tended to shift into my *left* visual field. This late evolution is important. It means that those color percepts in the left visual field are arising—spontaneously—somewhere over in the opposite, *right* side of my brain.

- A preferential increase of fMRI signal activity, down in my *right* fusiform gyrus, might be among the functional MRI correlates of these delayed luminous colors.

- The subtly blended color sequences are consistent with the microanatomy of color receptors that other researchers have found in the visual cortex of our primate relatives.

- The lines of evidence reviewed here converge toward a novel working hypothesis: A more open access into *allocentric* processing pathways could play a useful role in some mechanisms of neuroplasticity that gradually evolve during long-term meditative training. This chapter's hypothesis becomes the preamble for the notion to be explored in the next two chapters:

- Greater access to these *other*-referential innate resources—including those relayed through the ventral processing stream in the *right* hemisphere—could have the potential to access more *intuitive capacities* than did those exaggerated top-down functions that one's dominant *ego*centric processing networks had imposed during earlier decades.

The first section in this chapter spans decades. It begins with a neurologist's observations of visual phenomena made when he was only a novice meditator. Color plates following page 122 illustrate how, after 35 years of meditation, some of these phenomena underwent a shift over into the left visual field. The second section discusses these longitudinal observations and comments on their changing nature. The third section considers the mechanisms of the findings and their potential implications for health professionals and meditators in the society at large.

Observations over Decades

How the Colors and Luminosity Began

In 1998, I used the words "yellow-green" and "blue-purple" to describe the hues that had been entering my vision regularly during open-eyed meditation in dim light. [ZB: 374, 379] Throughout that interval of 14 years, I had grown accustomed to the way the colors had entered chiefly the *central* and lower regions of the visual fields, whether my eyelids remained open or partly closed.

I accepted that this color imagery clearly fell within the old Japanese term *makyo*. This term implied that the colors were by-products of meditation and would drop away with time. Indeed, I noticed them less and less. I had always been strongly influenced by colors as a child and was an occasional weekend watercolor painter.[2] Therefore, their tendency to persist could be dismissed as idiosyncratic. Importantly, *no* tendency to shift toward either field had been evident before 2009. The basic meditative setting and conditions described next have remained essentially unchanged for over three decades.

The Stable Conditions under Which Color and Luminosity Phenomena Have Been Recurring for Decades

Upon awakening, the light from three overhead 60-watt bulbs is switched on, the routine morning ablutions begin, followed by 15 minutes of simple yoga and setting-up physical exercises. Now, under the light from a single overhead 40-watt bulb, a conventional Zen approach begins: with sitting posture erect and eyelids open, I gaze down gently at an angle of 30 degrees toward a 5-millimeter dark spot 3 feet away on a pale blank wall. No specific goal has been set to see or do something. I simply remain aware of lower abdominal breathing movements and of whatever else transpires.

Within the first 5 minutes, the usual diffuse haze of faint greenish colors emerges. It begins lower down and ascends to occupy *both* sides of the visual field. During the next 25 minutes or so, it then evolves to include most of the following phases. (The asterisks identify which color changes lateralized since 2009.)

The Phases of Color Evolution during the Current 30-Minute Period of Meditation

- During the first 10–15 minutes, thoughts recede. Though still gazing toward the spot, my eyes diverge slightly, allowing external visual clarity to become increasingly unfocused. As vision blurs and softens, the early mottled hues of this faint haze gather substance. They now register as shades of yellow-green and/or blue-green throughout the full extent of the visual field's original gray background.

* After the first 10–15 minutes of settling in, this symmetrical greenish haze coalesces and *undergoes a distinct shift to the left of the midline of gaze* (see color plate 2).

* Whether this lateralized process had occupied the entire left half of the (homonymous) fields at onset or had begun down in the left lower quadrant, the area of greenish color now intensifies as it tends to coalesce into the *left upper quadrant* (see color plate 3).

• During the next phase, a faint gray haze intermediate between red and pink develops throughout the visual fields symmetrically. Inside a dark peripheral zone, it coalesces in the midline into a circular area of pink-purple color that has a soft-edged circumference (see color plate 4).

A soft wave of mental relaxation and physical ease sometimes accompanies the initial appearance of a bluish-pink-violet hue in its center.

* Waxing and waning during the following minutes, this previous round and soft-edged midline area that blends pink to purple colors can also drift over to the *left* and coalesce into the *left upper quadrant* (see color plate 5).

* Each phase becomes *more translucent* as its color becomes increasingly saturated, lateralizes to the left, and later coalesces into the left upper quadrant. There, the maximum zone of illumination is often reached closer to the circumference and nearer the 11 o'clock than the 10 o'clock position.

Each phase of these soft-edged color progressions from yellow-green through reddish-pink-purple usually lasts from many seconds to several minutes. However, neither this outline of sequences since 1974 nor the changes since 2009 are necessarily stereotyped. Cycles of unlateralized blotchy, shifting darker blue-green colors or pink-purple colors may mingle with thin, hazy washes of yellow-green and aquamarine or reddish pink throughout the entire visual field. No shades of blood red have been observed similar to the vivid red band seen in photographs of the spectrum of sunlight out at its long wavelength end.[3]

General Discussion of the Phenomena

Their Nomenclature and Nature

These color phenomena are not some kind of synesthesia.[4] [ZBR: 232] Synesthesias occur when *two* different sensory avenues blend into one unified mode of "cross modality perception." For example, numbers or letters can then take on particular colors.

It would help to have a unique diagnostic label, one that could further separate these two different conditions. One such term might be "meditators aurora." Aurora was the name the ancient Romans gave to their goddess of the dawn. It was Aurora's faint colors, glowing *just above the horizon*, that heralded the Sun, about to rise from below. Accordingly, in keeping with its Latin origin, *aurora meditatorum* suggests itself.

To be sure, more subtle colors emerge during meditation than we can see unfold in the dramatic displays of the aurora borealis. Notwithstanding, the spontaneous shifting colors and luminosities of *aurora meditatorum* present a scientific challenge. Which basic mechanisms cause these phenomena to arise spontaneously from the brain's vast array of *endogenous* visual functions? The colors do share one fact with other benign hallucinations: no discrete external stimulus causes them to emerge. Unlike formed hallucinations, they do not exhibit edged characteristics. Unlike hypnagogic hallucinations, no overt drowsy intervals necessarily precede their onset. Indeed, because this meditator has been stimulated by his early morning routines, he feels awakened and remains a wakefully observant witness.

Note that no *I* is prominent in the foreground of this scene. No person is trying deliberately to produce visual imagery by concentrated top-down attempts to focus attention during some kind of trance. Indeed, it is when I relax and open up into the greater degrees of bare awareness during *receptive* styles of meditation that these spontaneous color phenomena become more vivid. By the time that washes of the early thin hazes and left-lateralized visual phases begin to emerge, my original soft gaze has become *unfocused,* and the 5-millimeter dark spot on the wall has faded from view.

Commentary on the Additional Observations That Developed since 2009 (see asterisks)

The early haze of soft colors still *began* as centrally and symmetrically as before. Now, however, their distinct *luminosity* was apparent against the gray background. It infused the colors increasingly as they became more saturated, shifted to the left, and coalesced into the *left* superior visual field (see plates 2, 3, and 5). Had this conspicuous left shift into the *left* field occurred in this overt manner in earlier decades, it would have been obvious to any visually attuned neurologist. [ZBR: 174–175, 306–312, 410–420]

The real aurora borealis is seen more vividly against a black sky on dark nights before the moon rises. In a similar manner, the color and luminosity phenomena can be appreciated more readily in the darkness created by allowing the eyes to *drift slowly and gently upward*, in parallel. The extra darkness occurs because the pupils are now hidden under three-quarter-closed eyelids. [MS: 74–91] Plates 2–5 illustrate the results following this procedure. *Without straining*, this technique allows the colors and luminosity to stand out more clearly against the resulting dark gray–black background. This approach preserves a gap at the bottom through which the stimulus effect of ambient light still enters through the lowest edge of the field. This desirable aspect of standard Zen practice remains a useful way to minimize drowsiness. [ZB: 582] The colors and luminosity are usually more intense during gentle up-gaze than gazing down below eye level, even when similarly darkened conditions of partial eyelid closure are maintained.

Throughout these last five years, from 2009 to 2013, repeated observations during meditative retreats confirm that the left-lateralized cycles of translucent colors arrive sooner, become more vivid, and last longer during the later parts of each retreat than during the first days. The phenomena did not arise on mornings characterized by a sluggish arousal from sleep and general inattentiveness. Nor did they occur if the previous day was characterized by mental and physical depletion. At last, the inquisitive neurologist decided to address the seemingly obvious "What?" question. *What* was causing this long-delayed visual shift to the left? Neuroimaging studies began at this point.[5]

Functional MRI Correlates?

Regions of special interest were six pairs of sites in the brain that were the most color-selective. These sites were found by Beauchamp et al. in 1999 when they studied how normal subjects respond when shown a variety of different *external* colors.[6] During my first study in the 3 Tesla MRI scanner, *before* I began to meditate—and *before* any spontaneous colors arose—the total volume of pooled activity (voxels) in these 12 sites was statistically the same on the right and left sides. This data profile shifted once the luminous colors coalesced into the left upper visual quadrant. Now, the profile of my *spontaneously* active brain regions closely resembled the local maxima found when those *non*-meditating subjects in the 1999 study were actually being stimulated by *external* colors. Now the fMRI signal activity increased down in my *right* posterior collateral sulcus and fusiform gyrus. There, it reached a level almost twice that (98% more than) found in the same region on the left side. Moreover, this localized, *right*-sided fusiform activity was also 68 percent greater than that found over in the opposite, *left* mid-fusiform gyrus and was 38 percent greater than that in the *left* occipital V-1 cortex. Figures 11.1 and plate 1 illustrate an important point about the location of this right-sided fusiform region of visual association cortex. The fusiform gyrus (FG) lies along the *ventral* stream of *the right allocentric* processing pathway. Preliminary research to identify the predominately right-lateralized cortical correlates is ongoing.

Potential Mechanisms and Practical Implications

Each basic mechanism involved in colors, or meditation, or light is individually complex. When they interact, their complexities become daunting. Therefore, this section must narrow the scope of its discussion to five subheadings: (1) color generation phenomena, (2) the dynamic retinal/cerebral origins of color sequences during meditation, (3) the tendency of later evolving colors to coalesce on the *left* and into the left upper visual field, (4) the co-arising luminous background, and (5) potential mechanisms related to intuitive processing functions. Pointed questions [•] will again be inserted to sharpen key aspects of the discussion. The research reports selected indicate techniques that can yield useful answers in the future.

Color Generation Phenomena; Recent EEG, Neuroimaging, and Optical Imaging Studies

- How does vision change when normal subjects gaze into a uniform, homogeneous, blank visual field (Ganzfeld)?

After several minutes, the luminance of the field diminishes. Its diffuse, blotchy inhomogeneities now resemble a "cloudy fog."[7] The interesting finding is in *how* the EEG shifts, 20–60 seconds *before* these normal subjects develop a wide variety of hallucinations. The particular EEG profile suggests that these shifts occur in the deep feedback loops that normally link the thalamus and the cortex into their usual oscillating circuits. (see chapter 11)

- When a Zen meditator settles into a prolonged relaxed awareness, which brain regions become active—and less active—in ways that might correlate with the generation of colored percepts?

In 1988, after I had been meditating daily for (only) 14 years, a deoxyglucose PET scan monitored my brain during a prolonged, 2–3-hour period of relaxed, meditative awareness.[8] [ZB: 282–283] Sections at multiple levels of this scan revealed substantially greater net metabolic activity in the *right* cerebral hemisphere, including the inferior occipito → temporal region of the right fusiform gyrus. In contrast, both right and left *medial prefrontal* regions appeared *de*activated.[9] In addition, all language-related cortical regions on the left showed a relative deactivation. This was in keeping with the way my internal word-thoughts in the scanner had been dropping off to a very low level (see chapter 9).

Functional MRI research since 1988 has increasingly correlated these *medial* prefrontal regions (mPFC) with a variety of autobiographical functions. These are referable to the *I-Me-Mine* operations of our psychic sense of Self (see chapters 2, 3). Therefore, these major reductions of prefrontal activity in my PET scan tend to confirm the generally passive and openly receptive nature of my bottom-up awareness during this *extended* interval while I was engaged in the practice of a predominately receptive, *non*concentrative form of silent meditation.

During this new millennium, functional MRI researchers uncovered another crucial finding: when normal subjects are seemingly resting, their *medial* frontoparietal Self-referential regions also undergo *slow, spontaneous fluctuations* in amplitude. These occur a mere two to four times a minute. Importantly, these very slow medial spontaneous fluctuations often correlate *inversely* with another set of very slow waveforms of activity. These arise—simultaneously—in the dorsal and ventral *attention systems* over the *lateral* aspect of each hemisphere.[10]

Recall that chapter 3 also discussed the same kind of reciprocal seesaw relationship between the networks representing our Self versus those devoted to attention. However, that inverse relationship was observed *acutely*. It happened each time the brain was reacting to a brief external stimulus. Clearly, the spontaneous and the reactive observations have significant implications for meditators: Innate mechanisms in the brain are poised to deactivate the Self when attentive functions are activated.[11] [MS: 74–91] We continue to discuss the pivotal consequences of these dynamic inverse relationships in the later sections of this chapter.

- How does visual perception change when a normal subject is deprived of external light?

An artist chose to be blindfolded throughout a three-week period. During her first two days, she reported simple, vivid, elementary, brilliant red and yellow hallucinations.[12] Thereafter, these faded in intensity. Functional MRI signals increased during her hallucinations, in the *left* lingual gyrus and in the *right* parahippocampal gyrus. The *left* lingual signal cluster was said to overlap with other *left*-sided sites. These occurred in her secondary visual area (V-2), ventral posterior area, and that ventral area referred to simply as "V-4." Not until the other normal subjects in a separate study had first undergone dark adaptation for 45 minutes did gentle transcranial *magnetic* stimulation of their occipital cortex finally cause them to see light flashes (phosphenes).[13]

- Do discrete receptor sites exist in the normal visual cortex that represent greater local sensitivities for particular colors?

High-resolution optical imaging techniques began by mapping monkey V-2 cortex.[14] When these primates fixate on a single external color, their peak response to this color occurs in myriad arrays of tiny cortical sites. Each is usually less than 0.5 millimeters in diameter. Although these sites are separable, their borders frequently overlap those of certain other adjacent colors. *This overlapping occurs in a distinctive, sequential manner.*

For example, suppose researchers show the monkey a purple color. Instantly, the corresponding purple-sensitive (**P**) receptor regions respond within its V-2 cortex. Their circumferences often overlap with one or more adjacent sites. The closest next site responds when a blue color (**B**) is shown. Moreover, when this monkey is then presented with the next single external hues—green, yellow, orange, or red—similar overlapping tendencies continue. Indeed, these next four successively adjacent color receptor sites again tend to follow in that particular topographical order: **G, Y, O, R**.

The authors call this a "hue-dependent proximity relationship." The same trend also exists in the primary visual (V-1) cortex.[15] Here again, separable brain response sites occur each time the monkey is shown single purple, blue, green, yellow, orange, or red hues. These overlappings again tend to follow the preceding pattern of sequences.

- Why does this spectrum of reactive color sites in the brain seem familiar?

We see these same sequences emerging, from left to right, when a glass prism splits white daylight into its rainbow-like bands of color! The reddish-purple wavelengths of light are split the most, followed next by the bluish colors. These first (violet) bands emerge *in this order* off at the *short* wavelength end of the visible color spectrum. This region extends from 370 to 470 nanometers. Soon, green will enter (at around 500), to be followed by bright yellow (at around 580). After orange, the *pure* reds will finally emerge, far out at the *long* wavelength end of the spectrum (around 700 nanometers).

- So, why do we see *pink*?

In *dorsal* V-4 of monkey cortex, many clusters react to different colors, degrees of preference for luminance, and degrees of saturation.[16] These sites tend to coincide in overlapping, spatially orderly sequences. Here, pink responses seem to represent superimpositions of bright *white* or lesser *red* sensitivities, *not* isolated pink receptor sites per se. In contrast, separate *dark red*–preferring patches appear to represent the dark red hue, rather than overlappings of separately activated red and black sites.

The Dynamic Retinal/Cerebral Origins of Color Sequences during Meditation

- Can the complex operations that begin with retinal rods and cones in the eye influence other mechanisms farther back in a meditator's brain that generate images spontaneously?

Retinal layers in the eye respond differently both to illumination *and* to darkness. When we normally adapt to light or to dark, the results influence our cone color pathways.[17] Intricate color-contrast phenomena further shape what we perceive. While rods are responding to the photons of light, their signals also influence certain cone pathways that are sensitive to shorter wavelength colors. Once we become fully adapted to bright light, our eye becomes most sensitive to yellow hues. However, in only dim light (including that cast by only one 40-watt bulb) a meditator's initial color sensitivities for yellow can gradually shift toward the left (e.g., green ← yellow). This left shift (toward green) leads in the direction toward color sensitives that can experience hues from yellow-green toward lighter blue.

Jan Purkinje (1787–1869), a pioneering physiologist, lived in an era spared from such scientific intricacies of modern color interpretation.[18] However, he was a keen observer of the changes that occurred in his color vision during long meditative walks outdoors. As dusk deepened, he saw blue flowers and green leaves appearing brighter than before (in dim light, his color sensitivities would be shifting more to the left, toward the green and blue (blue ← green) *middle* wavelengths of light. In contrast, purple flowers (representing the short wave length extremity of the visible spectrum) or red flowers (representing the long wave-lengths) appeared more subdued.

This meditator also witnesses other rapid shifts involving lesser degrees of blotchy color *contrast phenomena*. These phenomena develop in seconds when humans are adapting to the dark.[19] However, the purpose of plates 2–5 is to depict the *major* soft-edged areas and color sequences. These evolve *incrementally* over a much slower time course of 1, to 5, to 15 minutes or so. This slower timetable coincides with the ways some parts of the meditator's brain (and the contractions of the smooth ciliary muscle that had initially focused his lens on fine details) have been settling into a relaxed attitude of more divergent, unfocused, open awareness. During these later minutes, the meditator will have been gradually letting go of two cognitive functions: (1) the earlier minimal fronto ↔ parietal executive routines that had enabled him to pay the first steps of focused, top-down attention, and (2) the earlier discursive word-thought streams of interior language.

At this point, the discussion leaves the retina of the eye and returns to the dynamic mechanisms that express *aurora meditatorum* farther back in the recesses of the brain. Here, an important category of mechanisms could help sponsor these spontaneous visual events. Their mechanisms are *dis*inhibitory.

- What does disinhibitory mean?

Disinhibitory means that the brain's lower hierarchical levels become activated because they have just been *released* from prior top-down inhibitory restraints. The concept that higher centers had imposed these restraints was part of John Hughlings Jackson's interpretation of release phenomena.[20] Our prefrontal cortex is a large high-level region that exercises these ongoing controlling functions on lower levels. Could its dorsal and medial regions that represent Self-centeredness also be the candidate sources when a release occurs from higher inhibitory controls? Could such a release then allow visual functions to become reactivated downstream in the posterior visual regions of an aging meditator's brain? This hypothesis is supported by the serial fMRI changes described by Erb and Sitaram (see chapter 9, note 7). Other studies show that the medial prefrontal cortex does become more readily *deactivated* when the brain undergoes its normal process of aging between the third and seventh decades.[21]

The Tendency of the Later-Evolving Colors to Coalesce into the Left Visual Fields

Chapter 3 emphasized that our right hemisphere expresses a dominant role in attention. [SI: 29–43] It is also easier for normal subjects to detect external stimuli when researchers deliver these stimuli into their subjects' *left* visual fields.[22] What accounts for this attentive dominance of the right hemisphere? At least at the cortical level, much of it appears referable to the ways that the bottom-up functions of its *ventral* attention networks link our *right* temporoparietal junction (TPJ) with the *right* inferior frontal gyrus (iFG).

- Do other physiological biases of our right hemisphere favor information that enters it from up in this left upper quadrant of our visual fields?

Yes. Some of these normal physiological biases emerge when our sensory-perceptive and motor-activity functions combine their two levels of operation.[23] Subtle interactive biases enable us normally to perform tasks most efficiently in the left upper quadrant. In order to detect this improved efficiency, certain experimental conditions prove optimal. Researchers in Heilman's team at the University of Florida place the visual target higher *up* and *out* to the *left*. Here the target lies within the more favorable sensory domain up in this *left superior* visual field, *and* it is also placed at distances increasingly farther away from an outreaching hand.

In a separate study, when an external blue color was presented up in the left *superior* visual quadrant of a patient, it evoked fMRI signals from a large irregular area down in this patient's opposite *right* fusiform gyrus.[24] A yellow color presented to this patient's left *lower* visual quadrant preferentially evoked responses from another region just posterior to the first. Which external color—among all 26 shown—evoked the maximal fMRI response from this patient's brain? Notably, it was the *blue-purple color* at the short wavelength end of the spectrum.

- Could this author-meditator have sustained a silent stroke in 2009? Could such a lesion have damaged those left-sided brain pathways that would normally project colors into his right visual fields?

In theory, such a lesion might explain why a person would experience the color and luminance phenomena only in those opposite, left visual fields that had been spared. However, neither the clinical history nor structural MRI scans support this hypothesis. No focal lesion or other unusual pathological changes were evident in the structural scans that were routinely performed for incidental research control purposes in 1986, 2009, and 2011.

The Co-arising Luminous Background

- Why does a glow infuse the colors, enabling them to stand out brighter against the dark gray background?

Luminance is inherent in those same neural pathways that relay color-coded message impulses back from the cones in our retina. When these retinal impulses arrive back in V-2 and V-4 cortex, their responsive receptor sites are also color-preferring *and* luminance-preferring.[25] Moreover, special tests reveal that our *left* upper visual quadrant normally shows a second curious subliminal bias.[26] When we look at an object, this covert bias leaves us with the visual impression that some prior hidden *external* source of light *already exists.* Where is it coming from? *From up above, and off to the left.*

This subtle source of light does more than seem to illuminate the object from that direction. *It enables the object to cast shadows.* Detailed psychophysical and fMRI research suggests that this normal illumination bias arising from up above and to the left originates during the *early* stages of visual processing in the back of the brain. Moreover, this normal illumination bias, referred in a bottom-up manner, is consistent with *ventral* stream processing.

- So, these pages indicate that the meditator later experiences spontaneous colors and that they are increasingly saturated and luminous the more they become referable to this left superior visual quadrant. Might such a localized visual bias express a normal background hum, as it were? Could these left-sided and superior quadrant events be reflecting the later release into the meditator's overt awareness of innate processing functions in lower pathways that normally begin in the opposite right inferior occipito → temporal cortex?

Such a proposal could be consistent with the overt empirical visual observations just described. It is also in accord with the normal *right*-sided preponderance of his PET scan during meditation and with the several sources of fMRI data commented on. Various lines of evidence indicate that the normal brain can have several substantially biased asymmetries of the usual resting activity among the *lower* visual regions on the right side. The arrow-headed line in figure 3.1 illustrates the ventral trajectory of some of these crucially important parallel processing networking functions. These brain functions are served by distributed systems along the "southern" visual pathways that can also access our allocentric frame of reference. Figures 11.1 and plate 1 illustrate how these early visual pathways on the lower *right* side will correlate with visual phenomena that emerge into consciousness in the opposite, *left* upper visual fields.

- *Viewed in the context of the spontaneous colors that arise during meditation, why do these other-referential ventral processing pathways become of special interest?*

The arrow-headed line in figure 3.1 passes through the long right fusiform gyrus (FG). In this specialized visual association region, we do more than integrate codes for color sensitivities. We also decode the separate identities of individual human faces and process the form of objects. The close proximities among these three crucial adjacent functions might now be relevant to an additional seemingly lateralized human bias. Part cultural, part psycho-physiological, it was disclosed during a survey of 659 paintings hanging in the Louvre in Paris: Artists who painted portraits during the thirteenth to nineteenth centuries often represented the light that illuminated their subjects' faces as having arisen from *one* direction.[27]

- Is there evidence that this illumination tended to arrive from a source external to the left side of their canvas?

Yes. The illumination appeared 8.6 times more often from the left than from the right. In contrast, artists who painted landscape scenes were only 2.9 times more likely to depict these landscapes as having been illuminated by light arising from this left side. Artistic and photographic conventions evolved during subsequent centuries. [MS: 81, 210]

Potential Mechanisms Related to Intuitive Processing Functions

Our rigid Self-centeredness causes big problems for ourselves, for others, and for the ecosystems that we are all responsible for. Imprisoned in the axis of its fixed belief system, our privileged Self seems isolated from the rest of the turning universe, feeling no responsibility for others' well-being.

Given the consequences of this restricted point of view, the late spontaneous visual phenomena described herein are not necessarily minor ephemera. Rather, they may be regarded as clues that might provide fresh perspectives for a planet suffering from a litany of Self-inflicted woes. Various lines of evidence keep informing us: subtle sources of illumination can arrive from elevations just above our old Self-limited mental horizon. Yes, their deep mechanisms still seem obscure, yet might they also have some potential to shed light on issues of paramount interest to humanity in general?

At the barest minimum, let such a fresh perspective reassure other members of the author's local Zen group. They are two men in their mid-40s. One is a professor of psychology who likens his slow play of colors to those of a lava lamp. The other is a retired marine. Having meditated regularly for the past five years, each person has a new understanding. Yes, their continuing to visualize colors during meditation might seem unusual, but it is *not* abnormal. Notably, the soft yellow-green and blue-purple colors seen by each meditator chiefly occupy the *central* fields and do not lateralize.

A recent local addition is a woman who has meditated regularly in the Vipassana tradition for the past 13 years. She meditates with her eyelids closed, as does one of the two men in the Zen group. She recalls her initial imagery as having been more of a deep blue and black in color. In recent years, yellow, green, and a variety of more vivid colors have developed in "circular swirls." More colors develop in the later minutes of each sitting as she becomes more relaxed. The colors emerge only in the center and lower half of her visual field.

Chapter 13 looks beyond these meditative phenomena toward other implications of regaining a fresh perspective.

13

A Way Out of the Grand Delusion

A human being is a part of the whole, called by us "Universe," a part limited in time and space. He experiences himself, his thoughts and feelings as something separated from the rest—a kind of optical delusion of his consciousness.

Albert Einstein (1879–1955)[1]

• Why does everyone suffer from the same refractory "optical delusion" that Einstein once captured in this memorable phase? Why can't we see beyond our separate Self/other delusions into the unifying reality of the Big Picture?

This imbalance begins with an actual physical separation: our skin's outer layer serves to separate Self from other. This defines the first, *somatic*, boundary of our *I-Me-Mine* operations (see chapter 3). However, our major troubles arise from much deeper levels. They are rooted in subconscious *psychic* longings and loathings. Limbic networks do more than attach the anxieties of our psyche to every Self-centered physical frame of reference. Limbic habit energies also keep driving us to see that other world outside only through a lens warped by our own emotional biases. [SI: 49–83; 85–121] Therefore, each time our intrusive Self-referent brain reaches out to clutch something it longs to possess in that space out there, it reinforces its own deep-seated "optical delusion." Why? Because it has been wired and conditioned to frame each question in the same covetous egocentric terms: *"Where is that object in relation to ME?"*

• Did Einstein suggest a constructive solution, explain how we could liberate ourselves from this delusion?

Yes. He accomplished this in one sentence. Its formula condensed some of the elegant earthshaking simplicity of E = mc². He said we could "free ourselves from this prison by widening our circle of compassion to embrace all living creatures and the whole nature in its beauty."[2]

Widen our circle of compassion? Doesn't such a widening expand our other-referential horizons? Doesn't this really mean a wide-open embrace of the fellow creatures that share this *other* world, this vast global space beyond our own elbows? If so, then one way to start is by cultivating the practices that help us *let go* of Self-centered preoccupations.

• How can we learn to appreciate the beauty in Nature?

By returning often to reclaim our birthright, the innate beauty of our ancestral home, the world outdoors. Chapter 4 and appendix A suggest ways to do just this.

More about the Implications of the Allo-pathways for Wordless Intuition

About the time that Einstein died in 1955, the Greek-derived word—*allocentric*—was starting to seep into

English discourse. We have seen that *allo-* is a prefix. It simply refers to "other," just as *ego* is a common way to refer back to our own Self. So, *allo-* now usefully describes the normal functions of many other subordinate networks in our brain. What is significant is the special way these networks initially process the world outside our skin. They frame it *anonymously, on its terms, "out there."* They do not insist that such a world must always pass first through the lens of our ego and then be subjected to our personal filters "back here."

Once researchers and readers at large grasp these sharp contrasts with *ego* processing at an intellectual level, the distinctions can be of great conceptual benefit. However, it is difficult to hold on to every conceptual implication of allocentric processing. This is especially true if one keeps relying entirely on word-thought logic and cannot release, even for a moment, one's fixed belief in the sovereignty of Self.

Immanuel Kant (1724–1804) led the West toward one way of understanding the other-referential mode. He introduced the concept of *Ding an sich*. This meant *the thing in itself*, the object as *it* exists "out there," *before* it undergoes further processing by our senses. [ZBR: 361–371] The notion of the thing in itself, out there, helps liberate us from that old, in-turned optical delusion that had always held us in solitary confinement. We are now left freer to perceive and appreciate that other major values are inherent within the spacious Big Picture. Later we might even begin to realize how to *behave* in accord with "the way all *other* things really are."

We can be reminded by one of Buddha's teachings how to hold on to this comprehension: use only broad, sturdy leaves, like those of a lotus, to build your container of understanding (see chapter 4). The next time you are near a genuine lotus leaf, let your fingers feel how thick and sturdy it is. After this direct experience, you will appreciate the basis for his teaching.

> • Why has the prefix allo- acquired the potential to encompass all interrelationships implicit in other things "out there"? And why could such an allo-concept provide an accurate perspective of reality that seems inherently more objective?

Keep reminding yourself: *allo*centric processing views scenes *anonymously*. The **A** pathway in figure 11.1 and plate 1 is both **A**llocentric and **A**nonymous. This perspective is emancipated. Such an overview begins free from every unfruitful *subjectivity* that would otherwise cling to your *ego*centric Self. One result of this jailbreak is an all-encompassing non-dual frame of reference. Perception is no longer distorted by so many Self-centered attachments. [ZBR: 333–371] The next time you are near a lotus pond, notice how high a lotus bloom can rise on its stalk out of the water. Similarly, a more liberated consciousness begins to open up from its elevated, universal perspective to consider *ecological* issues more intuitively. [ZB: 141–145] The more the old Self shrinks, the more comprehensive and compassionate can be this unsullied view of the Big Picture.

> • Back in the gritty, mud-spattered realities of daily life, when do we access the allo-pathways along this lower watershed of temporo ↔ frontal networks?

We access them each time our brain seeks an answer to its perennial question *"What is this?"* (see figure 3.1). This simple technique—asking "What?"—is a time-honored tradition. It began with Ch'an wordplay in the Tang Dynasty.[3] [ZBR: 201; MS: 63, 72–73] Especially will it be from contributions along the *ventral* visual stream of the right hemisphere that some of these innate capacities begin to express themselves. They have a global responsibility. Their job is to identify, anonymously and without recourse to words, which object is *out there* on both sides of the *whole* external environment.

It is rare that we pause to appreciate two other interpretive feats accomplished by these covert interpretive networks. First, they automatically decode what this object *means*. Second, their connections help infuse it with a reasonably accurate sense of reality. In this regard, Shunryu Suzuki has articulated what happens in these networks during a program of meditative training: they begin to reflect increasingly veridical truths, comprehended intuitively (see chapter 10 epigraph).

> • But given our prior "optical delusion"—the nearsighted egocentric mode that dominates these subordinate allocentric pathways—how could meditative practices help restore a more appropriate balance to the ways our brain interprets the supposedly objective reality of its perceptions?

Evidence reviewed in chapter 3 emphasizes the *complementary* attributes of the concentrative and receptive styles of meditation. [SI: 35–39, 109–117; MS: 42–52, 53–139] Therefore, it is essential to keep cultivating *both* approaches when you embark on the long-term approach to training your attentiveness. During your daily life practice, their two physiologies need to co-evolve in a *balanced* manner that becomes increasingly selfless. This is easier to do outdoors in Nature than indoors, where myriad multitasking artificialities keep distracting one's attentiveness. [ZB: 664–667]

> • Then why do these pages emphasize chiefly the right hemisphere's temporo-frontal intuitive functions while deemphasizing those overactive thought streams on the left side that are involved in language?

There is nothing new about this right-sided emphasis that favors intuitive functions over language. It is one way to redress a prevailing cultural imbalance. [SI: 150–152] For centuries, Zen masters in China, Korea, and Japan have objected strenuously to elaborate word-thoughts and concepts. They understood that each thought structure could exert a negative influence that interfered with the spiritual Path (see chapters 5, 6). In China, three centuries *before* the Common Era, the message advocated in the Tao Te Ching was already clear: "Those who know, do not speak; those who speak, do not know." [ZB: 12]

Soto Zen master Shunryu Suzuki (1904–1971) continued to articulate this empirical rationale: "To open your innate nature and to feel something from the bottom of your heart, it is necessary to stay silent . . . Staying silent will open your intuition . . . The way to study Zen is not verbal."[4]

Rinzai Zen traditions place a major emphasis on the particular refinement of intuition called insight. [SI: 123–188] At our first meeting, Kobori-Roshi (1918–1992) introduced me to the importance of *prajna*. [ZB: 545–549] He also taught that "in the deepest realm of Zen meditation there is no single word." [ZBR: 389] He did so for empirical reasons: word-thoughts seem to get in the way of *prajna*'s flash of insight-wisdom. Ineffability placed first on William James's short list when he enumerated the chief characteristics of a religious/mystical experience. Even more incisive is the old Japanese Buddhist phrase *gongo dodan*. It means "the path of words has been cut." [ZBR: 358, 360]. No words!

By definition, insight *happens* instantly. It is not driven by our logic-tight sequences of deliberate, wordy thought. Does any current research into the pros and cons of language support those early warnings by Tang Dynasty Ch'an masters that word-thoughts could block the flash of insight in their trainees?

Bergen et al. gave a simple first task to their normal subjects: listen to words that were being spoken in the form of short recorded sentences.[5] The whole meaning of each sentence hinged on where each event could have taken place in the extrinsic environment. The two possibilities were either higher *up*, or lower *down*. For example, in some sentences the subjects could hear an up-word (sky) being spoken. Other sentences would specify a down-word (e.g., grass).

The subjects' next task was a simple visual discrimination: They indicated by a button press whether they saw a circle or a square. Each visual target appeared either at a higher, or lower place on the computer screen. They could see each ○ or □ clearly, during a long 200 millisecond interval. Some subjects took 30 milliseconds *longer* to signal this discrimination. What caused this slowing? Why had they hesitated? The delay occurred when they saw either this square, or this circle, in that very *same* upper, or lower location. This was the same place in space that had just been inferred by that up-or-down word-language inserted into the prior sentence.

Something was amiss. Something about the way these early spatial nouns or verbs had entered into the subjects' neural processing was interfering with their subsequent performance, not helping it. When did these prior spatial words cause greater interference delays? When both the visual and auditory processing converged during those tasks that were chiefly referable to the *upper* visual fields. These greater upper-field hesitations are consistent with the possibility that word inferences were being entangled more among some (lower) networks that could have been extending their potential links among allocentric processing channels (see plate 1 and figure 11.1).

How do mere words interfere with other brain functions, directly or indirectly? Could entanglements that arise among language networks (perhaps especially in our left hemisphere) sometimes compete for neural resources with nearby intuitive processing mechanisms? Could some loose thought structures, (protothoughts, as it were), become roadblocks preventing our free access to insights that might otherwise help us express innate degrees of selfless insight-wisdom?

Researchers have different ways to demonstrate the latent power of words. For example, they can present their subjects with words that are either risky or safe. Then they can measure the way the subjects respond in either a Self-centered or an other-centered paradigm.[6] Under these experimental conditions, it turns out that the subjects' normal EEG and fMRI responses are *less* efficient (averaging 34 seconds slower in the EEG data) during a context in which egocentric entanglement could occur than they are during a context in which allocentric involvement could occur.

- What about other ways to improve brain functions, not hinder them?

Recent neuroscience research provides other intriguing links between preconscious problem solving and creative intuition. [MS: 145–155] The collective weight of such evidence leads us toward the following premise. Suppose that certain meditative practices do allow our *lower* temporo ↔ frontal networks to escape from the sticky cross-talk of Self-imposed, wordy distractions. After such a pregnant silence deepens, a testable working hypothesis could then ask the following question: Could other resources available along the "southern" pathways be liberated to engage in the wide-open, free-associative creative play that helps improvise our most adaptive insights? Could such an effortless flow of messages among these lower networks enable the latent musical traces in the brain of a Louis Armstrong to *play themselves*?

Seeking answers to such seemingly far-out questions, we will keep exploring the brain's subconscious avenues. In part V, this journey leads us to glimpse the outlines of new research horizons.

Part V

Peering into the Future

What we do know is the greatest hindrance to our learning what we don't know.

Claude Bernard (1813–1878)

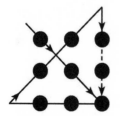

New Research Horizons

> The essence of things is just this. If even one thought appears, that is already a mistake.
>
> Zen Master So Sahn (1520–1604)[1]

> While my inner monologue unrolls, I have the impression of not being free.
>
> Hubert Benoit[2]

This chapter serves as a reminder: thoughts are an integral part of daily life. Thoughts are as natural as clouds in the sky. However, excessive thoughts distract from the clarity of awareness. From its inception, the Path of Buddhism has sought the balance of a Middle Way.

Concise Advice about "No Thinking"

We had not met before. This preliminary interview took place before the retreat started. The two of us had just sat down in facing chairs. The Zen Roshi spoke first. "Remember this," he said. His next six words supplied the essence of the mental attitude I would need during the week-long Zen retreat:

"No doctor. No God. No thinking."

The advice stripped this new student of all professional vanity. It negated any possible need (that even a Unitarian might retain) for some lingering theological attachments. It epitomized the Rinzai Zen approach to meditation: let go of discursive thoughts!

Discursive Word-Thoughts

To Hubert Benoit, the French psychologist, each person's Self-centered world was "the world of speech." The evidence was obvious: Every word-thought is verbal in nature. More-over, each word-thought conveys only relative meaning, not real, tangible meaning. Therefore, at least from a Zen perspective, his 1973 book invited us to "let go" of this strong primary attachment to language. In its place, he advised readers to cultivate other "automatisms of divergence."

This first proposal—to "let go"—might seem to restate some of the Buddha's early advice to Bahiya about letting go of attachments. We observed how Zen masters during later centuries incorporated this teaching into their training methods (see chapter 5). In this twenty-first century, how does such age-old psychological advice translate into neural terms? The counsel in these pages is straightforward: Abandon unfruitful Self-centeredness; free more lower pathways from being entangled with egocentric word-thoughts. As a result, you will open them up for more allocentric processing. But what did Benoit mean by "divergence"? And which of its "automatisms" were to be cultivated?

Divergence in the Context of Meditation and Creativity

Things that diverge spread apart from a common point of origin. When divergent thinking branches out it increases the number of creative options. On the other hand, too much diversity interferes with the next process of selecting which option is best. So, what absolute requirements do creativity and meditation each seem to share? At a minimum, they both require (1) flexible alternations between narrowly focused attention skills and global awareness skills, and (2) precise timing of each such skill set on the leading edge of just the right kinds of convergent and divergent processing, respectively.[3] [SI: 109–112] All along, our fluid intelligence performance improves when there is less cognitive and emotional dissonance, rather than more.

Williamson and colleagues conducted a pilot study of five adults who averaged 41 years of age.[4] None had meditated previously. The researchers wondered, How would a well-taught eight-week course of mindfulness-based stress reduction (MBSR) influence these subjects' divergent and convergent reasoning? The authors preferred the Torrance test for its dual capacities to examine both the visual and verbal domains of creativity. In brief, they found that verbal creativity and flexibility improved significantly; the trend toward nonverbal creativity was less pronounced.

Yet, students are introduced to a lot of new verbal instruction and to language in general during any such course. How much does all this exposure influence their subsequent verbal performance? Dotan Ben-Soussan et al. studied 27 women, nine of whom were enrolled in a particular whole-body physical training practice.[5] This motor task is called Quadrato. Its verbal instructions are precise, simple, and delivered by audiotape. The tape directs the trainees to take only a single step. However this step might take them forward, or backward, or to the left, right, or diagonally. This five-step, at random unpredictability creates a climate of attention plus uncertainty. The trainees performed this audio-directed random task for 7 minutes within a square space on the floor. The space measured only 20 inches (50 centimeters) on each side. Thereafter, all subjects were tested using the Alternate Uses Task for creativity. In contrast to the creative performance of the two control groups, the Quadrato subjects significantly increased their ideational *flexibility* (but *not* their ideational fluency). They also increased their frontotemporal alpha EEG coherence bilaterally.

Colzato and colleagues also used Guilford's Alternate Uses Task as a way to assess the productivity of divergent thinking, and used Mednick's Remote Associates Task to assess the results of convergent thinking.[6] The 19 meditators in their study had already practiced a mixture of concentrative and receptive forms of meditation for an average of 2.2 years. The task for each subject was to spend only 35 minutes a day (on each of three separate days) *either* in concentrative meditation or in receptive meditation or in a baseline control condition. Receptive meditation did improve the subjects' divergence on the Alternate Uses Task, as expected. However, both types of meditation improved *mood*. Why did the researchers wonder whether the energizing influence of mood might account for some of their subjects' productivity in *divergent* thinking? Because positive mood (accompanied by increased fMRI signals in the anterior cingulate cortex) has been reported as occurring during those intervals when normal subjects solve problems insightfully.[7] [SI: 19–20]

Takeuchi and colleagues studied the creative performance of 159 young adults in a university population.[8] They correlated the subjects' fMRI data with their responses on a separate divergence-type test (similar to the Torrance test employed by Williamson et al.). Subjects who scored higher on divergent thinking had greater degrees of resting connectivity that linked their medial prefrontal cortex with their posterior cingulate cortex. When an external task captured these particular subjects' attention, this medial (*"attention off"*) network region deactivated less than it did in the controls.

Abraham et al. issued an appropriate caveat when they surveyed the literature. They acknowledged how difficult it is to conduct meaningful neuroimaging research on a topic as complicated as creativity.[9] They designed their fMRI study to emphasize a process that they called "conceptual expansion." Their 19 university students worked to perform an Alternate Uses Task under the pressure of time constraints. Under these timed conditions, their subjects' task-induced conceptual expansion correlated with greater *left*-sided activation in their anterior inferior frontal gyrus (BA 45/47), their lateral frontopolar cortex (BA 10), and in the medial aspect of both anterior temporal poles (BA 36) (see figure 3.1).

Ellamil et al. conducted a landmark study of visual creativity in 15 subjects. These students, averaging 22 years of age, were specializing in art and design at a local university in Vancouver, BC.[10] The students had a novel, practical task. It was to design an actual book cover using an fMRI- compatible drawing tablet. The researchers distinguished between divergence at the start of the task, when several ideas were *first* being generated, and the processing during *later* intervals, when ideas were being critically evaluated and selected.

When the students were first generating novel ideas, they recruited two medial temporal lobe regions: the hippocampus on the right side and the parahippocampus on both sides. Later, during the phase of evaluation/selection, they jointly activated the standard executive and default networks. In addition, they also activated the left anterior insula plus both temporal polar regions (L>R). [SI: 31, 160-161, 238]

Harré and colleagues took a different tack.[11] They wondered why experts could solve intricate problems of great complexity. Their theory: experts would have gradually developed transformations farther back within "the early sensory region of the brain." It was these proposed changes that would give experts an *implicit* "preprocessing" advantage. Elsewhere, the term *preattention* has served to identify the leading edge at the tip of this preprocessing. [SI: 139–141]

• Why is the word implicit applied to these covert steps in perceptual learning?

Because the perceivers are not aware of two things: (1) They do not know exactly *what* they have learned, (2) They do not comprehend *how* their prior years of training could have transformed their thoughts and behaviors. In short, implicit learning happens *subconsciously*. And it remains there, out of sight and out of mind, until propitious circumstances liberate it. [MS: 136, 155, 171]

To test their theory, Harré et al. analyzed the actual performance records of many expert professionals who were playing against amateurs during 18,000 games of GO. In this oriental game of skill, two players compete by moving their marble-like pieces on a board. The winner is the player who annexed the most territory. Formal analysis of this mountain of data supported the existing hypothesis: these experts appeared to have developed their preprocessing skills by using what might be called perceptual templates. Each such *gist*, confirming covert perceptual expectations, helped them instantly categorize *whole complex scenes*.

Supporting evidence about such games of GO comes from the diffusion tensor image (DTI) study by Lee and colleagues at Seoul National University.[12] This new imaging technique exposes the brain to a shifting magnetic field. The resulting displacements create measurable shifts in the ways water molecules diffuse through the micro-architecture of white matter. The authors' 16 GO experts averaged 12 years of training. The 19 controls had no special training or interest in such games. In brief, at two sites in their white matter the GO experts showed the most consistent *increases* in their fractional anisotropy (FA). These sites were in the *right* frontal/subcortical and *left* inferior temporal regions. With regard to the temporal lobe themes discussed earlier (see chapters 11, 12), these two temporal lobe regions notably included the fusiform gyrus and the inferior longitudinal fasciculus. The increased FA values in these two inferior temporal regions were interpreted as consistent with the kinds of neural template mechanisms that could provide GO experts' with the instant decoding they needed during early visual processing.

Chess expertise seems to involve a horse of a different color. In Tübingen, Germany, the eight chess experts (in the top 1 percent) studied by Bilalic et al. had faster reaction times than did the 15 chess novices.[13] They also had greater fMRI activations in the following four regions: the junctional region where the lateral parietal, temporal, and occipital lobes all come together (see figure 2.1); the supramarginal gyrus (L); and medial regions like the retrosplenial cortex and the parahippocampal cortex (see figure 3.1).

Differences between the Right and Left Temporal and Frontal Lobes

Chapter 13 deferred a key question: Could our right and left temporal lobes perform remarkably useful functions in ways sometimes so different, indeed *so ill-timed*, that such a lack of flexibility might cause them to work at cross-purposes? Surely, our left temporal lobe has many practical multimodal functions to perform, not just the specialized role it plays in language processing.[14] Indeed, as the GO studies indicated, when these processing streams ramify farther forward toward the anterior pole of the temporal lobe, their normal associative capacities seem to resonate among template networks in subtly intelligent ways. The net results illustrate the wide variety of our other higher-order pattern recognition and interpretive functions. [ZB: 247–253; ZBR: 152–157]

Neurology began the old-fashioned way. It was a way that said, If you want to find out how the normal brain works, notice which clinical deficits occur after a discrete region of gray matter was damaged. Nowadays, researchers are asking, What symptoms occur when the *left* anterior temporal lobe cortex is merely *disorganized* briefly? Investigators can now use transcranial *magnetic* stimulation (TMS) to create such a temporary, *unilateral* disorganization. In normal volunteers, TMS can cause a brief loss of normal high-level temporal lobe conceptual functions.[15] The nature of the resulting 10-minute deficit confirms what researchers expected to find: our left anterior temporal lobe seems to serve normally as a conceptual hub. Normally, a sense of semantic meaning emerges as this high-level decoding matrix processes the information that reaches it from transcortical and subcortical sites.

In 2006, Han and colleagues at Beijing University employed a different approach.[16] They wanted to study the normal functions of the *right* temporal lobe. [SI: 135–138] They used functional MRI to monitor 12 subjects who were being shown a series of static film clips. They had extracted these isolated frames from various parts of a short movie. Their subjects' task was to answer this action-based, visual question: Do you recognize any logical plot underlying this sequence of separate visual scenes? Three *right*-sided regions increased their fMRI signals only when the subjects linked these separate visual episodes into one coherent plot. These regions were the right middle temporal cortex (BA 21), the right posterior superior temporal cortex (BA 42), and the right inferior postcentral gyrus (BA 1, 2, 3). The regions did not co-activate when random episodes fell into no meaningful sequence.

Asari et al., at the University of Tokyo Medical School, preferred inkblot responses. They presented their 68 normal adults with ten different Rorschach inkblot stimuli.[17] Simultaneously, they monitored these subjects' fMRI signals and their spontaneous verbal responses. Which site was significantly activated whenever the subjects voiced singular, novel responses to these ambiguous figures? The polar cortex of the right anterior temporal lobe.

Dense anatomical connections link this region at each anterior temporal pole with the amygdala, with the inferotemporal cortex more posteriorly, and with the nearby orbitomedial prefrontal cortex. Notably, connectivity analyses suggested that activity in the subjects' amygdala (L>R) was enhancing the degrees of connection that would link their left anterior prefrontal cortex with their right temporal pole. However, this activity in their amygdala also had a different role to play in the back of the brain. It usually appeared to *reduce* the connectivity between this right temporal pole and those regions farther back in their occipitotemporal cortex. The two sets of findings are interpretable and complementary: (1) Our personal memories, our imagination and perceptions seem to respond in complex ways to emotional messages arising from the amygdala, and (2) simultaneously, the nearby temporal pole could act to integrate this information into novel projective responses, the kinds that infuse imagination into processing.

In 2012, Cohn et al. also wished to test the capacities of normal subjects to detect visual coherence and incoherence.[18] They chose static visual images that held a special appeal for their American subjects. These sequences of single frames were extracted from the popular "Peanuts" comic strip. Notice that none of these images contained words. The subjects' reactions were monitored using visual event-related potential (VERP) responses. In brief, the results suggested that visual coherence arrived when a sensitive *left*-lateralized anterior neurocognitive mechanism became involved. This waveform arrived 300–400 milliseconds after the visual stimulus. The wave complex appeared to be reacting in a "pattern-predictive" manner at the same time that two mental themes converged. One theme represented the larger structure of an emerging, global, coherent narrative. The other component seemed to involve lesser events that could represent discrete sources of meaning. The anterior location of this particular VERP waveform is a point of further interest. It could be consistent with the possibility that the nearby inferior frontal *and* temporal regions on the left side were pooling some joint resources. Such a combination could help to infuse a larger narrative meaning into a series of images even though no actual words were attached to any of those separate visual frames. [ZBR: 213–214]

> • But is it always useful to cling to only one fixed meaning that might arise from some hub over in one temporal pole and nearby frontal region?

Why not *think outside the box*, loosen up such high-level concepts, and create a different narrative structure, one that can access other options? [SI: 123–188] For example, let's start with the important region around the left anterior temporal lobe hub. Suppose this hub were to become *less* active, whereas at the same time those other higher-level functions on the right side became *more* active. Now what could happen?

This could have seemed a far-out question even as Chi and Snyder prepared to answer it at the University of Sydney, in Australia.[19] Notice that the technique they chose delivered a particular kind of gentle stimulation to the brain. This method involves the transcranial passage of *direct current* (tDCS). This is *non*-magnetic stimulation at *low* amperage (1.6 milliamperes). When the cathodal (minus) DC electrode is placed on the scalp over the *left* anterior temple, the resting potentials of nerve cells are rendered *less* likely to fire in the underlying left anterior temporal *lobe*. However, by placing the anodal (plus) electrode on the scalp over the subject's *right anterior temporal lobe*, the nerve cell excitability of this right anterior temporal lobe region is facilitated. These reciprocal modulations occur *simultaneously*. They create less activation on the left but more activation on the right. An extensive literature supports the basic principles involved in this line of research.[20–22]

The normal subjects had to solve difficult insight problems while they were receiving tDCS and for many minutes after it stopped. These tasks use matches to indicate Roman numerals. Each problem must be solved by moving only one match stick. For example, try to change this false statement (11 equals 6) into a true statement by moving only *one* match:

$$XI = III + III$$

Why is this task so hard to solve? We have already limited our options. We have set up several rigidly conditioned restraints. One of the places we stay stuck is in a conventional logic-tight construct. It asserts that once an X is crossed, it must stay crossed. Who says so? Whose mental sets become so flexible that they can envision sliding one of these matches over a bit? Who can cut free from their ingrained force of habit, allowing this X to *diverge* into a more open V? During tDCS, three times as many normal participants could become more open-minded. They did solve such problems, in contrast to control participants who had received only sham stimulation. [SI: 183–186, 298]

In brief, what the subjects needed to do was to let go of their prior conventional constraints. Their imagination needed to open up, to embrace fresh insights and novel meanings. Single solutions happened to arrive after their *right* anterior temporal lobe circuits were not only gently facilitated but also potentially liberated. From what? Liberated from prejudgments, inhibitory constraints, and distractions previously imposed by ill-timed contributions from their left anterior temporal lobe. Could these complications be related to cross-talk received from some of the left side's extensive language-entangled functions?

This same direct current stimulation (tDCS) technique was then applied to other normal subjects during a second experiment.[23] Their task was to solve the much more difficult nine-dot problem. How can anyone solve this task? The only way is to literally think outside the box (see the illustration at the start of part V). But *word*-thinking is not the way to proceed. Why not? Because our intrusive Self, following convention, imposes another rigid *conceptual* constraint. Its boundary rules caution, "*Stay inside* the box." Silently, we obey our old, habitual mind-sets. No participants could solve this tough problem before they were stimulated or while being exposed to the sham control conditions.

When could 14 out of the 33 participants arrive at the correct solution? When the passage of direct current tended to reduce the functions of their *left* anterior temporal lobe at the same time that this current was facilitating the functions of their *right* anterior temporal lobe. It need not be assumed that every change occurring during tDCS or lingering for a hour or so thereafter must be confined solely to events generated at this cortical level.[24, 25]

These new tDCS observations reopen old discussions. When each of us pursues our highly individualistic approach to creative problem solving, how do our right and left hemispheres blend their dynamic positive and negative contributions? When we are faced with a formidable problem, do we have a single, well-defined goal? Is it to perform a quick, flexible, critical, yet balanced appraisal while seeking only one best solution? [SI: 153–158] If so, then we must keep shifting skillfully, flexibly, *at just the right times*, avoiding not only premature attachments to each fresh option but also overcritical rejections.

With one swift stroke, Isaac Newton (1642–1727) used a glass prism to split white daylight. Six rainbow-like bands of color emerged. Today's neuroimaging researchers are trying valiantly to untangle the six interwoven strands of creativity. Yet no comparable system on the technical horizon has this elegantly simple capacity to split creativity into its six interactive themes. They are interest, preparation, incubation, illumination, verification and exploitation.[26]

> • Could long-term meditators develop enduring changes in the pathways that interconnect the diverse gray matter regions in their brains?

Luders et al. first reviewed the latest literature relating to this large crucial topic. Then they described the results of their own study of meditators at UCLA, aided by diffusion tensor imaging (DTI).[27] Their 27 subjects were much *older* than meditators in the usual neuroimaging study. They averaged 57 years of age. Moreover, these meditators had been practicing for a very long time—an average of 23 years—and represented three major traditions of Buddhist practice. The results were contrasted with the DTI data found in the white matter of an equal number of age-matched normal controls.

The meditators showed a *generalized* increase in this DTI index of connectivity. The evidence was present in 20 separate white matter tracts. The increase was especially noteworthy in two major connection pathways that link the functions of their frontal and temporal lobes. One major path was on the left side: the superior longitudinal tract where it traverses the superior temporal gyrus. The other major path was the uncinate tract. It connects each inferior frontal lobe with its corresponding medial temporal lobe. This uncinate tract was involved on both right and left sides. Moreover, increases also occurred in two white matter tracts *within* the left temporal lobe itself: in the inferior longitudinal fasciculus and in that same branch of the left superior longitudinal fasciculus that courses farther into the left superior temporal gyrus. These two left-sided increases correlated with the subjects' increasing age, not with how long or how frequently they had practiced.

> • Was such evidence of neuroplasticity, when measured only at a single endpoint after two decades of meditation, accompanied by any pertinent psychological evidence? More specifically, were individual meditators more mature in their intra- or interpersonal relationships?

No data from that cross-sectional survey nor personal data supplied in this book testify either to the original immature baseline status or to the mature adult status of each person's psychological nature. All during these decades the meditators were exposed to the cumulative effects of four relevant mechanisms: (1) meditative nurture, (2) aging processes in general, (3) the usual kinds of maturation, and (4) the kind of Jamesian maturation that helps build extra character when we deliberately confront real-life daily experiences and seek to surmount other major challenges (see chapter 7). In fact, we do not know precisely which inhibitory, disinhibitory, and excitatory mechanisms had changed which psychophysiological attribute during any subject's decades of development.

Ample room remains for rigorous future longitudinal research. We still need to clarify what lay practitioners and monastics actually do when they meditate;[28] how the effects of implicit learning can be explained on the basis of each individual meditator's mechanisms of neuroplasticity; and how the resulting reorganizations in each brain can become overtly manifest daily in measurable degrees of that person's authentic, real-life, selfless compassion.[29] [MS: 42–52; 53–139]

- Can the mechanisms underlying selfless insight really be linked with those that release the covert networks of allocentric intuitive processing? If so, can such links clarify why spontaneous color phenomena could lateralize into the left visual field of an aging meditator?

A plausible sequence of relatively small conceptual steps could be involved. It happens that there are nine such steps in a working hypothesis, condensed elsewhere.[30] [MS: 169–177] The way to link them might seem reminiscent of those steps which resolve the standard nine-dot problem. For example, the first stroke follows the course of a diagonal line from the left-lateralized colors that points down toward their sites of origin in the opposite right lower temporal-occipital lobe (see chapter 12). From there, it could take only a small intuitive leap outside the box to realize the creative implications of that arrow line of allocentric processing shown in figure 3.1. Its trajectory leads us to an important realization: remarkable parallel, intuitive capacities are distributed among our temporal and frontal lobe networks. A wealth of connections from here are poised to engage the rest of the brain in further integrated interactions. [SI: 123–188]

For example, the latest controlled study by Luders et al. included 50 long-term meditators.[31] Their average duration of practice was exceptionally long: 19.8 years. Significant increases in grey matter volume were found in the subiculum and were slightly greater on the right side. This subregion of the hippocampus sends major projections to the mamillary body of the hypothalamus. These messages relay up through the anterior thalamic nucleus to the cingulate gyrus. [ZB: 180–189] This article refers to the episodic memory functions attributed to the subiculum. These are the kinds of remembrances that could be relevant to the mechanisms that enable long-term meditators to cultivate *re*mindfulness. [ZBR: 99–108; SI: 96–97; MS: 109, 162]

New research horizons continue to open up in front of us every day. In no way could tDCS have been foreseen back in eighteenth-century Italy, on that day when Luigi Galvani just happened to see a frog's leg twitch as it responded to a nearby electrical charge.[32] Today's developments in direct current research appear to have galvanized a fresh view of the future. How will electromagnetic energies next be used, selectively, in techniques that change the resting potentials of inhibitory and excitatory nerve cells inside our brain? How will they be *mis*used? Stay tuned.[33]

15

Resources of Enduring Happiness; Opening to "Just This"

Meditation is not about sitting quietly in the shade of a tree and relaxing in a moment of respite from the daily grind; it is about familiarizing yourself with a new vision of things, a new way to manage your thoughts, of perceiving people and experiencing the world . . . One can *become* enduringly free and happy, providing one knows how to go about it.

Matthieu Ricard[1]

Go forth to seek: the quarry never found
is still a fever to the questing hound.
The skyline is a promise, not a bound.

John Masefield (1878–1967)[2]

How *does* one become familiar with this new way of experiencing the world? We have been swept up into an era when it might seem possible to condense meditative training during a quick fix. Item: People who practice a kind of integrative body-mind training (IBMT) for only three to eleven hours can improve their executive attention and change some Self-control networks in corresponding regions of their brain.[3] [SI: 42–43] Zen maintains a longitudinal perspective. This chapter gives added weight to the first-person reports by seasoned professionals who have meditated for decades.

Matthieu Ricard, Ph.D., is preeminent in this respect. What does one do next, having been born to a prominent French philosopher father and an artist mother, after one begins a career as a gene-mapping biologist? One goes forth to seek something beyond the horizons of France. During the past four decades, Ricard became an exemplary Buddhist monk, practicing in the Tibetan tradition. He went on to play a key role both as a leading subject and as an interpreter in the pioneering neuroimaging studies of other skilled meditators by Richard Davidson, Antoine Lutz, and their colleagues at the University of Wisconsin. [ZBR: 396–398] When Matthieu Ricard devotes an entire book to the subject of happiness, readers discover the lived wisdom of a genuinely happy sage.

In his 2012 article, Ricard and colleagues distinguished between our short-term and long-term approaches to happiness (see table 1).[4]

Hundreds of human subjects undertook a series of psychological tests that confirmed the essential point of this table: durable happiness requires selflessness. One result of long-term meditative practice is attributable to the ways that it cultivates higher societal values and authentic meanings *beyond* our sense of Self. These meanings emerge incrementally in the course of our relationships with other people both inside and outside our local community of meditators (the *sangha*). Behavioral transformations evolve that no longer depend on advancing our own Self-interest or avoiding

Table 1
Measuring Happiness

	Fluctuating happiness	Authentic durable happiness
Role of Self Characterized by	Self-centeredness Longing for complex pleasures; Loathing displeasures	Selflessness A stable plenitude expressing affirmative resources and simplified needs
Valuing	Self-enhancement	Authentic meanings beyond the Self
Prevailing attitudes	Mine!	Ours

Adapted from Dambrun, Ricard, Despres, et al., 2012 (see note 4).

discomfort. The interpersonal lessons one learns in a Living Zen context endure in behavior. Their give-and-take aspects have been forged and tempered during a series of life's emotional ups and downs.

Multiple books and articles have tried to define other ingredients of happiness. Somehow, they overlook the comment in Udana 2.1 attributed to the newly enlightened Buddha: "Getting free of the conceit that 'I am' — this is truly the ultimate happiness."[5] A later wise man, the Stoic Seneca (4 B.C.E–65 C.E.) commented on the sense of liberation inherent in "the pursuit of wisdom." Apropos of such pursuits, we now have an article in *Time* magazine, entitled "The Happiness of Pursuit."[6] Perhaps this topic is periodically rediscovered because a sense of stimulation occurs when we undertake a quest. This fact is a clue that powerful neurobiological motivations underlie our search for novel stimuli.[7]

Emotions Move Us

Myokyoni wisely observed that the first step in Zen training is becoming familiar "with the workings of the emotional household." [MS: 125] To the present author, a decade ago, it seemed that real happiness often depended on how these emotional ups and downs, coupled with basic traits of character, could influence events for better or for worse.[8] Other important aspects of the emotions were reviewed on pages examining the Way of Zen Buddhism. [ZB: 347–352, 567–570, 648–653; ZBR: 239–265, 396–398; SI: 223–247; MS: 66, 143–145, 160–162]

But suppose one had to construct a short list of our major emotional responses, a list that was limited to the vernacular. Then, the first five might be oversimplified as mad, scared, sad, bad (revolted, disgusted), and glad. Notice the asymmetry: this ratio is four negative to one positive. If happiness depends just on the feelings associated with being glad, then it is not likely to last very long if all those negative emotions keep overcoming our better nature.

Panksepp's latest book contains *seven* emotional systems.[9] His list begins with seeking, a word that implies searching for something. The list continues with fear, rage, lust, care, grief, and ends with play. Even after we first identify our questing, instinctual appetitive drives with seeking (including the quest that motivates our hound), and then confirm that nurturing and play are positive, notice that the four remaining influences are negative. These powerful negative systems of fear, rage, lust and grief can still outweigh the effects of the positive systems by a wide margin.

From his Zen perspective, Thich Nhat Hanh placed being hostile-mad-enraged at the forefront of our emotional problems. In 1992 he said, "The absence of anger is the basis of real happiness, the basis of love and compassion."[10] But the deep layers of fear (being really scared) can be profoundly traumatizing. They are much more disturbing than the emotion that we usually feel when we are angry. To help dissolve such deep fears he prescribes first gently acknowledging them nonjudgmentally, and later analyzing their origins.[11] He relates the intensity of our "original fear" to the harsh transitional question we faced at birth: can this vulnerable newborn babe, ejected from its warm home into the cold world, inhale its own oxygen, exhale its own CO_2? Life hinged on the ways that our brain stem and hypothalamic survival reflexes solved this existential problem. [ZB: 232–235]

Clarity

James Ford is the minister of the First Unitarian Church in Providence, Rhode Island. An ordained Soto Zen teacher, he is the author of three books about Zen and Zen masters. His 2012 book bears the subtitle, *Field Notes from a Zen Life*.[12] In easily read pages, this seasoned observer shares what he has learned about the arduous spiritual Path during his last four decades. Helpful chapters clarify what Zen practice is and is not, describe what to look for in a Zen teacher, and culminate in seven key suggestions. These summarize the essence of any spiritual approach worth following in today's complex world.

The seventh suggestion is a prescription for ongoing mental *clarity* (chapter 2 in the present volume considers clarity an attribute of sage wisdom). Ford warns readers against the kinds of "techno-shamanism" that might mislead them into using psychedelics. How do the closing lines in his chapter describe the authentic Path toward this desirable ongoing clarity? It is an approach to "opening up," not "shutting down." Ford offers a simple explanation for this statement about the particular kinds of an *opening up* approach that can access genuine clarity: The quest "is not about abnormal experiences, but the most ordinary of them all, just this, just this."

D. T. Suzuki was in full agreement with this characterization of the basic ordinariness of Zen (see preface). And the origins of the words "*just this*" can be traced back to the earliest Buddhist sutras (see chapter 1).

Aspects of Openness, Including Some Caveats

We live in a permissive culture. It openly invites people to experiment with potent drugs. [ZBR: 291–302; SI: 267–268] A recent report from Johns Hopkins University is instructive.[13] [ZB: 436–438] Its 52 psilocybin-naive volunteers (average age 46) were well-educated (54 percent had postgraduate degrees). Moreover, 90 percent were regular participants in religious services, discussion groups, prayer, or meditation. In their baseline (self-reported) personality assessment, openness ranked the highest (average score 64) among the standard domains that psychologists use to take an inventory of one's personality.

- What is Openness?

We were introduced to this word back in chapter 2. There, the asterisk preceeding openness identified it another important quality associated with the mature attitudes of a sage. This openness implies a warm welcome—hospitality with open arms. One's attitudes are no longer hostile, inturned, insular. Psychologists include six subdescriptions in this standard personality inventory of openness. They include such attributes as: active imagination, aesthetic appreciation of art and nature, depth of emotional feelings, interest in theoretical and abstract ideas, tolerance for a range of lifestyles, and interest in learning new hobbies.

Openness feels good. Most people aspire to open their hearts to others, to empathize in ways that seem to express their native virtues of compassion. [ZB: 648–653] It might be anticipated that those university-educated participants who volunteered for this study would tend to rank themselves high in these six potential attributes when researchers asked them to assess their own personalities.

These adult subjects then completed *either* one eight-hour, double-blind session on *oral* psilocybin (30 milligrams/70 kilograms body weight) in a fully supportive setting, *or* four similar sessions (on separate days) when their daily *oral* doses ranged from 5 to 30 milligrams/70 kilograms. Thirty of the subjects who received the high dose of psilocybin went on to satisfy their researchers' criteria for having a "complete mystical experience." The other 22 subjects did not.

The subjects' reports indicated that they had experienced further increases in openness while on this drug. These increases correlated with the degree to which these mystical experiences had just been evoked. The increases did not correlate with each subject's prior report of a baseline level of openness.

- What happened later on?

During the follow-up evaluations 16 months later, only those same 30 subjects who had earlier undergone a complete, short-term, evoked mystical experience reported that their induced increases in openness had persisted. This self-assessment becomes more important because, by this later date, openness reports were back near the baseline screening levels in the other group of subjects who did not undergo such an experience. The persistence of increased openness is in contrast to the natural decline that is observed in self-reports obtained from the aging adult population. It also exceeds that reported by patients whose depression had been reversed successfully while they received antidepressant drugs.

Researchers in future studies are encouraged to go beyond the obvious limitations of self-report measures, to seek hard objective evidence indicating that actual *trait* changes are expressed in transformed openness *behavior*. When this is accomplished, by applying rigorous psycho-physiological and other behavioral tests, it will emulate the hard-nosed example set by Zen masters in past centuries. Their exacting attitude has been *"Show* me, don't tell me" (see chapter 5).

It is not clear what the short-term and long-term structural and functional MRI findings might be that could serve to complement the data of this oral-dosage study. [ZBR: 300] Nor is it clearly established that all the complex acute mechanisms evoked by a rapid *intravenous* dose of psilocybin[14] are relevant to the very different setting and comfortable conditions maintained during this oral-dose experiment.

Considerable latitude exists among the six personality subdescriptors that are included in openness. Given this variability, it could be a thorny task for researchers to localize such openness to a few specific neuroimaging sites. For example, one recent neuroimaging study was based on the structural MRI and DTI data of 265 Norwegian adults. It was conducted at a single point in time. It found no reliable neural associations with the trait of openness.[15] However, a recent *longitudinal* structural MRI study was designed to follow 274 normal Japanese adults, aged 24–75, over a six-year interval.[16] Lesser degrees of atrophic change were found in the right inferior parietal lobule of those adults whose self-reported personality traits were consistent with more openness. This large lobule is packed with a complex array of association functions. [ZB: 244–247; ZBR: 148–152] Among them are our normal capacities to attend to the orderly timing of events during visual processing, and to help us distinguish between our own Self and other persons. [SI: 194–196]

Letting Go of the Deep Layers of Self Facilitates Opening to "Just This"

Chapter 1 introduced us to the Udana, and to the way the Buddha distilled his pithy message of selflessness for two old men, Bahiya and Malunkya. Chapter 3 then began to examine the neural correlates of meditating selflessly. Let's return now to an earlier thesis by Thich Nhat Hanh. He said that we must first drop off our pervasive negative emotions (become less angry and fearful) before real happiness begins to ensue. What other evidence supports it?

During kensho, multiple agitations referable to the pejorative aspects of the Self are extinguished. They vanish from lived experience for at least a short time afterward. These profound egocentric subtractions do not simply cut off those six high-level descriptors that psychologists use to inventory an open personality. [ZBR: 200] Indeed, kensho's acute deletions appear to amputate one's motivational legs, as it were, at the Self's two most fundamental levels of dynamic behavior: they cut off all impulses that might drive one to advance or start to retreat. These acute subtractions—of approach behavior (+) and aversive behavior (–)—sever the expressions of one's deepest, most polarized longings and loathings. [ZB: 607–608] The teachings confirm that insight-wisdom at this deep level means being liberated from both polar excesses: from bliss *and* pain (see chapter 1).

Existential Aspects of Zen Training

Sitting mindlessly in one's cozy armchair, it is difficult to *feel* the distinctive impulses and primal survival codes that drive one's approach behavior to seek oxygen, water, food, sex, or drugs that stimulate specific receptor sites. However, rigorous meditative retreats help one recognize how powerfully these appetitive drives compel our behaviors. [ZB: 138–140] Carl Jung knew that formidable resistances would greet any such quest that probed our subterranean depths. [ZB: 129–137] The outlines of such a task are barely glimpsed, let alone recognized, during an abbreviated eleven-hour or eight-week introduction to meditation.

During the long-term ancient Path that leads out of their grand delusion, trainees must keep learning how to harness and gentle the deeply contending instincts of their imperious (yet fearful) Self. [SI: 218] LeDoux[17] and Denton et al.[18] recently examined these deep survival circuit functions that empower our primordial, instinctual, appetitive emotions. Every day, these networks help us manage our deepest visceral comforts and discomforts even as our implicit fear of dying still lurks quietly in the background.

Not until kensho arrives, much later on this long Path, does the trainee comprehend what it feels like to be cut so free from the bonds of primal fear itself that the ensuing deep peace "passeth all understanding."[19] The words, "just this" or "suchness" serve to remind us that words are but feeble attempts to express the ineffable attributes of this brief state. [ZBR: 357–387]

Roots of Primal Fear

Certain persons cannot feel normal fear when they reach adult life. Why not? Because these rare patients have developed a chronic progressive degeneration of their amygdala.[20] Under which special conditions can these adult patients again experience fear? When they volunteer to accept a challenge approximating the situation that they faced at birth: an experimental panic attack. This is induced by breathing an excess of carbon dioxide. These CO_2 experiments illustrate that some deep primal fears could normally enter through avenues other than the amygdala. If we are to exclude such standard limbic system sites as the amygdala and the hypothalamus, what other normal gateways exist where inhibition could cut off some maladaptive roots of our Self?

The periaqueductal gray (PAG) in the midbrain is an obvious candidate. It must be added to the standard limbic and paralimbic sites involved in our normal fight or flight responses. [ZB: 217–218, 233–235, 657–658; ZBR: 15, 243–244] The recent human fMRI studies by Buhle et al. indicate that aversive stimuli (pain and negative visual images) normally activate this central gray region.[21] Moreover, we normally co-activate this core brain stem region along with the anterior mid-cingulate cortex, merely by anticipating that negative consequences loom ahead.[22]

But the large omni-Self constellation is not limited to only these several deep sites. Approach and retreat behaviors link into multiple, diverse regions. For example, suppose you are a researcher who would like to positively motivate your experimental subjects to approach a goal. Kinnison et al recruited their volunteers by offering them a potential reward of 20 dollars.[23] Where did the various reward cues induce increased fMRI signals in these subjects? In 22 nodal regions of a very large network. Just at the cortical level alone, these sites included the anterior insula, medial prefrontal cortex, and middle frontal gyrus. Subcortically, this omni-network included the midbrain, caudate, putamen, and nucleus accumbens.

To elicit their subjects' instincts to retreat, the researchers wielded the threat of subjecting them to an actual electric shock. After their subjects became fearful, the experimenters then used neutral cues to condition these subjects to anticipate this aversive threat. When these conditioning cues arrived, they prompted increased fMRI signals from 16 nodal regions. Cortically, these included the anterior insula (again), the inferior frontal gyrus, and the medial prefrontal cortex (again). Subcortically, this cue conditioned network included the thalamus, the bed nucleus of the stria terminalis [ZBR: 468] and the basal forebrain [ZB: 167, 260, 269]. Notably, cues that induced the fearful threat of an impending shock also *reduced* the functional connectivity that linked several cortical regions. This finding points toward one of the mechanisms which can enable emotional stress to interfere with our normal cognitive performance.

Subtle Preludes to Major Openings

The introduction mentioned what happened just before the author dropped into the states of internal absorption and kensho. On each occasion he first let go, passively abandoned himself to circumstances, then briefly glanced up.

> • What happens when one lets go, gives up, abandons plans, surrenders the sovereign Self, accepts whatever consequences might ensue?

In each surrender, the person reaches an extremity of Selfhood. Minutes before the start of the episode of internal absorption, the nerve-compression paralysis of my left leg had proven that my sitting practice was flawed. [ZB: 467–472] All willpower had then dissolved passively, releasing a mode of simple acceptance.

Just before the episode of kensho, that same meditator (who would consider it unthinkable to be late for the first morning sitting) had made an error and had taken the wrong train on his way to the retreat. Clearly, this person was no longer in full control of events that might happen next. [ZB: 536–539]

Neither prelude was felt as an occasion for Self-chastisement. Rather, each one was simply accepted as a matter-of-fact illustration of incompetence.

A working hypothesis might suggest that these submissions of the psychic Self had contributed little openings that happened to coincide with other, deeper shifts. These could have been developing incrementally during the previous days when meditation was being practiced more frequently. [SI: 113–117]

Commentary

A Living Zen practice gradually establishes the primacy of affirmative, realistic attitudes over unwholesome appetitive drives. When openings of various sizes to "just this" are repeated, they gradually dissolve your grand delusion of being an absolute sovereign Self. The ancient sutras contained an original prescription for "just this." As you keep refilling this prescription, let your long-term approach be regular meditation, not medication.

In Closing

Zen does not teach to destroy all the impulses, instincts, and affective factors that make up the human heart, it only teaches to clear up our intellectual insight from erroneous discriminations and unjustifiable assertions; for when this is done, the heart knows by itself how to work out its native virtues.

Daisetz T. Suzuki (1870–1966)[1]

D. T. Suzuki authored 26 books in English on Zen and allied topics. Given how much they contain, he may reasonably be considered to have been practicing a longitudinally ripened form of Living Zen before he died at the age of almost ninety-six.[2] His first attempts to meditate in a Zen setting were discouraging. Lucky for us, he persisted.

If you have been meditating for a while, try to remember how strange it seemed when you first sat down to practice. Chapter 4 could serve as a reminder: Siddhartha was only a beginner when he first sat under a rose-apple tree as a young child. May similar remindful moments keep springing up in your future. Let them help you recall how to meditate, to introspect, to discover why you're so biased, to then follow your best intentions, and to relate to others more fruitfully.

Pause. Suspend those cultural pressures that would urge you to buy the latest personal electronic device, keep looking down while you manipulate it. Let moments of reflection allow you to raise your sights above eye level. Look out into those elevated dimensions of space that lie above the horizon. Now is an appropriate time to renew your interests in meditating more regularly. Decide to meet fresh challenges on this ancient Path—to climb difficult mountains after mountains. Each time you do, you could be developing significant new dimensions of your character, as William James had foreseen.

Perhaps gazing far out toward the horizon on one side will allow you to tap into a more structured, conservative kind of outlook.[3] Maybe you will then be reminded to adhere to traditional precepts. Some have withstood the test of millennia. If gazing far out toward the horizon on that other side recalls a more open, liberal outlook, then may the long history of the Way remind you: new potentials emerged each time meditation evolved in a new cultural setting, enabling its practitioners to let go of biased concepts and institutional rituals long outgrown.

So, make time to go outdoors into the natural world. Here you can easily reclaim your native attentiveness and train it in a balanced, ongoing manner. Here, it will be simpler to elevate your gaze, let go of word-thoughts and concepts, uncover fresh intuitions.

The following sentences condense the bottom-line message of each previous chapter:

* *"Just this"* means that *no you* intrudes into clear consciousness.

* Your sovereign sense of Self learns to become less intrusive after years of submitting daily life experiences to mindful introspection.

* Meditation cultivates attentiveness. Attentiveness includes the kind of globally receptive, other-referential awareness that operates subconsciously. *Allocentric* is another word that describes such an open, other-referential awareness.

* Stay in touch with your own deep affinities with the trees and plants, rooted in the Earth, that also undergo their own natural cycles of growth, decay, and regrowth.

* *"Just this"* points toward the direct experience of insights that convey wisdom, wordlessly.

* Birds capture our attentiveness. On rare occasions, bird songs can trigger an awakening.

*   "The more unconscious one keeps in the matter, the more likely one is to succeed." (William James)

*   Zen practice means detaching from thoughts. (Foyan Quingyuan)

*   Remindfulness is a kind of "lowly listening." It serves, in the Emersonian sense, as our natural source of intuitive "guidance."

*   Awareness matures over the decades. Its early, strong *I-Me-Mine* orientations evolve toward gentler, more adaptive, *You-Us-Ours* attitudes of allocentric and ecocentric identification.

*   Gazing up and out there into the distance can create a beneficial influence on one's perspective.

*   Decade after decade, the brain's innate resources keep learning and transforming intuitive functions.

*   Meditation offers ways to transform our "optical delusion" of consciousness. Einstein used this phrase to describe the Self-centeredness that keeps each infinitesimal Self imprisoned, unmindful of this incredibly vast universe.

*   Creativity resembles meditation, to the degree that with great flexibility they both deploy convergent and divergent attentive processing mechanisms.

*   An authentic enduring happiness becomes possible when Self-centeredness yields to selflessness, and affirmative attitudes govern one's maladaptive emotions.[4]

Remember: as you cultivate the clarity of mindfulness and re-mindfulness on your journey, Living Zen becomes the actual daily life practice of opening up to directly experience the basic oneness you share with the ordinary, wondrous world. Just this. Then, increasingly, the innate neural expressions of kindness, intuition, compassion, and gratitude can become embodied subconsciously in your everyday activities.

Appendix A

The Forest as a Sanctuary for Re-creation

One impulse from a vernal wood
May teach you more of man,
Of moral evil and of good,
Than all the sages can.

William Wordsworth (1770–1850)[1]

One of the Buddha's favorite places to sit was at the base of a tree. In that era of large forests, one could live a relatively simple life as a monk or nun, be an active member of a sangha, and still find places in the forest wilderness where one could retreat to meditate in solitude.[2] Nowadays, people who commune with Nature outdoors keep rediscovering that trees and other natural scenery possess inherent healing properties. [ZB: 664–667; MS: 53–60]

Wordsworth's affinities for the fresh foliage of springtime were appreciated centuries earlier in China. An old Ch'an story describes an event when Lin-chi was a younger monk.[3] He is out in the forest, planting young pine trees, when he is confronted by his formidable master, Huang-po (d. 850). The master asks, "Why are you planting so many pine trees way out here on the mountain?" Lin-chi replies, "First, to improve the natural setting that leads up to the main temple gate. Second, to leave a landmark to benefit future generations." He then stamps his hoe on the ground vigorously, exhaling loudly. At this point, Huang-Po, impressed, predicts, "Under you, my lineage will flourish throughout the world."

This came to pass. Lin-chi (J. Rinzai) (d. 866) and his followers went on to found the Rinzai school of Zen. In homage to him, the planting of pine trees continues as an annual tradition in some Rinzai centers. The ceremony is called *Saisho*. Its Kanji character stands for "Planting the Pine." In the climate of China, early Ch'an would flourish among monks who could grow their own food. Most were farming the fields (*nong chan*) not residing in the forest.[4] Any kind of gardening work/play is recommended. It is an excellent way to stay in touch with the earth. It also reinforces a simple reality: all growing things go through natural developmental cycles.

Taking Nature Walks among the Trees

D. T. Suzuki wrote a long book chapter extolling the "Japanese Love of Nature."[5] With regard to Nature, it becomes of interest to note how he would later describe an alternate state experience to Albert Stunkard.[6] It happened one day while Suzuki was taking a walk between tall rows of old cryptomeria trees (*C. japonica*). Someone (perhaps a monk) had planted these magnificent evergreen conifers in earlier centuries. Their tall columns now lined the avenue that led up to the Mountain Gate of the Rinzai Zen temple of Engaku-ji.[7] "As I walked up the steps," said Suzuki, "I became aware that I was the same as the trees at which I was looking. It was not that I had ceased to be myself, but I had become the trees as well." [ZBR: 335–357]

By 1982 the Japanese Ministry of Agriculture, Forest and Fisheries had come to a decision: it needed a new term to describe the forest recreational activities that it was making available to all Nature-lovers. The term it coined, *Shinrin-yoku,* refers to the actual practice of "taking in all the atmosphere of the forest." Currently, at least four dozen official Forest Therapy trails exist to encourage the urban population of Japan to engage in this therapeutic practice of hiking in the forest.

This practice means total *immersion* in a forest. Indeed, it is now commonly spoken of as forest bathing.[8] A series of scientific reports have since documented the beneficial effects associated with this immersion. These have chiefly been inspired by the senior author, Yoshifumi Miyazaki of Chiba University. In a recent review, readers can discover the evidence collected from 420 subjects at 35 different forest park sites throughout Japan.[9] The "forest bathers" showed the expected improvements over their urban control group in such Self-reported improvements as mood and feelings of well-being. At rest, they also showed a 5.8 percent decrease in heart rates, a 12.4 percent decrease in salivary cortisol levels, and decreased urinary levels of catecholamine. A subgroup of middle-aged hikers also showed a substantial acute increase (56%) in natural killer cells (NK) followed by a more prolonged increase (23%). Natural killer cells are one index of heightened immune function against cancer.[10]

Emerson was aware that he felt nourished when he took the long view that led far out to the distant horizon. Moreover, his essay entitled "Nature" contained the following metaphor about immersion: "We go out daily and nightly to feed the eyes on the horizon, and require so much scope, just as we need water for our bath."[11]

In a 2008 study, Berman and colleagues reported that normal students improved their attentive performance scores after they walked outdoors through the tree-lined Ann Arbor Arboretum. [MS: 60, 206–207] Berman and others recently conducted a similar study of 19 patients who were diagnosed with a moderately severe depressive disorder.[12] Before these patients actually started out—either on their 50-minute nature walk or on their control walk through the city streets of Ann Arbor—they were asked to take on an added psychological task. This task was to ruminate on a prior personal experience, an emotional event that was very negative and was still unresolved. Despite this burden, the 2.8-mile nature walk through the Arboretum generated a substantial increase in their mood, and their memory span also increased.

The dynamic, mood-enhancing restorative attributes of green space have now been documented using five-channel *mobile* EEG recordings.[13] The results on the 25-minute walk through green space in Edinburgh differed from the two other walks that went through urban shopping and busy commercial streets.

Our inherent affinities with trees and Nature keep inviting us to rejoin them, become immersed, and be restored.

Appendix B

Potentially Useful Words and Phrases

> It is better to know some of the questions than all of the answers.
>
> James Thurber (1894–1968)[1]

Earlier pages, here and elsewhere, have explored the power of silence. [ZB: 633–636] Research committees are not likely to fund grant applications devoted to silence per se. Committees require you to identify explicit topics and label them with meaningful words that describe conceptual details on multiple pages. At the fertile interface between Zen and the brain, new words and phrases keep bubbling up to the surface. Some of these might be useful in helping to generate testable hypotheses. Among the samples cited here, research is already finding potential psychophysiological correlates in a few instances.

Achronia

Achronia defines the absolute lack of any notion about time. One's own personal time drops out during the selflessness of kensho-satori. Time no longer exists as a general concept. [ZBR: 38–381, 465, 539] Within this zero state of time, consciousness is also beyond any notion of time*less*ness. Less-ness might convey the notion that time was still a quality that was then felt to be missing. No such sense of lost time exists within achronia. Instead, the horizon of consciousness opens out beyond all prior boundary notions. Neither past nor future exist. This total vacancy of time enters direct experience, nonverbally, as Eternity.

Attentive Processing

Attentive processing is a generic term. Why does the word *attentive* precede *processing*? This particular order serves as a useful reminder: our very first milliseconds of attentiveness are incisive. Attention is the sharp point, the arrowhead, out at the very tip of our arrow-shaft of processing. Once this point impales the intended target, the processing of the target can then proceed. So, attentive processing specifies that attention serves this vanguard role. [MS: 154–155]

Awareness usually refers to a less intense level of attentiveness. However, this attentiveness remains globally sensitive. Its ambient receptivity can detect any faint stimulus. [ZB: 496] Event-related potential research suggests that bare awareness might take only a fourth or fifth of a second to detect the mere presence of such a simple stimulus. In contrast, attentive processing can take perhaps twice as long when the subject's task is to completely identify a stimulus that is more complex. [ZBR: 185, 190; SI: 14–15; MS: 19] A bare awareness that attends to external stimuli is characteristic of our forms of bottom-up processing. However, an internal awareness also remains poised to react when subtle interoceptive cues arise from inside our own body. [MS: 83, figure 7]

Another term, *intention*, is also important, because it refers to our memory-based attitudes of mind. Some intentions remain so clearly registered in mind that they help keep our voluntary, top-down goals online for a short time. [MS: 14, figure 1] Often, however, our so-called best intentions are like long-range resolutions that we hope to keep online *subconsciously*. There, held in the recesses of long-term memory, their affirmative guidance systems remind us which goals to seek and how to behave.

Aurora Meditatorum

This term refers to the spontaneous appearance of colors that arise during meditation against a background of illumination. The way these epiphenomena arise and lateralize suggests some late implications of long-term meditative practice (see chapter 12).

Doing-Time

Doing-time operates preconsciously. It estimates how much we can actually *do* in a particular short interval of time. [ZB: 562–563; ZBR: 376–377] For example, it first surveys that unforgiving distance between two curbstones on either side of the traffic-filled street. Meanwhile, it scans our autobiography for details recording our past performance. We are then silently informed how fast our Self must run in order to cross this gap safely. All the dynamic correlates involved in this insightful realization and its yes/no decision have yet to be documented.

However, recent research establishes that (1) connections between the left cerebellum and the right superior temporal sulcus (STS) sponsor our visual perception that *another* person's body is moving,[2] and (2) the posterior inferior frontal gyrus becomes activated during the inhibitory phase of our own go/no-go decisions,[3] as does our subthalamic nucleus. [MS: 136] Extensions of such techniques make it theoretically possible to clarify how several Self-centered reflexive functions enter into the intuitive mechanisms of doing-time operations.

I-Me-Mine

This triad summarizes three key operational components of the Self. [ZB: 43–47, 50–51, 145, 569] Notice how they interact in a situation when, for example, *My* attitudes emerge into *My* opinions about politics and then govern how *I* "should" react to some other person whose aggressive political opinions have just injured *Me*. [SI: 110, 207–211] Meditation can help our youthful *I-Me-My*opias to become more far-sighted in later decades.

Functional MRI is being used to uncover many autobiographical aspects of the *I* and the *Me*. [SI: 53–83] Less is known about every possessive attachment by the *Mine*.[4] This intrusive Self clings vigorously to every tangible and intangible possession that it owns. These passionate attachments are concealed within the fixed opinions established by our personal and cultural belief systems. Caveats abound when meditators are being studied. [SI: 110]

Harris and colleagues conducted an informative fMRI study of such belief systems.[5] They presented their 14 normal adults with a range of factual statements. These statements were expressed visually in words or numbers, e.g., "Eagles are common pets"; "There is probably no actual Creator God"). Their subjects could then respond in one of three ways: (1) I *believe* this (implying that *I* accept this fact as true); (2) I *dis*believe this (meaning that *I* reject this fact as untrue); and (3) I'm *uncertain* (*I'm* still checking).

When the subjects believed that a given statement was true (in terms of *their* personal frame of reference), the BOLD signal activity increased in their ventromedial prefrontal cortex, L>R. However, during their rejections, prominent activations occurred in their left inferior frontal gyrus and in their anterior insula on both sides. During uncertainty, activation increased in the anterior cingulate gyrus. Moreover, a deactivation occurred in the caudate nucleus that might be interpretable as a potential exercise of behavioral restraint on their part.

Just This

The two words happened to join when I was improvising a home remedy for my own mindlessness and distractibility during meditation. [ZBR: 33–37] "Just this" became a useful way to follow the breath in and out until a thought-free phase of bare awareness ensued. During those years, I was not aware that the phrase "just this" could be traced far back into the Buddhist history of China and Japan [SI: 11–13] or Korea (see chapter 13), let alone to the pithy words attributed to the Buddha in ancient India (see chapter 1).

I have since heard from several experienced meditators who, having read about this simple "Just this" technique, or having observed me demonstrating it, also found it helpful.[6]

So, this phrase has now taken on several optional levels of silent meaning. Here are some examples. One can:

1. Let *just* become a silent label for breathing *in*, while *this* evolves through several steps to become a silent label for breathing *out*.

2. Let this silent usage then drop out by itself during meditation. What remains is simply the bare, wordless awareness of breathing movements.

3. Later, allow the phrase to become a distant, accurate metaphor when referring to "just this" experience, namely, entering into the actual phase of clear silent awareness that neither hears nor knows such words.

4. Later, let the phrase evolve into a metaphor with even subtler resonances. Such an impression might be consistent with the soft realization that "Just this" clear, selfless awareness—right *here* and *now*—is a moment of immanence, an integral part of the immense Big Picture. [SI: 199]

5. Continue to allow the phrase and its usages to remain within the ordinary interpretations of neurobiology and Buddhist history, free from potential metaphysical extensions.[7]

Moodlight

Moodlight refers first to a soft eerie emotion. It is what any person might normally *feel* out in a quiet cemetery alone, on a cool dark night, at a time when the full Autumn moon provides the sole source of illumination. In this instance, the term serves simply to establish that one's inner subjective *mood* is in a particular emotional category. This differs from the more objective, optical-visual perception of the actual moon*light* that is shining from such an external moon.

Yet a feeling comparable with moodlight may gather momentum during the rare occasion when an unparalleled vacancy of Self arrives in kensho. [ZBR: 415, 432–440] The psychophysiological correlates of normal moodlight have not yet been documented, nor have they been studied in the core of the state of awakening called kensho.

Promethean Hyperpraxia

This term refers to several distinctive, creative liberations of behavior in the Zen context. On these occasions, the kinds of normal skilled movements released are enhanced both in their quality and quantity. [ZB: 674–677] In the first two instances, the liberations develop acutely, either at the close of the state of internal absorption [ZB: 508–510], or at the close of the state of kensho [ZB: 544, 611].

The third instance refers to an incremental, decades-long development. This is the kind of swift, efficient behavior that evolves as experienced meditators move along the Path toward the *stage* of ongoing enlightened traits. [ZB: 668–674] Each one of these several liberations of the person's habitual behaviors is noteworthy in itself. For example, many preclinical studies show that the normal release of nitric oxide (NO˙) has functional consequences (potentially important for behavior) in the caudate nuclei, putamen, and substantia nigra. [ZBR: 279–288; SI: 260–261; MS: 138] The hope is that future investigations of this free radical gas, and of dopamine and related neural messengers, will extend the clinical research horizons of these intriguing preclinical results.

Remindfulness

This word itself serves as a reminder: complex, autonomous, affirmative, covert memory skills are poised silently, subconsciously online, to accomplish Self-correcting overview functions, consistent with our best intentions (see chapter 2). These functions are included in *sati* (Pali) and have affinities with the qualities of *samprajanya* (Sanskrit).

Trait Tectonics

This phrase points toward the *deep* transformations of behavior traits that evolve in the brain's subterranean levels on the long-term meditative Path of Zen training. [ZB: 625–697; ZBR: 389–401]. These must be distinguished from those changes caused by aging.[3]

Common Acronyms Used in Brain Research

Techniques Used in Studying the Brain[1, 2]

DCM	Dynamic causal modeling
DTI	Diffusion tensor imaging
EEG	Electroencephalography
fMRI	Functional magnetic resonance imaging
fNIRS	Functional near-infrared spectroscopy
LORETA	Low-resolution brain electrotomography
MEG	Magnetoencephalography
MRS	Magnetic resonance spectroscopy
PET	Positron emission tomography
RTfMRI	Real-time functional magnetic resonance imaging
Structural MRI	Structural magnetic resonance imaging
tDCS	Transcranial *direct current* stimulation
TMS	Transcranial *magnetic* stimulation
VERP	Visual event-related potentials

Acronyms Used in Describing Functional Anatomy

Applicable to the Lateral (Outer) Brain Surface (see figures 2.1, 2.2)

FEF	Frontal eye field
IFG	Inferior frontal gyrus
mFG	Middle frontal gyrus
pIPS	Posterior intraparietal sulcus
TPJ	Temporoparietal junction

Applicable to the Medial (Inner) Brain Surface (see figure 3.1)

aCC	Anterior cingulate cortex
FG	Fusiform gyrus (on the undersurface of the temporal lobe)
mPFC	Medial prefrontal cortex (with dorsal, anterior, ventral and orbital subdivisions)

pCC	Posterior cingulate cortex
PPA	Parahippocampal place area
PRECUN	Precuneus
RETROSPLEN	Retrosplenial cortex
sPL	Superior parietal lobule

Applicable to the Brain Stem (see figure 2.1)

LC	Locus ceruleus
PAG	Periaqueductal gray (central gray)

Appendix D

Elephants in the Living Room

> Enlightenment is the shedding of all delusions, errors, and no-
> tions . . . the voiding of everything that obscures truth and
> prevents it from revealing itself.
>
> Soko Morinaga-Roshi (1925–1995)[1]

An elephant entered into the ancient Udana collection of
sutras.[2] Different blind men examined separate parts of this
elephant in one of the better-known stories that the Buddha
used in his teachings. Each blind man came to a different
conclusion. When neuroimaging researchers examine the
brain today, they may disagree but no longer seem blindfolded. Appendix C indicates that they now have access to
3-D visual brain mapping resources without parallel. Yet the
literature still seems unready to acknowledge that large
pachyderms remain present in plain sight. Consider a few
examples of questions still outstanding:

• Attention regions undergo both fast reactive shifts and slow
spontaneous cyclic shifts. Each of attention's peaks coincides
with reciprocal changes in the activity of Self-centeredness regions. The peaks and valleys shift in *opposite* directions. Which
deep mechanisms mediate these normal, widespread, reciprocal shifts between cortical activation and deactivation? How
do deeper thalamo ↔ cortical connections enable our frontoparietal and cingulo-opercular control networks to normally
communicate effectively with the default system?[3] [SI: 98–108,
237–239]

• How do these underlying mechanisms govern the shifts that
enable allocentric attentive processing to prevail anonymously
and meaningfully during states of kensho-satori? [SI: 109–117]

• How can we normally register a discrete personal event in our memory, then consolidate it into our extensive autobiography? It cannot become part of *our* personal story *unless* we simultaneously integrate our personalized sense of Self into the immediate topographical details of an actual locale. These scenic details represent where such an event, as we say, actually "took place." Each such memory represents coherent linkages, a merger that integrates a person, a time, and a place. An innate, subconscious Self-othering process seems to be linking networks of the anterior prefrontal cortex with their posterior parietal counterparts. Major co-activations occur both medially and in the angular gyrus. [SI: 58–59, 72, 74]

• Which objective neuropsychological test procedures most accurately assess not only the normal surface layers of the *I-Me-Mine*[4, 5] but also those deep primal dimensions at the existential core of our psychic and somatic Self-centeredness? (see chapter 15)

• How do such comprehensive psychological test procedures change, *longitudinally*, in carefully selected subjects? For example, how do they change in those subjects who (1) are reasonably stabilized patients after having sustained *discrete* structural damage to certain regions? Regions of particular interest are parts of their medial prefrontal cortex, or parts of their medial posterior parietal region, or parts of their extended amygdala on one or both sides; (2) are meditators, and have just undergone an acute loss of Self-centeredness during kensho-satori? [SI: 206–207]; (3) are long-term trainees and exemplify the exceptional *stage* of ongoing enlightened traits? [ZB: 637–645] To reach such an advanced stage means that they continue to manifest appropriate degrees of sage wisdom, especially simplicity, stability, and authentic compassion. [SI: 211–215]

A recent review article expands on these and other related topics.[6]

References and Notes

Epigraph

Hippocrates, vol. 2, trans. W. Jones, Loeb Classical Library no. 148 (London: Heinemann; Cambridge, MA: Harvard University Press, 1923).

Preface

1. D. Suzuki, *Living by Zen,* ed. C. Humphreys (London: Rider, 1972), 37.

2. J. Masefield, The Ending (Poems from "The Wanderer"), in *The Collected Poems of John Masefield* (London: Heinemann, 1923), 923, available at dspace.wbpublibnet.gov.in:8080/jspui/bitstream/ 10689/1483/23/Chapter%2020_928%20-%20969p.pdf.

3. The dorsal attention system is represented symmetrically. Each dorsal network responds attentively, in a top-down voluntary manner, to the opposite side of the environment. In contrast, the ventral attention system is predominately *right*-sided. Its networks respond attentively, in a reflexive, global manner, to either side or to both sides of the environment, L>R. This system acts as a circuit breaker, helping to reorient the dorsal system to a more relevant target. [SI: 29–34].

4. D. Suzuki, *Zen and Japanese Culture* (Princeton, NJ: Princeton University Press, 1959). Suzuki devoted 66 pages to the chapter entitled "Love of Nature" (329–395). The Japanese edition was published in 1938.

5. T. Merton, *Zen and the Birds of Appetite* (New York: New Directions, 1968), ix. The "birds" in Merton's title are not the kinds of real birds discussed in chapter 6. Instead, Merton was using birds as a metaphor to remind us of all those intellectual and spiritual hungers that hover like buzzards around the topic of Zen. Circling greedily, they long to clutch something exotic and strive to possess it. To Merton, these acquisitive forms of spiritual materialism are among the human "birds" that represent our appetitive drives. Contrast this with the Living Zen presented in this book. It stands for the simplified, uncluttered awareness that unfolds when all such overly Self-centered appetites are governed by more wholesome attitudes.

6. The word *horizon* has taken on different meanings in different cultures. See M. Inwood, *A Heidegger Dictionary* (Oxford: Blackwell,

1999), 98. In Greek, *horos* first implied a boundary that was limiting. However, for Masefield, and for the purposes of this book, the skyline at the horizon serves not as an absolute boundary but as a potential opening toward a promising future. When Husserl was developing his theories about perception, he spoke of *der Horizont*. In this context, one's own perception of an object's various aspects might be conceptualized as the inner horizon. Yet this same object also exists in multiple other relationships with the rest of the whole world, far out beyond us. Those outward extensions toward infinity might be conceptualized as that object's outer horizon.

For Heidegger, each topic (e.g., Nature, Zen) had its own conceptual horizon-like boundary. In order to analyze the philosophical distinctions that separate these two constructs, Nature and Zen, we must first step *outside* each of their two separate horizons. Only from such a vantage point can a new paradigm supply the necessary overarching perspective.

In this book the author explores the neural (not philosophical) dimensions of spatial relationships. Here, words reflect neurobiological explanations. On these pages, the egocentric frame of reference is a perspective that is overtly Self-centered. In contrast, the allocentric frame of reference is covertly other-referential.

7. Trial-and-error lessons teach us how to leap safely across a wide brook: take a few steps, just far enough back to gather momentum for a running jump.

8. J. Austin, Meditating Selflessly at the Dawn of a New Millennium, *Contemporary Buddhism* 2012; 13: 61–81.

By Way of a Personal Introduction

1. H. Thoreau, *Walden, or, Life in the Woods* (Garden City, NY: Anchor/ Doubleday, 1973), 7. Originally published in 1854.

2. R. Emerson, The Poet, in *Essays and English Traits*, ed. C. Eliot, Harvard Classics (New York: Collier, 1909), vol. 5, 173. Originally published in *Essays: Second Series* (1844).

Part I: Epigraph

H. Thoreau, Solitude, in *Walden, or, Life in the Woods* (Garden City, NY: Anchor/Doubleday, 1973), 113. Originally published in 1854.

Chapter 1 Two Old Men Consult the Buddha

1. S. Suzuki, in D. Chadwick, *Zen is Right Here: Teaching Stories and Anecdotes of Shunryu Suzuki, Author of Zen Mind, Beginner's Mind* (Boston, MA, Shambhala, 2007), 50.

2. Samyutta Nikaya (SN) 35.95, Malunkyaputta Sutta: To Malunkya-putta. All translations from the Pali by Thanissaro Bhikkhu are available at Access to Insight, accesstoinsight.org/tipitaka/. Here, the term *putta* refers to a person who is descended from an earlier person named Malunkya.

3. Majjhima Nikaya (MN) 63, Cula-Malunkyovada Sutta: The Short-er Instructions to Malunkya, trans. T. Bhikkhu, available at Access to Insight, accesstoinsight.org/tipitaka/.

4. Majjhima Nikaya (MN) 63, Cula-Malunkyovada Sutta, M i 426–432, in *In the Buddha's Words: An Anthology of Discourses from the Pali Canon*, ed. B. Bodhi (Boston: Wisdom, 2005), 230–233.

5. B. Nanamoli and B. Bodhi, trans., MN 63, in *The Middle Length Discourses of the Buddha: A New Translation of the Majjhima Nikaya* (Boston: Wisdom, 1995), 533–536. The following pages 537–541 contain the Mahamalunkya Sutta. That sutra (MN 64) identifies personalized viewing as the first of the five fetters. Personalized viewing is interpretable as entirely Self-referential viewing. Albert Einstein would call this the "optical delusion" of our Self-con-sciousness (see chapter 13). The other four fetters are doubt, rigid adherence to rules and observances, sensual desire, and ill will. It is one thing to know *about* these fetters at an intellectual level. Only by transforming the maladaptive networking functions between the limbic system, striatum, and cortex can we begin to be emancipated from all five fetters. Other formulations list the five hindrances as desire, ill will, sloth and torpor, and ruminating about guilt and doubt.

6. The translators have not specified the chronology of the sutras dis-cussed in this chapter. Buddha may have seen Bahiya before Malunkya, because the brief utterances, or Udanas, tend to be of earlier origin than many other sutras. See B. Bodhi, ed., *In the Bud-dha's Words: An Anthology of Discourses from the Pali Canon* (Boston: Wisdom, 2005), 13. For a short critical survey of the history of the Pali canon, see C. Hartranft, Did the Buddha Teach Satipatthana? *Insight Journal* 2011 (May 17); 35: 4–10.

7. Udana 1.10. Bahiya Sutta: Bahiya, trans. T. Bhikkhu, available at Access to Insight, accesstoinsight.org/tipitaka/. Bahiya's ques-tion—Is a sage someone who comprehends the universe as the Self?—turns out to echo in later centuries. In China, Shih-t'ou (700–790) became enlightened when he was triggered by a similar passage in the scriptures. This passage had been written over three centuries earlier by the Taoist monk Seng-Chao (378–414), a Ch'an antecedent who worked with Kumarajiva. [ZBR: 330].

8. Thich Nhat Hanh locates Savatthi as near modern Saheth-Maheth. This city is in northern India near Nepal, far from the coast. Such a great distance could be a measure of Bahiya's motivation. See Thich Nhat Hanh, *Path of Compassion: Stories from the Buddha's Life* (Berkeley, CA: Parallax Press, 2012), frontispiece map.

9. Was this an oblique reference to Malunkya, added to the early Udana by monks in later centuries?

10. Nor, for example, would they specify some 33 synonyms for Nirvana, words that over the centuries would find their way elsewhere into the Samyutta Nikaya 43, 1–44.

11. The sutras do not inform us of an important fact: how the body language associated with Bahiya's awakening manifested and confirmed this clinical diagnosis.

12. Shodo Harada-Roshi, *The Path to Bodhidharma: The Teachings of Shodo Harada-Roshi,* ed. J. Lago, trans. T. Storano (Boston: Tuttle, 2000), 162. The fullness of enhanced allo-processing is what enters experience when the ego drops off (see chapter 3).

13. D. Suzuki, *Zen and Japanese Culture* (Princeton, NJ: Princeton University Press, 1959). This painting, by Mu-Ch'i, is a treasure in the collection at Ryoko-in, the subtemple at Daitoku-ji, where Nanrei Kobori-Roshi introduced me to Zen. The painting reflects the major influence that Chinese culture and Ch'an had on Zen. Green persimmons start out distastefully astringent. Only slowly do they become sweet. [ZB: 649] Suzuki chose these ripening persimmons to be his frontispiece, the first of 69 glossy plates. This placement suggests that he understood the incremental aspects of Zen training and did not intend to be held solely to his oft-quoted statement, "Without *satori* there is no Zen" (218).

Chapter 2 Neuropsychological Aspects of the Attentive Self

1. S. Freud, The Dissolution of the Oedipus Complex (1924), in *The Standard Edition of the Complete Psychological Works of Sigmund Freud,* ed. J. Strachey (London: Hogarth Press, 1961), vol. 19, 173–182.

2. S. Sahn, *The Compass of Zen* (Boston: Shambhala, 1997), 234.

3. A. Baldassarre, C. Lewis, G. Committeri et al., Individual Variability in Functional Connectivity Predicts Performance of a Perceptual Task, *Proceedings of the National Academy of Sciences* 2012; 109(9): 3516–3521. This task required an average of 5,600 practice trials (!) before the subjects achieved an accuracy of 80 percent. The original data set from the earlier study was reanalyzed in this latest report.

4. A. Martin, K. Barnes, and W. Stevens, Spontaneous Neural Activity Predicts Individual Differences in Performance, *Proceedings of the National Academy of Sciences* 2012; 109(9): 3201–3202.

5. Y. Sasaki, J. Nanez, and T. Watanabe, Advances in Visual Perceptual Learning and Plasticity, *Nature Reviews Neuroscience* 2012; 11(1): 53–60.

6. This discussion is expanded in J. Austin, *Meditating Selflessly: Practical Neural Zen* (Cambridge, MA, MIT Press, 2011), 6–12, 198–199. 13, 201–202. 1–3. A recent review emphasizes the functional anatomy of the ventral attention network and cites 121 references. See B. Kubit and A. Jack, Rethinking the Role of the rTPJ in Attention and Social Cognition in Light of the Opposing Domains Hypothesis, *Frontiers in Human Neuroscience* 2013; 7(323): 1–18, doi: 10.3389/fnhum.2013.00323. This article points out that several functions are represented within the large heterogeneous region currently called the right TPJ. [ZBR: 416, 418, 421; SI: 21–26, 278] For example, the evidence confirms that (1) the supramarginal gyrus is activated during attentive target detection, and (2) the locus for a reorienting shift resides at a more posterior site between it and the angular gyrus, a well-recognized lateral component of the task-negative "default network." Moreover, some normal abilities to overcome an excessively Self-referential bias are represented in the right supramarginal gyrus, according to G. Silani, C. Lamm, C. Ruff and T. Singer, Right Supramarginal Gyrus is Crucial to Overcome Emotional Egocentricity Bias in Social Judgments, *Journal of Neuroscience* 2013; 33(39): 15466–15476. Clearly, additional high-resolution research must separate the several functions that earlier studies attributed to the nearby superior temporal sulcus (R>L). [SI: 41, 136–137, 142, 212].

7. M. van de Nieuwenhuijzen, A. Backus, A. Bahramisharif, et al. MEG-based Decoding of the Spatiotemporal Dynamics of Visual Category Perception. *Neuroimage* 2013; 83:1063–1073.

8. The way the moon's image is reflected, mirror-like, on water was part of an ongoing early dialogue. [ZBR: 268–269, 348] People were developing theories about perception at the sensory level centuries before researchers began to speculate about the motoric and other attributes of mirror neurons in the primate brain. [SI: 76–78].

Chapter 3 Neural Correlations of Meditating Selflessly

1. This is a condensation of John Blofeld's translation, found in *Zen Sourcebook: Traditional Documents from China, Korea, and Japan,* ed.

S. Addiss with S. Lombardo and J. Roitman (Indianapolis: Hackett, 2008), 42.

2. T. Merton, *Zen and the Birds of Appetite* (New York: New Directions, 1968), 47. The allocentric perspective is difficult to put into words. [SI:55–64] However, Merton's sentence happens to describe a crucial point: this implicit, covert, other-referential awareness is "already there." However, *we are not aware that it exists*, because it is basically anonymous.

3. K. Kim and M. Johnson, Extended Self: Medial Prefrontal Activity during Transient Association of Self and Objects, *Social Cognitive and Affective Neuroscience* 2012; 7(2): 199–207. (See also appendix D.).

4. Elsewhere, throughout numerous sutras, the Buddha had time to explain the finer details of his comprehensive eightfold prescription for letting go of our unwholesome, maladaptive, Self-centered attachments. In some instances, these releases could occur suddenly during alternate states of consciousness. Bahiya's abrupt awakening represents such an event. However, other similar unbindings occur incrementally. They, too, release Self-referent attachments and transform a meditator's traits. These "intelligent wisdoms" arrive gradually when one applies the trial-and-error, "live-and-learn" approach of careful mindful introspection to daily life events, discovering that their ups and downs are impermanent. [ZB: 641–645].

5. G. Gainotti and F. Ciaraffa, Is 'Object-Centered Neglect' a Homogeneous Entity? *Brain and Cognition* 2013; 81: 18–23.

6. Recent evidence suggests that our normal upward (vertical) bias during a (global) line-bisection task can increase when we superimpose a focal attention component. For a discussion of these issues, see A. Falchook, M. Mody, A. Srivastava, et al., Vertical Line Quadrisection: "What" It Represents and Who Gets the Upper Hand, *Brain and Language* 2012 (Dec 19), doi: 10.1016/j.bandl.2012.11.003 [Epub ahead of print].

7. C. Doeller, C. Barry, and N. Burgess, From Cells to Systems: Grids and Boundaries in Spatial Memory. *The Neuroscientist* 2012; 18(6):556–566.

8. This explanation requires us to consider potential mechanisms that act at still deeper levels to enhance the meaning inherent in these frontotemporal allo-functions. Allo-contributions that resonate with meaning could be amplified by shifts in the thalamus that release cortical networks along this lower "What is it?" path-

way. The study in note 9, below, reviews the kinds of anticorrelated shifts that could simultaneously cause overactive intrusions by the psychic Self to drop out of consciousness.

9. M. Lee, C. Hacker, A. Snyder et al., Clustering of Resting State Networks, *PLoS One* 2012; 7(7): e40370, doi: 10.1371/journal.pone.0040370. This fMRI study uses a "fuzzy-c-means clustering algorithm" that has significant advantages over other methods, including independent component analysis. Its figures 4, 7, and 8 illustrate that humans are entangled in language functions. The figures show that our clusters of language networks extend their reach into the caudate nucleus bilaterally, the medial frontal lobe, and the inferior temporal lobe. Therefore, in order to reach genuine interior silence of the Huang-po variety the brain's usual priorities must be substantially reordered within multiple linked cortical and subcortical networks. The study in note 10, below, emphasizes this point.

10. A. Rapp, D. Mutschler, and M. Erb, Where in the Brain Is Nonliteral Language? A Coordinate-Based Meta-analysis of Functional Magnetic Resonance Imaging Studies, *Neuroimage* 2012; 63(1): 600–610. A meta-analysis suggests that nonliteral forms of language (metaphors, idioms, irony) are also mostly (68%) left-lateralized. Long-term meditative training can help to reduce the intrusions of both literal and nonliteral language (see chapter 14). This could relieve other adjacent normal functions of the inferior frontal and superior temporal gyri on either side from entanglements that would compromise their capacities to infuse more efficient attentive processing through allocentric pathways.

11. J. Austin, The Thalamic Gateway: How the Meditative Training of Attention Evolves toward Selfless Transformations of Consciousness, in *Effortless Attention: A New Perspective in the Cognitive Science of Attention and Action,* ed. B. Bruya (Cambridge, MA: MIT Press, 2010), 373–407; J. Austin, Selfless Insight-Wisdom: A Thalamic Gateway, in *Measuring the Immeasurable: The Scientific Basis of Spirituality* (Louisville, CO: Sounds True, 2008), 211–230. During states of consciousness when the person's covert cortical inhibitory pathways that had served prior egocentric ends are themselves being blocked (on either side), these releases from inhibition could have secondary *dis*inhibitory effects. The result would be to release some excitatory functions on the other side. These excitations could potentiate further amplifications of meaning that are arising from functions already being unleashed along the

"southern" allocentric pathway by deeper mechanisms that were primary in the thalamus (see chapter 13). [SI: 180, 270].

Chapter 4 Buddhist Botany 101

1. S. Suzuki, *Not Always So: Practicing the True Spirit of Zen,* ed. E. Brown (New York: HarperCollins, 2002), 82–83.

2. Excerpt from Utopia, in *Wistawa Szymborksa. Poems New and Collected 1957–1997* (Orlando, FL, 2000), 173. Reprinted by permission from Houghton Mifflin Harcourt Publishing Company. This poem, "Utopia," written in 1976, helps explain why Szymborska received the Nobel Prize for literature two decades later.

3. B. Bodhi, ed., *In the Buddha's Words: An Anthology of Discourses from the Pali Canon* (Boston: Wisdom, 2005), 64. This story originates in the Majjhima Nikaya 36, Mahasaccaka Sutta, I 240–249. The exact dates of major events in the life of the Buddha remain subject to interpretation.

4. N. Taylor, ed., *Taylor's Encyclopedia of Gardening, Horticulture and Landscape Design,* 2d ed. (Boston: Houghton Mifflin, 1948), 333. The Samyutta Nikaya (15: 1) identifies the Indian subcontinent as the land of the rose-apple tree (*Jambudipa*). See B. Bodhi, ed., in reference 3, above: 37, 427, note 18.

5. Available at forestgeneration.com/rose-apple.html. This website notes that the rose-apple tree has entered into numerous legends. Among them is the following misconception: "The Rose Apple is said to be the golden fruit of immortality, and Buddha is said to have experienced enlightenment while sitting under a Rose Apple Tree."

6. Udana 1.1, Bodhi Sutta: Awakening (1), trans. T. Bhikkhu, available at Access to Insight, accesstoinsight.org/tipitaka/.

7. J. Snelling, *The Buddhist Handbook: A Complete Guide to Buddhist Schools, Teaching, Practice, and History* (Rochester, VT: Inner Traditions, 1991), 22–24.

8. N. Foster and J. Shoemaker, eds., *The Roaring Stream: A New Zen Reader* (Hopewell, NJ: Ecco Press, 1996), 138–144.

9. R. Aitken, *The Morning Star: New and Selected Zen Writings* (Washington, DC: Shoemaker and Hoard, 2003), 200–207. See also Thich Nhat Hanh, *Path of Compassion: Stories from the Buddha's Life* (Berkeley, CA: Parallax Press, 2012), 72. By at least the Tang Dynasty, Buddhist artists were aware that this brightest morning star was in fact one of the known planets. Dating to the year 879 is a silk painting discovered in the Dunhuang Caves. It portrays this planet, Venus, as a goddess. Garbed in a flowing silk robe, she is playing

a lute. She is identified further by the rooster on her head. It stands poised to announce her arrival at the first hint of the dawn's early light. See *Treasures of Dunhuang Grottoes*, rev. 1st ed. (Hong Kong: Polyspring, 2002), 248–250. See color pictures 219 and 220.

10. Itivuttaka 27, Iti 19–21, in *In the Buddha's Words: An Anthology of Discourses from the Pali Canon*, ed. B. Bodhi (Boston: Wisdom, 2005), 176–177.

11. J. Snelling, *The Buddhist Handbook: A Complete Guide to Buddhist Schools, Teaching, Practice, and History* (Rochester, VT: Inner Traditions, 1991), 23.

12. S. Huntington and J. Huntington, *Leaves from the Bodhi Tree: The Art of Pala India (8th–12th Centuries) and Its International Legacy* (Seattle: Dayton Art Institute and University of Washington Press, 1990).

13. *The Shambhala Dictionary of Buddhism and Zen* (Boston: Shambhala, 1991), 25.

14. These early historical connections with Sri Lanka remind us of our indebtedness to countless monks in the Theravada Buddhist tradition. They preserved many oral teachings of the Buddha and the early Indian patriarchs in the Pali language, the ancient vernacular dialect related to classical Sanskrit.

15. Thich Nhat Hanh, *Your True Home: The Everyday Wisdom of Thich Nhat Hanh*, ed. M. McLeod (Boston: Shambhala, 2011).

16. J. Steuber, ed., *China: 3000 Years of Art and Literature* (New York: Welcome Books, 2008), 180.

17. K. Yamada, *The Gateless Gate: The Classic Book of Zen Koans* (Boston: Wisdom, 2004), 6. Master Wu-men Hui-k'ai (1183–1260) became enlightened by the sound of a drum while standing one day near the Dharma hall. He compiled the book of koans (The Mumonkan) known as the Gateless Gate. The gating influence of the reticular nucleus is of interest in this regard (see chapter 11).

18. D. Suzuki, *Studies in Zen*, ed. C. Humphreys (New York: Delta, 1955), 12, 45. D. T. Suzuki regards this dialogue of the Buddha and Mahapitaka Brahmaraja as probably having been invented by a later Chinese teacher whose alleged goal was to justify the belief that a particular sequence of 27 Indian patriarchs had preceded Bodhidharma. The Pali sutras do not connect this Flower Sermon story with one particular flower.

19. *The Shambhala Dictionary of Buddhism and Zen* (Boston: Shambhala, 1991), 156.

20. Samyutta Nikaya (SN) 56.31, V 437–438, in *In the Buddha's Words: An Anthology of Discourses from the Pali Canon*, ed. B. Bodhi (Boston: Wisdom, 2005), 360.

21. N. Taylor, ed., *Taylor's Encyclopedia of Gardening, Horticulture and Landscape Design,* 2d ed. (Boston: Houghton Mifflin, 1948), 276. The simsapa tree, *Dalbergia sisu,* is named after the Swedish botanist Nils Dalberg.

22. Samyutta Nikaya (SN) 56.32, V 442–443, in *In the Buddha's Words: An Anthology of Discourses from the Pali Canon,* ed. B. Bodhi (Boston: Wisdom, 2005), 362–363.

23. S. Vogel, *The Life of a Leaf* (Chicago: University of Chicago Press, 2012), 163–169. A protective hydrophobic coating is available commercially. It has been given the name Lotusan.

24. Anguttara Nikaya (AN) 3.34, Hatthaka Sutta: To Hatthaka, trans. T. Bhikkhu, available at Access to Insight, accesstoinsight.org/tipitaka/.

25. Anguttara Nikaya (AN) 7.70, IV 136–139, in *In the Buddha's Words: An Anthology of Discourses from the Pali Canon,* ed. B. Bodhi (Boston: Wisdom, 2005), 206.

26. R. Aitken and K. Tanahashi, trans., The Genjo Koan, *Buddhadharma* 2012 (spring), 31–33. This is the first chapter of *Shobogenzo,* Zen Master Dogen's principal work.

27. Anguttara Nikaya (AN) 4.36, Dona Sutta: With Dona, trans. T. Bhikkhu, available at Access to Insight, accesstoinsight.org/tipitaka/.

28. Majjhima Nikaya (MN) 106, Anenja-sappaya Sutta: Conducive to the Imperturbable, trans. T. Bhikkhu, available at Access to Insight, accesstoinsight.org/tipitaka/.

29. Red Pine, trans., *The Lankavatara Sutra. A Zen Text. Translation and Commentary* (Berkeley, CA: Counterpoint, 2012), 21–41. This sutra, rooted in Yogachara Buddhism, is alleged to have been considered so important to Bodhidharma that he gave it to Hui-k'o, the second Ch'an patriarch in China (487–593). Visionary epiphenomena are not emphasized in Zen. [ZB: 374–391].

30. The diamond Sutra (Vajrachchedika Sutra) also teaches that objects appearing real to us are still projections of our own mind. See *The Shambhala Dictionary of Buddhism and Zen.* (Boston, Shambhala, 1991), 57. A view more comfortable in neuroscience is that our brain usually reconstructs images based on information that its receptor systems are receiving from the world outside, and our imagination takes off from there.

31. Thich Nhat Hanh, *Path of Compassion: Stories from the Buddha's Life* (Berkeley, CA: Parallax Press, 2012), 223, 227. Kusinara corresponds with modern Kushinagar.

32. Digha Nikaya (DN) 16, ch. 6, Maha-parinibbana Sutta: The Great Discourse on the Total Unbinding, trans. T. Bhikkhu, available at Access to Insight, accesstoinsight.org/tipitaka/.

Part II: Epigraph

S. Sahn, *The Compass of Zen* (Boston: Shambhala, 1997), 349.

Chapter 5 A Glimpse of "Just This" in Tang Dynasty China (618–907)

1. A. Ferguson, *Zen's Chinese Heritage: The Masters and Their Teachings* (Boston: Wisdom, 2000), 183–184. This master is Yunyan Tansheng (780–841). He was a close friend of Daowu Yuanzhi (769–835). [SI: 12] The two brother monks seem likely to have shared in that era's wordless comprehension of what "just this" really signifies. (See also note 3, below.).

2. T. Cleary, *Book of Serenity: 100 Zen Dialogues* (Boston: Shambhala, 2005), case 49, 206–209.

3. When Ferguson's book *Zen's Chinese Heritage* discusses another master, Yaoshan Weiyan (751–834), it further clarifies the inexpressible issues condensed into the words "just this" and "thusness" (107–110, 150). For example, on page 150, Master Yaoshan says, "I have a single phrase that I never said to anyone." At this point Daowu Yuanzhi stands up and says, "I follow you." Later, another monk asks Master Yaoshan, "How is this single phrase spoken?" Yaoshan replies, "Without words." (See also chapter 13, note 2.).

Chapter 6 Avian Zen

1. H. Thoreau, *Walden, or, Life in the Woods* (Garden City, NY: Anchor/ Doubleday, 1973), 233. Originally published in 1854. Thoreau, like Stevenson, suffered from tuberculosis.

2. D. Chadwick, ed., *Zen Is Right Here: Teaching Stories and Anecdotes of Shunryu Suzuki, Author of "Zen Mind, Beginner's Mind"* (Boston: Shambhala, 2007), 107.

3. Source unknown; often attributed to Paul Valéry.

4. J. Covell, *Zen's Core: Ikkyu's Freedom* (Elizabeth, NJ: Hollym International, 1980).

5. B. Joeng and H. Gak, trans., *The Mirror of Zen: The Classic Guide to Buddhist Practice by Zen Master So Sahn* (Boston: Shambhala, 2006), xviii.

6. S. Bodian, The Taboo of Enlightenment, *Tricycle* 2004; 14: 44–47, 108–111. This article contains Bodian's interview with Adyashanti,

a.k.a. Steve Gray. My interview occurred privately on October 24, 2012, when we both attended a conference.

7. N. Foster and J. Shoemaker, eds., *The Roaring Stream: A New Zen Reader* (Hopewell, NJ: Ecco Press, 1996), 260–266.

8. R. Aitken, Personal verbal communication, 2001.

9. A. Ferguson, *Zen's Chinese Heritage: The Masters and Their Teachings* (Boston: Wisdom, 2000), 88–90.

10. T. Cleary and J. Cleary, trans., *The Blue Cliff Record* (Boston: Shambhala, 2005), 275–278. Here, this same master is referred to as Ching Ch'ing. Jingqing is more familiar for using the patter of falling rain as an auditory test stimulus. Some styles of meditation begin by using single words (uttered silently) to label, and thus to interrupt, the strong impulse to engage in long trains of unfruitful thoughts. [SI: 9] In Zen, the word labeling of in-breaths and out-breaths serves only as a temporary expedient. The impulse to think words drops out by itself when you settle down and allow it to do just this. [ZBR: 33–37].

11. A. Grimstone, ed., K. Sekida, trans., *Two Zen Classics: Mumonkan and Hekiganroku* (New York: Weatherhill, 1977), 273–277.

12. R. Richardson, ed., *The Heart of William James* (Cambridge, MA: Harvard University Press, 2010), 150–151. James was referring to Stevenson's account of the legend.

13. Stevenson's account of the legend occurs in "The Lantern-Bearers," an essay first published in 1888 in *Scribner's* magazine and in *Across the Plains* in 1892. See R. Stevenson, *Across the Plains: With Other Memories and Essays* (New York: Scribner's Sons, 1905), 183–205.

14. R. Richardson, ed., *The Heart of William James* (Cambridge, MA: Harvard University Press, 2010), 182. James knew that heart disease would shorten his own life.

15. A. Ferguson, *Zen's Chinese Heritage: The Masters and Their Teachings* (Boston: Wisdom, 2000), 367–370. Like other early Zen masters, Yongming chose to die sitting cross-legged in an upright position.

16. J. Greene and M. Herter Norton, trans., *Letters of Rainer Maria Rilke: 1910–1926* (New York: Norton, 1969), 369–370. This description is a transcript from Rilke's notebook, written during 1906–07 while he was wintering on the Isle of Capri.

17. C. Beck with S. Smith, *Nothing Special: Living Zen* (San Francisco: HarperCollins, 1995), 227.

18. Both Thanissaro Bhikkhu and John Ireland used "just this" as the pivotal phrase in their separate translations of Udana 1.10. Available at accesstoinsight.org/tipitaka/.

19. S. Keen, *Sightings: Extraordinary Encounters with Ordinary Birds* (San Francisco: Chronicle Books, 2007), 45.

20. *The Sound of One Hand: Paintings and Calligraphy by Zen Master Hakuin*, Kiku-an Collection, 2011. Exhibition at Los Angeles County Art Museum.

21. R. Aitken, *The Dragon Who Never Sleeps: Verses for Zen Buddhist Practice* (Berkeley, CA: Parallax Press, 1992). cf this gatha on page 31.Aitken-Roshi gathas are an excellent way to practice living Zen.

Chapter 7 Homage to William James

1. *The Heart of William James,* ed. R. Richardson (Cambridge, MA: Harvard University Press, 2010), 140. This quotation is preceded by the kind of practical advice from James that can help us understand some of the as-if mechanisms involved in the Buddhist practices of *metta* (loving-kindness): "*Become the imitable thing,* and you may then discharge your minds of all responsibility for the imitation." Other brief quotations are found on pages 11, 82, 110, 132, 139, 140, 141, 202, 271.

2. R. Wiseman, *The As If Principle: The Radically New Approach to Changing Your Life* (New York: Free Press, 2012). This principle dates back millennia.

3. W. James, *The Varieties of Religious Experience* (New York: Longmans, Green, 1902; 1925). "Religion and Neurology" was the title of the first of the 20 earlier lectures that would grow into this book.

4. D. Brooks, The Neural Buddhists, *New York Times,* May 13, 2008, available at nytimes.com/2008/05/13/opinion/13brooks.html?_r=0. [MS: xv].

5. B. Hölzel, S. Lazar, T. Gard, Z., et al. How Does Mindfulness Meditation Work? Proposing Mechanisms of Action from a Conceptual and Neural Perspective, *Perspectives on Psychological Science* 2011; 6(6): 537–559; P. Malinowski, Neural Mechanisms of Attentional Control in Mindfulness Meditation, *Frontiers in Neuroscience* 2013; 7: 8, doi: 10.3389/fnins.2013.00008.

6. A brochure outlines Professor Harold Roth's Contemplative Studies Program at Brown University. It begins by citing James's well-known endorsement of "the faculty of voluntarily bringing back a wandering attention" (*The Principles of Psychology* (New York: Holt, 1890), 463). This familiar quotation closes with a sentence by James that is less well known: "An education which should improve this faculty [of attention] would be the education par excellence." James was critical of the higher education in his era, believing that it had caused much grievous national harm. This can be appreci-

ated from the way he refers to the "Ph.D. octopus" and the "Mandarin disease" (*The Heart of William James,* ed. R. Richardson (Cambridge, MA: Harvard University Press, 2010), 238–246.).

7. C.-M. Tan, *Search Inside Yourself: The Universal Path to Achieving Success, Happiness (and World Peace)* (New York: HarperCollins, 2012). Chade-Meng Tan has been teaching meditation to the staff at Google since 2007.

8. J. Watson, Marines Studying Mindfulness-Based Training, *AP--The Big Story,* January 19, 2013, available at bigstory.ap.org/article/marines-studying-mindfulness-based-training.

Part III: Epigraph

Hu Shih, Notes on Zen, in *Anthology of Zen,* ed. W. Briggs (New York: Grove Press, 1961), 31. Master Tao-sheng played a leading role in founding the early Nirvana school of sudden enlightenment that was developing in China before Bodhidharma arrived.

Chapter 8 Recent Clinical Information

1. T. Cleary, *Zen Essence: The Science of Freedom* (Boston: Shambhala, 1989), 41.

2. N. Kapur, Paradoxical Functional Facilitation in Brain-Behavior Research: A Critical Review, *Brain* 1996; 119: 1775–1790; N. Kapur, *The Paradoxical Brain* (New York: Cambridge University Press, 2011).

3. "Whenever a thought comes into your mind, you simply let the thought go and return to that open silent attending upon the depths. Not because thinking is bad, but because it pulls you back to the surface of yourself." C. Bourgeault, *Centering Prayer and Inner Awakening* (Lanham, MD: Cowley, 2004), 6.

4. N. Etcoff, P. Ekman, J. Magee, and M. Frank, Lie Detection and Language Comprehension, *Nature* 2000 (May 11); 405: 139, doi: 10.1038/35012129.

5. J. Taylor, *My Stroke of Insight: A Brain Scientist's Personal Journey* (New York: Viking, 2008). It would be of interest to have a more precise neuroanatomical description of the nature and extent of this complex underlying, anomalous vascular lesion. This could help clarify more than the primary basis for the acute symptoms. It could also help explain what could have been the much earlier *dual developmental* consequences of such a vascular anomaly. For example, how had this lesion reshaped the functions of the adjacent regions on that left side? And, had any potential compensatory functions developed in the right hemisphere?

6.	The neurology group at Johns Hopkins University has studied the results of the ordinary kinds of left hemispheric stroke damage that do not cause Nirvana-like symptoms. Their data raise the possibility that some left sided functions might normally have a more subtle general role in local, *other*-relational forms of spatial attention processing. See J. Kleinman, M. Newhart, C. Davis, et al. Right Hemispatial Neglect: Frequency and Characterization following Acute Left Hemisphere Stroke, *Brain and Cognition* 2007: 64: 50–59. Perhaps some regions exist in the intermediate zone between the "northern" and "southern" pathways (e.g., functions within the inferior parietal lobule). If so, these might normally be more involved in Self-referential processing, leaving the still more ventral temporo-occipital regions to be normally involved as discussed earlier, in the usual forms of allocentric processing. See also chapter 2, note 6.

7.	Why could it take a very large and deep lesion to completely disable all the normal components of a patient's ventral attention system? See the fMRI study by M. Lee, C. Hacker, A. Snyder et al., Clustering of Resting State Networks, *PLoS One* 2012; 7(7): e40370, doi: 10.1371/journal.pone.0040370. Many *subcortical* nuclei of the basal ganglia and thalamus are included in the cluster of sites that comprise our normal ventral attention system. These other constituents of this ventral attention system now appear to include more than the temporoparietal junction and the inferior frontal gyrus (as before) but also the cingulo-opercular network and the anterior insula. These two regions are part of the Salience II network (see chapter 9). (See also the Kubit and Jack reference in chapter 2, note 6.).

	This important study by Lee and colleagues has three major implications. Its text and figures 4 and 8 illustrate the following: (1) Our *dorsal* attention network serves as the vanguard of cortical attention processing; these highest-level focusing functions can plausibly unfold at more nearly conscious levels when we engage in top-down concentrative forms of meditation; (2) Our *ventral* attention network, given such extensive thalamic and basal ganglia components, is poised not only to help awareness instantly detect subliminal events (including internal signals and information received during introspection) but also to react to them quickly. This can occur during those deep, reflexive shifts that are consistent with mini-insights. These deep pivotal *subconscious* insightful functions can arise within reach of both the reticular nucleus of the thalamus and the habitual, experience-based operations of the basal ganglia. [MS: 135–139] The intuitive results could enter into the kinds of implicit learning, remindfulness, and other adaptive behaviors that emerge spontaneously during a long-term program of training that emphasizes receptive forms of meditation; (3) One large, complex macrosystem now includes the following *three* components: (a) the so-called *default mode network;* (b) the *frontoparietal control network,* including the caudate nucleus; and (c) the *language network.* Consider the consequences of having these particular three parts linked into one large constellation. Cross-talk among these three components could help explain why it is normally so characteristic of our psychic Self to manifest these three strong tendencies: (a) to engage in monkey-mind wandering; (b) to be preoccupied with its top-down compulsive plans to control future events; and (c) to engage in social chatter. Notably, the triad of components included in this meganetwork can also *de*activate to different degrees when triggering stimuli activate the dorsal and/or ventral attention systems. Triggering stimuli usually *de*active the default and dorsal attention networks the most, whereas the language and ventral attention networks normally deactivate the least.

8. The Lankavatara Sutra (cited in chapter 4) provides two important messages: (1) our normal imaginative capacities are substantial; (2) they can be driven in artificial ways. Why do both messages serve as an important preamble for discussing the next case report? Because a disorganized brain can further stimulate one's imagination, prompting one's perceptions to yield false impressions of "reality." [SI: 145–146] The resulting vivid dream-like productions then become so convincing that anyone can be misled into highly-rationalized metaphysical, occult interpretations. [ZB: 164–169, 443–452; ZBR: 184, 279–286; MS: 36–37, 193–195] A recent clinical example is the engaging story of a "special kind of Near-Death Experience" (NDE). It is narrated by a gifted academic neurosurgeon, Eben Alexander, who fortunately survived a rare, near-fatal E. Coli meningitis. See *Proof of Heaven. A Neurosurgeon's Journey into the Afterlife.* (New York, Simon and Schuster, 2012).

My sympathies extend to other authors who encounter major resistance in trying communicate unusual, ineffable experiences to their colleagues in neuroscience or to those on a spiritual path. [ZBR: 450–452] That said, one may hope that, over time, this meningitis patient will remain open to consider other patho-physiological explanations for his NDE story, beyond the short list begun in his appendix B. If so, then several alternatives might ultimately coalesce near his existing hypotheses. For example, contributions from the limbic nuclei of the thalamus could be extended beyond his hypothesis 2. The existing hypothesis 7 would first assume that all of the patient's neo-cortical regions were rendered equally and totally dysfunctional. Second, it would exclude important subcortical regions from possibly becoming so disinhibited secondary to this cortical damage that they could be the source for unleashing impressions of "ultra-real" mental processing. In this regard, the appendix (A) contains no relevant neuroimaging evidence that documents the actual locations, degrees, and sequences of brain damage. Lacking this important cortical and subcortical information, the possibility remains that the damage initiated by the meningitis was not uniform.

Questions arise. Could *somatic* processing functions have been more damaged over the dorsal, fronto-parietal, cortical surface? Such a disproportionate *dorsolateral* involvement might contribute to the reasons why this witness described becoming "completely free of my bodily identity" during all of his near-death experience (page 77). If lesser degrees of damage had occurred to the lower cortical processing streams then some of their *less*-damaged, *ventral* allo-centric functions might have been relatively spared. These lower pathways could contribute some temporal lobe pattern-recognition psychic functions and covert assessments of meaning toward what a desperately-ill patient could misinterpret as emergent "trans-earthly knowledge" (page 82).

With respect to the existing hypothesis 9, normal subcortical pathways lead into the pulvinar nucleus of the thalamus from the superior and inferior colliculi. [ZB: 240–247] These deep sensory resources provide covert avenues for infusing the gist of salience into auditory-visual processing. This blend could then be relayed up through the thalamus and further processed in some of the relatively-spared portions of fronto-temporal-parietal cortex. [SI: 27–29]

Could less obvious factors have stimulated dynamic, overactive neuromessenger receptor responses from the malfunctioning brain of this particular patient? Readers are informed that: he recently underwent a rigorous training program in order to achieve peak physical conditioning; there was a 'teen-age use of LSD and mescaline; potentially indelible memory traces could have been laid down during his unique exposure to *365* free-fall skydiving jumps in college. What is one to conclude about the inference that the image of an angelic blue-eyed girl during this "special NDE" (page 185) is reliable evidence of an occult glimpse into "another world"? Such a proposal might have been more intriguing had the patient recreated a painting of her actual features during the first months of his recovery. He would then have been able to compare such an image (recreated from the time of his illness) with that color photograph of his long-deceased, actual birth-sister. He did not see this picture until months later.

A near-death experience of "heaven" can be beautifully described, touch one's sentiments, and sponsor altruistic works. Does such an informal narrative suffice? Is it adequate scientific "proof" that "heaven" really exists? Or, does it reinforce age-old teachings about the vast imaginative capacities of the human brain that are applicable to a patient's over-stressed, dysfunctional brain? When the academic neurologist, Ernest Rodin, underwent his near-death experience during anesthesia, he experienced not "heaven" but the absolute certainty that he had died. Only in retrospect could he convince himself that these deathly certainties had all been a delusion. [ZB: 448; MS: 36–37] For a readable approach to terminal issues, written by a Zen teacher who has had decades of bedside experience, see: J. Halifax. *Being With Dying. Cultivating Compassion and Fearlessness in the Presence of Death* (Boston, Shambhala, 2008). For an evaluation of near-death experiences co-authored by a seasoned psychiatrist, see: P. Fenwick and E. Fenwick. *The Art of Dying. A Journey to Elsewhere* (London, England. Continuum 2008).

9. A. Rapp, D. Mutschler, and M. Erb, Where in the Brain Is Nonliteral Language? A Coordinate-Based Meta-analysis of Functional Magnetic Resonance Imaging Studies, *Neuroimage* 2012; 63(1): 600–610. This meta-analysis suggests that our normal nonliteral forms of language (metaphors, idioms, irony) are also mostly (68%) lateralized to the left side of the brain. The ways these nonliteral forms of language involve the resources of our inferior frontal and superior temporal gyri on either side could further interfere with the adjacent networks that allow clarity to emerge from our allocentric attentive processing pathways.

Chapter 9 Mindfulness Starts as Present-Moment Awareness

1. Dalai Lama, *Beyond Religion: Ethics for a Whole World* (Boston: Houghton Mifflin Harcourt, 2011), 170. With regard to the several

meanings of mindfulness, the Dalai Lama states, "The most important meaning of mindfulness is *recollection*" (109).

2. J. Kabat-Zinn, *Mindfulness for Beginners* (Louisville, CO: Sounds True, 2012), 152.

3. Ideally, only wholesome withdrawals would be made, in our best interests. And, by the way, it could help to be able to erase the disturbing emotions linked to some memory deposits (see chapter 11).

4. B. Shannon, R. Dosenbach, Y. Su et al., Morning-Evening Variation in Human Brain Metabolism and Memory Circuits, *Journal of Neurophysiology* 2013; 109(5): 1444–1456. The periaqueductal gray (PAG) in the pons must be distinguished from the locus coeruleus in all future studies. See J. Buhle, H. Kober, K. Oschsner et al., Common Representation of Pain and Negative Emotion in the Midbrain Periaqueductal Gray, *Social Cognitive and Affective Neuroscience* 2013; 8(6): 609–616.

5. W. Hasenkamp, C. Wilson-Mendenhall, E. Duncan, and L. Barsalou. Mind Wandering and Attention during Focused Meditation: A Fine-Grained Temporal Analysis of Fluctuating Cognitive States, *Neuroimage* 2012; 59(1): 750–760. Other associated regions were activated during disengagement. They included the lateral inferior parietal region and a small cluster involving the left inferior parietal lobe, the thalamus, and the body of the caudate nucleus. The 1.5+ second resolution of fMRI does not permit each of the four intervals to be measured in milliseconds. A noteworthy finding occurred among meditators who had more hours of meditation experience: their right ventromedial prefrontal cortex became *less active* and its reactivity was also *less* sustained. Why did this entire experiment show relatively less evidence of lower pathway activity and of bottom-up attentiveness? One explanation might be that tasks designed to continually require button pressing in the scanner are already very top-down and task-heavy. (See also note 16, below.).

6. A. Lutz, D. McFarlin, D. Perlman, and R. Davidson, Altered Anterior Insula Activation during Anticipation and Experience of Painful Stimuli in Expert Meditators, *Neuroimage* 2013; 64(1): 538–546. Eleven of the experts and 13 of the 14 controls were Caucasian. Long hours of sitting meditation offer many opportunities to learn how to adapt to pain of deep origins. The usual cingulo-opercular dimensions of the so-called salience network may differ in reports from different laboratories.

7. M. Erb and R. Sitaram, Neuroimaging Experiments on Meditation, in *Zen in the Light of Science* (Perris, CA: Sunyata Meditation Association, 2010), 1–26, describes the calm, open-eyed, alert, and silently aware interval when all word-thoughts drop out. [SI: 103] This quiet interval has not been singled out for explicit study in the following reports:.

(1)   M. Allen, M. Dietz, K. Blair et al., Cognitive-Affective Neural Plasticity following Active-Controlled Mindfulness Intervention, *Journal of Neuroscience* 2012; 32(44): 15601–15610. An active control group was an important addition to the experimental design of this six-week study of mindfulness training.

(2)   J. Brewer, P. Worhunsky, J. Gray, Y. Tang, J. Weber, and H. Kober, Meditation Experience Is Associated with Differences in Default Mode Network Activity and Connectivity, *Proceedings of the National Academy of Sciences* 2011; 108(50): 20254–20259. The 12 experienced meditators in the mindfulness/insight tradition who averaged some 10,000 hours and >10 years of meditation experience showed less medial prefrontal and posterior cingulate activity than did the 12 naive controls. They also reported significantly less mind wandering during meditation. This study supports the medial prefrontal evidence of reduced activity in the present author's PET scan, obtained during receptive meditation in 1988 [ZBR: 203, SI: 243–244].

(3)   J. Grant, J. Courtemanche, and P. Rainville, A Non-elaborative Mental Stance of Decoupling of Executive and Pain-Related Cortices Predicts Low Pain Sensitivity in Zen Meditators, *Pain* 2011; 152(1): 150–156.

(4)   V. Taylor, V. Daneault, J. Grant et al., Impact of Meditation Training on the Default Mode Network during a Restful State, *Social Cognitive and Affective Neuroscience* 2013; 8(1): 4–14.

(5)   N. Farb, Z. Segal, and A. Anderson, Mindfulness Meditation Training Alters Cortical Representations of Interoceptive Attention, *Social Cognitive and Affective Neuroscience* 2013; 8(1): 15–26.

(6)   D. Lehmann, P. Faber, S. Tei, et al. Reduced Functional Connectivity between Cortical Sources in Five Meditation Traditions Detected with Lagged Coherence Using EEG Tomography, *Neuroimage* 2012; 60(2): 1574–1586. The word *connectivity* is currently used in different ways to summarize findings obtained using very different techniques. The increased or decreased connectivity reported in many of the fMRI studies in this sample needs to be reconciled with the uniformly *reduced* connectivity in the delta and beta activity described in this important sLORETA study.

[ZBR: 190] The current literature tends to leave unexamined the inference that because their activities coincide in time, separate cortical regions must be linked by a functional *transcortical* connection. In decades past, it was customary to refer to the "pacemaker" attributes of the thalamus. These clearly were the source that took the lead in co-activating separate regions of the cortex. [ZB: 402–404; ZBR: 167–175]

(7)   E. Luders, P. Thompson, F. Kurth et al., Global and Regional Alterations of Hippocampal Anatomy in Long-Term Meditation Practitioners, *Human Brain Mapping* 2012 (Jul 19), doi: 10.1002/hbm.22153 [Epub ahead of print].

(8)   G. Pagnoni, Dynamical Properties of BOLD Activity from the Ventral Posteromedial Cortex Associated with Meditation and Attentional Skills, *Neuroscience* 2012; 32(15): 5242–5249.

(9)   Y. Tang, M. Rothbart, and M. Posner, Neural Correlates of Establishing, Maintaining, and Switching Brain States, *Trends in Cognitive Science* 2012; 16(6): 330–337. [SI: 42–43]

(10)   G. Desbordes, L. Negi, T. Pace et al., Effects of Mindful-Attention and Compassion Meditation Training on Amygdala Response to Emotional Stimuli in an Ordinary, Non-meditative State, *Frontiers in Human Neuroscience* 2012 (Nov 1); 6: 292, doi: 10.3389/fnhum.2012.00292.

(11)   B. Hölzel, E. Hoge, D. Greve et al., Neural Mechanisms of Symptom Improvements in Generalized Anxiety Disorder Following Mindfulness Training, *Neuroimage: Clinical* 2013; 2:448–458.

(12)   Y. Dor-Ziderman, A. Berkovich-Ohana, J. Glicksohn et al., Mindfulness-Induced Selflessness: A MEG Neurophenomenological Study. *Frontiers of Human Neuroscience* 2013; Sept. 24; 7:582. doi: 10.3389/fnhum.2013.00582.

8.   Research protocols followed during experimental tests of ordinary intuition/insight do not yet address the deep experiential issues presented by actual states of kensho-satori. [ZBR: 271–275; SI: 172–173] (See also appendix D in this book.).

9.   M. Erb and R. Sitaram, Neuroimaging Experiments on Meditation, in *Zen in the Light of Science* (Perris, CA: Sunyata Meditation Association, 2010), 1–26.

10.   R. Forman, Enlightenment Ain't What It's Cracked Up to Be, *Network Review* 2012 (summer), 12–14+. (scimednet.org.)

11.   Jeffery A. Martin has conducted interviews and psychological testing on more than 1,000 subjects who have undergone awaken-

ings of various kinds, often without prior formal meditative training. They range in age from 18 to the 90s. Their two predominant characteristics are a substantial sense of well-being and an increasingly less intrusive sense of Self. Almost all subjects were considered normal except for some evidence of depression or anxiety. We await further psychophysiological, neuroimaging, and postmortem studies on this population of mostly Caucasian, educated subjects in hopes of defining their neural correlates. See nonsymbolic.org/sing1.zip.

12. R. Forman, Enlightenment Ain't What It's Cracked Up to Be, *Network Review* 2012 (summer), 33. This form of therapy has plausibly contributed to his introspective acumen.

13. Consider the math. If you are only meditating for, say, 24 minutes a day, that's a mere one-sixtieth of the 24 hours in a day. To develop enduring neuroplastic transformations in behavior, you will need to engage in daily life practice [MS: 125–145] and endure meditative retreats [MS: 113–124].

14. D. Brown and J. Engler, A Rorschach Study of the States in Mindfulness Meditation, in *Meditation: Classic and Contemporary Perspectives,* ed. D. Shapiro and R. Walsh (New York: Aldine, 1984), 232–262.

15. C. Limb and A. Braun, Neural Substrates of Spontaneous Musical Performance: An fMRI Study of Jazz Improvisation, *PLoS One* 2008; 3(2): e1679, doi: 10.1371/journal.pone.0001679.

16. A. Engle and P. Keller, The Perception of Musical Spontaneity in Improvised and Imitated Jazz Performances, *Frontiers in Psychology* 2011; 2: 83, doi: 10.3389/fpsyg.2011.00083. It is difficult to interpret which cognitive and emotional qualities are entering into such decisions. The frontal regions are also involved in general problem-solving tasks. [SI: 238].

17. A very different study monitored 13 undergraduate classically trained pianists. Their task was to improvise melodies using the five keys on a fMRI-compatible keyboard. During these artificial conditions, the authors suggest that the pianists had been using a top-down processing strategy. Would this alone explain why the pianists also showed *de*activation of the right temporoparietal junction and the anterior cingulate gyrus? See A. Berkowitz and D. Ansari, Expertise-Related Deactivation of the Right Temporoparietal Junction during Musical Improvisation, *Neuroimage* 2010; 49(1): 712–719. [MS: 162].

18. D. Vago, Mapping Modalities of Self-Awareness in Mindfulness Practice: A Potential Mechanism for Clarifying Habits of Mind, *Annals of* the *New York Academy of Sciences* 2013; Oct 1. doi:10.1111/nyas.12270.

Chapter 10 Subconscious Background Qualities That Can Infuse Awareness

1. T. Cleary, *Zen Essence: The Science of Freedom* (Boston: Shambhala, 1989), 51.
2. S. Suzuki, *Not Always So: Practicing the True Spirit of Zen,* ed. E. Brown (New York: HarperCollins, 2002), 153.
3. M. Strick, T. van Noorden, R. Ritskes, et al. Zen Meditation and Access to Information in the Unconscious, *Consciousness and Cognition* 2012; 21: 1476–1481. Twenty minutes is a short time to meditate. Some aspects of working conscious performance may not reach their maximum until the hours between 7 p.m. and 9 p.m. [ZB: 338–347] These behavioral experiments do not distinguish between the effects that meditation might have on the subjects' sharp point of attention mechanisms per se versus the effects it might have on their next longer intervals of attentive processing.
4. D. Fair, N. Dosenbach, J. Church et al., Development of Distinct Control Networks through Segregation and Integration, *Proceedings of the National Academy of Sciences* 2007; 104: 13507–13512. The children were studied when they were ages 7–9 years.
5. A. Keil and A. Freund, Changes in the Sensitivity to Appetitive and Aversive Arousal across Adulthood, *Psychology and Aging* 2009; 24: 668–680.
6. G. Vaillant. *Triumphs of Experience. The Men of The Harvard Grant Study.* (Cambridge, MA Belnap/Harvard University Press, 2012). The pages from 51 to 53 condense the 7 major lessons of this prospective study. One key lesson is that development is a *lifelong* neuroplastic process. It continues into the later decades. This conclusion is relevant to the late onset of the shift of colors into the present author's left visual field: development is a lifelong neuroplastic process, continuing into the later decades. Vaillant's chapter 5 reviews aspects of this maturation (pages 144–189). His chapter 8 reviews the subconscious mechanisms used for adaptive coping, (261–291). Certain involuntary behavior traits are associated with becoming more mature. These later developments include altruism, foresight, humor, the sublimation of inappropriate

desires, and degrees of stoicism that enable one to endure uncomfortable situations. Rigorous Zen meditative retreats will test one's capacity for most of these attributes.

7. A. Manelis, L. Reder, and S. Hanson, Dynamic Changes in the Medial Temporal Lobe during Incidental Learning of Object-Location Associations, *Cerebral Cortex* 2012; 22(4): 828–837.

8. J. Blackstone, *The Empathic Ground: Intersubjectivity and Nonduality in the Psychotherapeutic Process* (Albany, NY: State University of New York Press, 2007); Z. Josipovic, I. Dinstein, J. Weber, and D. Heeger, Influence of Meditation on Anti-correlated Networks in the Brain, *Frontiers in Human Neuroscience* 2011; 5: 183, doi: 10.3389/fnhum.2011.00183.

9. R. Boyle, *What Is Awakening?* (New York, Columbia University Press, 2014, in press). Appendix 2 is a personal summary.

10. E. Gilbert, *Conversations on Non-Duality: Twenty-Six Awakenings* (London: Cherry Red Books, 2011). The narrative reported by Suzanne Foxton (see chapter 11) is based in part on this book. *Nonduality* is a term that is associated more with Advita Vedanta than with Zen Buddhism. (See also chapter 9, note 11.).

11. J. Summerfield, D. Hassabis, and E. Maguire, Cortical Midline Involvement in Autobiographical Memory, *Neuroimage* 2009; 44(3): 1188–1200.

12. Suppose you were a subject who was being tested during such a moment of recollection. Would you be 100 percent certain that you had *really* seen some movie or news clip? Or, was that event just something you imagined? When checking your memory, why might your search reach back into the posterior cingulate and precuneus regions? Because these medial posterior regions (and the adjacent retrosplenial cortex) contribute as co-active partners in a kind of personal Self-othering memory bank (see figure 3.1). How can this large interactive system link the time-place-person of an event into one discrete chunk of memory associations? Not without first combining relevant aspects of our psychic and somatic Self, then attaching these personal links to the array of incidental environmental details, and finally anchoring them with precision into each corresponding compartment of personalized time. Only this kind of intimate historical chronicle of adverbial/topographical details can firmly establish that each particular (*now*) event makes coherent meaning in terms of our own personal time clock and our own place in space. See J. Austin, The Thalamic Gateway: How the Meditative Training of Attention Evolves

toward Selfless Transformations of Consciousness, in *Effortless Attention. A New Perspective in the Cognitive Science of Attention and Action,* ed. B. Bruya (Cambridge, MA: MIT Press, 2010), 373–407. A pertinent episode of tachistoscopic quickening is described elsewhere. [ZB: 390–391] Each private slice of time includes some Self-othering sense of place.

13. F. Picard, State of Belief, Subjective Certainty and Bliss as a Product of Cortical Dysfunction, *Cortex* 2013; 49(9): 2494–2500. Detailed EEG and neuroimaging data would be useful to supplement the symptoms of the former state, beautifully described by the second patient in this article.

14. J. Austin, *Chase, Chance, and Creativity: The Lucky Art of Novelty* (Cambridge, MA: MIT Press, 2003), 108, 135.

15. W. Gallagher, *NEW: Understanding Our Need for Novelty and Change* (New York: Penguin, 2012).

Part IV: Epigraph

Wynton Marsalis told this story about the legendary jazz musician Louis Armstrong (1901–1971) on the Public Broadcasting System NewsHour television program on June 1, 2011. Video available at pbs .org/newshour/bb/entertainment/jan-june11/marsalisjazz_06–01.html.

Chapter 11 Reprocessing Emotionally Traumatic Imagery While Elevating the Gaze

1. M. Corbetta, Spatial Neglect and Attention Networks, *Annual Review of Neuroscience* 2011; 34: 569–599. Patients who suffer brain damage to their *right* ventral system pathways have several *global* problems. These include defects in becoming aroused, staying vigilant, detecting relevant targets, reorienting and disengaging their attention. Some of the positive symptoms that I experienced during internal absorption seem to be the physiological opposite of such negative symptoms. [ZB: 467–506] These contrasts suggest the hypothesis that the intensity of such positive phenomena during internal absorption could have been asymmetrical in origin. Thus, they could have arisen chiefly among the normal right-sided networks that have links with the *right* ventral attention system. This would not exclude other contributions from functions attributable to the dorsal attention system. Corbetta's authoritative review expands the boundaries of this ventral system. Its components now include modules on both the dorsal and ventral sides of the temporoparietal junction (TPJ), e.g., the supramarginal gyrus

(SMG) and the superior temporal gyrus (sTG), and the ventral frontal cortex (VFC). This ventral region can now include the insula, inferior frontal gyrus (iFG), and middle frontal gyrus (mFG) (see figure 2.1).

2. M. Arcaro, S. McMains, B. Singer, and S. Kastner, Retinotopic Organization of Human Ventral Visual Cortex, *Journal of Neuroscience* 2009; 29: 10638–10652. In their 2011 review, Kravitz and colleagues explain how the "where/what" distinction expanded in recent decades. See D. Kravitz, K. Saleem, C. Baker, and M. Mishkin, A New Neural Framework for Visuospatial Processing. *Nature Reviews Neuroscience* 2011; 12 (4): 217–230.

3. W. James, *Principles of Psychology* (New York: Holt, 1918), vol. 2, ch. 22.

4. J. Austin, How Does Meditation Train Attention? *Insight Journal* 2009 (summer); 23: 16–22, available at bcbsdharma.org/wp-content/uploads/2013/09/09SummerFullIssue.pdf.

5. J. Myers-Levy and R. Zhu, The Influence of Ceiling Height: The Effect of Priming on the Type of Processing That People Use, *Journal of Consumer Research* 2009; 34: 1–13.

6. L. Barsalou, Grounded Cognition, *Annual Review of Psychology* 2008; 59: 617–645.

7. L. Jia, E. Hirt, and S. Karpen, Lessons from a Faraway Land: The Effect of Spatial Distance on Creative Cognition, *Journal of Experimental Social Psychology* 2009; 45: 1127–1131. The conclusions were based on 197 students in an Indiana University introductory psychology class. Creative performance improved when their tasks involved associating to very distant locations. As the title indicates, these sites were imagined to be *faraway* over the global horizon, e.g., as far away as Greece or California. The three tests for creativity included one logical task and two tasks requiring visuospatial imagination.

8. N. Liberman, O. Polack, B. Hameiri, and M. Blumenfeld, Priming of Spatial Distance Enhances Children's Creative Performance, *Journal of Experimental Child Psychology* 2011; 111(4): 663–670. Fifty-five children were studied.

9. S. Fuller, R. Rodriguez, and M. Carrasco, Apparent Contrast Differs across the Vertical Meridian: Visual and Attentional Factors, *Journal of Vision* 2008; 8: 1–16.

10. D. Bayle, B. Schoendorff, M. Hénaff, and P. Krolak-Salmon, Emotional Facial Expression Detection in the Peripheral Visual Field,

PLoS One 2011; 6(6): 1, doi: 10.1371/journal.pone.0021584. These larger cells are part of the magnocellular system.

11. G. Borst and S. Kosslyn, Fear Selectively Modulates Visual Mental Imagery and Visual Perception, *Quarterly Journal of Experimental Psychology (Colchester)* 2010; 63: 833–839.

12. B. Strange, M. Kroes, J. Fan, and R. Dolan, Emotion Causes Targeted Forgetting of Established Memories, *Frontiers in Human Neuroscience* 2010; 4: 175, doi: 10.3389/fnbeh.2010.00175.

13. C. Wu, M. Libertus, K. Meyerhoff, and M. Woldorff, The Temporal Dynamics of Object Processing in Visual Cortex during the Transition from Distributed to Focused Spatial Attention, *Journal of Cognitive Neuroscience* 2011 (Dec); 23(12): 4094–4105.

14. P. Kanske and S. Kotz, Positive Emotion Speeds Up Conflict Processing: ERP Responses in an Auditory Simon Task, *Biological Psychology* 2011; 87: 122–127.

15. M. Arcaro, S. McMains, B. Singer, and S. Kastner, Retinotopic Organization of Human Ventral Visual Cortex, *Journal of Neuroscience* 2009; 29: 10638–10652. These visual response fields overlap heavily with the parahippocampal place area (PPA). [ZBR: 74; SI: 72–73].

16. A. Lane, K. Ball, D. Smith, et al. Near and Far Space: Understanding the Neural Mechanisms of Spatial Attention, *Human Brain Mapping* 2013; 34(2): 356–366. During tests for far space, the target was 56 feet away. During tests for near space, the target was thirty times closer, only 22 inches from the subject.

17. W. Huijbers, C. Pennartz, D. Rubin, and S. Daselaar, Imagery and Retrieval of Auditory and Visual Information: Neural Correlates of Successful and Unsuccessful Performance, *Neuropsychologia* 2011; 49(7): 1730–1740.

18. This large network is often called the default network. [SI: 226] To meditators, its significance lies less in its name than in the crucial empirical fact: regions involved in our autobiographical functions tilt in the opposite direction from those regions involved in our attentiveness. [ZB: 201–203; SI: 103–121].

19. W. Huijbers, C. Pennartz, R. Cabeza, and S. Daselaar, The Hippocampus Is Coupled with Default Network during Memory Retrieval But Not during Memory Encoding, *PLoS One* 2011; 6(4): e17463, doi: 10.1371/journal.pone.0017463. Would similar evidence be found using intracerebral recordings or sLORETA techniques?

20. Z. Saygin, D. Osher, J. Augustinack, et al. Connectivity-Based Segmentation of Human Amygdala Nuclei Using Probabilistic (MRI) Tractography, *Neuroimage* 2011; 56(3): 1353–1361.

21. N. Axmacher, A. Do Lam, H. Kessler, and J. Fell, Natural Memory beyond the Storage Model: Repression, Trauma, and the Construction of a Personal Past, *Frontiers in Human Neuroscience* 2010; 4: 211, doi: 10.3389/fnhum.2010.00211.

22. C. Waugh, B. Frederickson, and S. Taylor, Adapting to Life's Slings and Arrows: Individual Differences in Resilience When Recovering from an Anticipated Threat, *Journal of Research in Personality* 2008; 42: 1031–1046. Resilience restores the tipped Bodhidharma doll to its original erect position. [MS: 103, 111] In contrast, the processes of post-traumatic growth enable one to grow *beyond* one's prior limits. See M. Plews-Ogan, J. Owens, and N. May, *Choosing Wisdom: Strategies and Inspiration for Growing Through Life-Changing Difficulties* (West Conshohoken, PA: Templeton Press, 2012), 27–39.

23. E. Diekhof, K. Geier, P. Falkai, and O. Gruber, Fear Is Only as Deep as the Mind Allows: A Coordinate-Based Meta-analysis of Neuroimaging Studies on the Regulation of Negative Affect, *Neuroimage* 2011; 58(1): 275–285.

24. T. Schmitz, E. De Rosa, and A. Anderson, Opposing Influences of Affective State Valence on Visual Cortical Encoding, *Journal of Neuroscience* 2009; 29: 7199–7207. "Broadening" needs to be defined in terms of the networks serving its separate visual field quadrants (see figure 11.1 and color plate 1).

25. B. Min, A Thalamic Reticular Networking Model of Consciousness, *Theoretical Biology and Medical Modeling* 2010; 7: 10, doi: 10.1186/1742-4682-7-10.

26. E. Carvalho-Netto, R. Martinez, M. Baldo, and N. Canteras, Evidence for the Thalamic Targets of the Medial Hypothalamic Defensive System Mediating Emotional Memory to Predatory Threats, *Neurobiology, Learning and Memory* 2010; 93: 479–486.

27. T. Fitzgibbon, B. Szmajda, and P. Martin, First-Order Connections of the Visual Sector of the Thalamic Reticular Nucleus in Marmoset Monkeys (*Callithrix jacchus*), *Visual Neuroscience* 2007; 24: 857–874.

28. B. Zikopoulos and H. Barbas, Pathways for Emotions and Attention Converge on the Thalamic Reticular Nucleus in Primates, *Journal of Neuroscience* 2012; 32(15): 5338–5350. Three subsections

in this article discuss a variety of relevant brain mechanisms involved in emotion and attention.

29. S. Christman, K. Garvey, R. Propper, and K. Phaneuf, Bilateral Eye Movements Enhance the Retrieval of Episodic Memories, *Neuropsychology* 2003; 17: 221–229; F. Shapiro, F. Kaslow, and L. Maxfield, *Handbook of EMDR and Family Therapy Processes* (Hoboken, NJ: Wiley, 2007); G. Hogberg, M. Pagani, O. Sundin et al., Treatment of Post-traumatic Stress Disorder with Eye Movement Desensitization and Reprocessing, *Psychiatry Research* 2008; 159: 101–108; I. Engelhard, M. van den Hout, W. Janssen, and J. van der Beek, Eye Movements Reduce Vividness and Emotionality of "Flashforwards," *Behavioral Research Therapy* 2010; 48: 442–447.

30. S. Lilley, J. Andrade, G. Turpin, et al., Visuospatial Working Memory Interference with Recollections of Trauma, *British Journal of Clinical Psychology* 2009; 48: 309–321.

31. F. Shapiro, *Eye Movement Desensitization and Reprocessing (EMDR): Basic Principles, Protocols, and Procedures,* 2d ed. (New York: Guilford Press, 2001), 66–67, 246.

32. D. Rubin and D. Berntsen, The Frequency of Voluntary and Involuntary Autobiographical Memories across a Life Span, *Memory and Cognition* 2009; 37: 679–688.

33. M. Leitch, J. Vanslyke, and M. Allen, Somatic Experiencing Treatment with Social Service Workers following Hurricanes Katrina and Rita, *Social Work* 2009; 54: 9–18.

34. W. Huijbers, C. Pennartz, D. Rubin, and S. Daselaar, Imagery and Retrieval of Auditory and Visual Information: Neural Correlates of Successful and Unsuccessful Performance, *Neuropsychologia* 2011; 49(7): 1730–1740.

35. E. Gilbert, *Conversations on Non-Duality: Twenty-Six Awakenings* (London: Cherry Red Books, 2011), 370–384. Renate McNay conducted this interview with Suzanne Foxton. Other audiovisual interviews of Foxton are available at nothingexistsdespiteappearances.blogspot.com. See also S. Foxton, *The Ultimate Twist* (Salisbury, UK: Non-Duality Press, 2011), 3.

36. In the fifteenth century, after the Zen monk Yoso Soi experienced kensho-satori, his later calligraphy indicates that he brushed in the Japanese term twice ("obvious obvious") next to his enso (moon-circle). This was to suggest how deeply the penetrating clarity of its insight-wisdom had transformed his consciousness of the way things really are. [ZBR: 443].

37. This upgaze is reminiscent of that witnessed in the interview described in chapter 6.

38. H. Thoreau, *Walden, or, Life in the Woods* (Garden City, NY: Anchor/ Doubleday, 1973), 113. Originally published in 1854.

39. L. Colzato, B. Hommel, W. van den Wildenberg, and S. Hsieh, Buddha as an Eye Opener: A Link between Prosocial Attitude and Attentional Control, *Frontiers in Psychology* 2010; 1: 156. Simple visual stimuli are being used as tests to measure the local versus global responses of the subjects in this study. The stimuli are squares and rectangles in different patterns. These behavioral tests were performed on two groups of matched Taiwanese subjects. One group was Buddhist, the control group was atheist. Neither group were meditators. Even so, the Buddhist group showed the more *global* visual attentional bias than did their matched atheist controls. An incidental finding is of potential research interest. In general, the residents of Taiwan rank relatively low (only #17) on the Hofstede Scale of International Individualism. This ego/ allo ranking means that the subjects tend to regard themselves as sharing in more of a larger *group* identity instead of existing as separate (egocentric) individuals. In contrast, a much higher sense of Self-identity is shown on this scale by residents who live in the Netherlands (#80) > Italy (#76) > Israel (#54) > and Japan (#46).

40. The author welcomes hearing from researchers who are prepared to give these issues further careful attention [facebook.com/james. haustin.1]. Readers inclined to dismiss all evidence in this chapter are invited to revisit earlier evidence: a casual glance upward toward a lightbulb occurred just before the plunge into internal absorption [ZB: 470]; a casual gaze up into the sky occurred immediately before kensho [ZB: 537]. Incidentally, it was by looking up, not down, that a nine-year old child first discovered mankind's ancient cave paintings at a Spanish cave called Altamira. See J. Austin, *Chase, Chance and Creativity. The Lucky Art of Novelty*, (Cambridge, MA; MIT Press, 2003), 80–86.

41. J. Austin, The Thalamic Gateway: How the Meditative Training of Attention Evolves toward Selfless Transformations of Consciousness, in *Effortless Attention. A New Perspective in the Cognitive Science of Attention and Action*, ed. B. Bruya (Cambridge, MA: MIT Press, 2010), 373–407.

42. J. Bays, *How to Train a Wild Elephant: And Other Adventures in Mindfulness* (Boston: Shambahala, 2011), 122–124. Moreover, she emphasizes "becoming aware of the color blue," a practice that

"opens up a new appreciation of the sky" (95–98). For further empirical evidence that the human visual cortex is especially responsive to colors at the blue end of the spectrum, see chapter 12, including its note 24.

Chapter 12 Spontaneous Color Imagery during Meditation

1. J. von Goethe, quoted in *The New International Illustrated Encyclopedia of Art,* ed. J. Rothenstein (New York: Greystone, 1968), vol. 6, 1121.

2. J. Austin, *Chase, Chance, and Creativity: The Lucky Art of Novelty* (Cambridge, MA: MIT Press, 2003), 78, 119.

3. *Webster's Third International Dictionary, Unabridged,* ed. P. Gove (Springfield, MA: Merriam, 1965), 447–449. A color plate appears in this dictionary between pages 448 and 449. It illustrates the normal solar spectrum of daylight and identifies its major bands of color in nanometers. The color wheel on this same plate also reminds meditators that purple is the complementary color of yellow-green. The actual names given to colors include "reddish purple" and eight shades of pink.

4. R. Walsh, Can Synaesthesia Be Cultivated? Indications from Surveys of Meditators, *Journal of Consciousness Studies* 2005; 12: 5–17.

5. J. Hegarty, J. Austin, T. Trull et al., approval 96108, Independent Review Board, University of Missouri, Columbia.

6. M. Beauchamp, J. Haxby, J. Jennings, and E. DeYoe, An fMRI Version of the Farnsworth-Munsell 100-Hue Test Reveals Multiple Color-Selective Areas in Human Ventral Occipitotemporal Cortex, *Cerebral Cortex* 1999; 9: 257–263. Nine of the 12 normal subjects in this study showed stronger color selectivity on the *left* side of their brains. For a distinction made between area 4 in the lingual gyrus and 4 alpha in the mid-fusiform gyrus, see D. Murphey, D. Yoshor, and M. Beauchamp, Perception Matches Selectivity in the Human Color Center, *Current Biology* 2008; 18: R250–251.

7. J. Wackermann, P. Putz, and C. Allefeld, Ganzfeld-Induced Hallucinatory Experience, Its Phenomenology and Cerebral Electrophysiology, *Cortex* 2008; 44: 1364–1378. EEG frequencies below 7 cycles per second are reduced, whereas alpha frequencies between 12 and 14 cycles per second are increased.

8. The research focus during the PET scan in 1988 was not on the first-person visual phenomena that arise during meditation; no serial visual observations were made at that time. With regard to this chapter's empirical observations, they appear scientifically

justifiable at least to the degree that they could stimulate further rigorous multidisciplinary investigations. However, the model epiphenomena described are in no sense intended to represent a substitute variety of imagery, one that might distract other Zen meditators from cultivating more traditional forms of practice. *Zazen is not about seeing colors.* It is remaining aware that they come and go, like everything else in life.

9. Subsequent fMRI reports from many laboratories have established that the *acute de*activation of (heterogeneous) regions involved in Self-referential functions tends to coincide with the acute activation of attentive functions, and vice versa. See J. Austin, The Thalamic Gateway: How the Meditative Training of Attention Evolves toward Selfless Transformations of Consciousness, in *Effortless Attention. A New Perspective in the Cognitive Science of Attention and Action,* ed. B. Bruya (Cambridge, MA: MIT Press, 2010), 373–407.

10. M. Raichle, Two Views of Brain Function, *Trends in Cognitive Science* 2010; 14: 180–190.

11. J. Austin, The Thalamic Gateway: How the Meditative Training of Attention Evolves toward Selfless Transformations of Consciousness.

12. R. Sireteanu, V. Oertel, H. Mohr, et al., Graphical Illustration and Functional Neuroimaging of Visual Hallucinations during Prolonged Blindfolding: A Comparison to Visual Imagery, *Perception* 2008; 37(12): 1805–1821.

13. B. Boroojardi, K. Bushara, B. Corwell et al., Enhanced Excitability of the Human Visual Cortex Induced by Short-Term Light Deprivation, *Cerebral Cortex* 2000; 10(5): 529–534. A formal longitudinal controlled study would be of interest to see how long-term meditation influences meditators' light and dark adaptation, spontaneous color phenomena, and spontaneous shiftings between illuminations and darkness.

14. Y. Xiao, Y. Wang, and D. Felleman, A Spatially Organized Representation of Color in Macaque Cortical Area V2, *Nature* 2003; 421: 535.

15. Y. Xiao, A. Casti, J. Xiao, and E. Kaplan, Hue Maps in Primate Striate Cortex, *Neuroimage* 2007; 35(2): 771–786.

16. M. Li, F. Liu, M. Juusola, and S. Tang, Perceptual Color Map in Macaque Visual Area V4, *Journal of Neuroscience* 2014; 34(1): 202–217. The monkey's *dorsal* V-4 *can* be studied. The calming effect of an external pink color apparently helped to quiet combative prisoners who were placed in pink-colored holding cells. See Alter, A.

Drunk Tank Pink. And Other Unexpected Forces That Shape How We Think, Feel, and Behave. (New York, Penguin 2013, 1–3; 157–180). We have yet to clarify which mechanisms link specific color receptors and percepts with particular states of emotion and relaxation in individual human subjects.

17. B. Conway, Color Consilience: Color through the Lens of Art Practice, History, Philosophy, and Neuroscience, *Annals of the New York Academy of Sciences* 2012; 1251: 77–94; F. Sjöstrand, Color Vision at Low Light Intensity, Dark Adaptation, Purkinje Shift, Critical Flicker Frequency and the Deterioration of Vision at Low Illumination, *Journal of Submicroscopic Cytology and Pathology* 2003; 35: 117–127.

18. R. Shapley and M. Hawken, Color in the Cortex: Single- and Double-Opponent Cells, *Vision Research* 2011; 51: 701–717.

19. A. Shepherd and G. Wyatt, Changes in Induced Hues at Low Luminance and following Dark Adaptation Suggest Rod-Cone Interactions May Differ for Luminance Increments and Decrements, *Visual Neuroscience* 2008; 25: 387–394. You can verify that isolated color-contrast phenomena are fugitive. First choose to focus on the *blue* sky in a painting on the wall, then close your eyes 10 seconds later. After your lids close, you soon perceive the contrasting *yellow* afterimage. This yellow occupies the same area as did the blue sky and then fades. During meditation, fugitive color-contrast phenomena occur as well as shifts between darkness and luminosity at border zones, but they are not within the scope of this chapter.

20. As discussed elsewhere [ZB: 379–380] each hemisphere is also partly restrained by subversive pathways of inhibitory control. These cross over from counterpart regions on the opposite side. How this complex system of checks and balances operates at subcortical and cortical levels is not yet clear. With reference to the stimulations mentioned in chapter 13, notice that certain parameters of local brain stimulation may engage the opposing functions of different excitatory and inhibitory nerve cells in unexpected ways.

21. S. Davis, N. Dennis, S. Daselaar, et al., Que PASA? The Posterior-Anterior Shift in Aging, *Cerebral Cortex* 2008; 18(5): 1201–1209.

22. J. Christie, J. Ginsberg, J. Steedman, et al., Global versus Local Processing: Seeing the Left Side of the Forest and the Right Side of the Trees, *Frontiers in Human Neuroscience* 2012 (Feb 22); 6: 28, doi: 10.3389/fnhum.2012.00028.

23. V. Drago, P. Foster, D. Webster, et al., Lateral and Vertical Attentional Biases, *International Journal of Neuroscience* 2007; 117: 1415–1424.

24. D. Murphey, D. Yoshor, and M. Beauchamp, Perception Matches Selectivity in the Human Color Center, *Current Biology* 2008; 18: R250–251. This patient had a seizure disorder and had subdural electrodes implanted over his right ventral temporal cortex. The authors' findings that blue perceptual responses are prominently represented in human visual cortex are echoed in an article by L. Jakobson, P. Pearson, and B. Robertson, Hue-Specific Color Memory Impairment in an Individual with Intact Color Perception and Color Naming, *Neuropsychologica* 2008; 46(1): 22–36. In this patient, who had major external trauma to the back of the head, color imagery and memory were spared for the blue/purple region of color space.

25. H. Lim, Y. Wang, Y. Xiao, et al., Organization of Hue Selectivity in Macaque V2 Thin Stripes, *Journal of Physiology* 2009; 102: 2603–2615. V2 corresponds with BA18 in humans.

26. P. Gerardin, Z. Kourtzi, and P. Mamassian, Prior Knowledge of Illumination for 3D Perception in the Human Brain, *Proceedings of the National Academy of Sciences* 2010; 107(37): 16309–16314.

27. P. Mamassian, Ambiguities and Convention in the Perception of Visual Art, *Vision Research* 2008; 48: 2143–2153. We are left wondering which subtle underlying right hemisphere physiologies might encourage an artist's brush to reach over to the left (and up) to render the direction of such illumination. Are these behavioral tendencies to be understood in the sensory domain (see note 25), or do they express combinations of sensory and motor biasing (see note 23)? How do physiological tendencies seep into our culture?

Chapter 13 A Way Out of the Grand Delusion

1. A. Einstein, Letter to Robert Marcus, February 12, 1950, available at lettersofnote.com/2011/11/delusion.html. Similar words are also quoted in W. Sullivan, The Einstein Papers: A Man of Many Parts, *New York Times*, March 29, 1972, 20, together with additional words (see next Einstein quotation in this chapter) attributed to Einstein but without a specific source.

2. Which of the several unusual anatomical features of Einstein's brain might correlate with the remarkable scope and depth of his insightful intelligence? Neuroscientists have speculated about this for decades. The latest data centers on his unusually thick corpus

callosum. [ZB: 358–367; SI: 25, 71–74] This unusual thickness is manifest in his genu, midbody, isthmus and especially in his anterior to mid-splenium. These findings, in the bridge that joins both hemispheres, suggest that Einstein's extraordinary cognitive skills could have represented contributions emerging from both sides of his brain, especially posteriorly. See M. Weiwei, D. Falk, T. Sun, et al., The Corpus Callosum of Albert Einstein's Brain: Another Clue to His High Intelligence? *Brain*, September 24, 2013, 1–8.doi.10.1093/brain/awt252.

3. T. Cleary, *Book of Serenity: One Hundred Zen Dialogues* (Boston: Shambhala, 2005), 210–214. Case 50 describes how old Xuefeng (822–908) pops out of the door to his hut and surprises two visiting monks by asking, "What's this?" Xuefeng's other names are Hsueh-feng (Chinese) and Seppo (Japanese). Later, Master Yen-t'ou (828–887) spoke to one of these visiting monks, saying, "It was too bad that I hadn't told Xuefeng [his brother monk] the 'last word' " (hinting that the last word was "just this"). Four centuries later, in case 13 of the Gateless Gate, Master Wu-men Hui-k'ai (1183–1260) comments in a poem about any such wordplay: "The 'last word' or the 'first word'—*IT* is not a word!" (See also chapter 5, note 3.).

4. S. Suzuki, *Not Always So: Practicing the True Spirit of Zen*, ed. E. Brown (New York: HarperCollins, 2002), 69, 75.

5. B. Bergen, S. Lindsay, T. Matlock, and S. Narayanan, Spatial and Linguistic Aspects of Visual Imagery in Sentence Comprehension, *Cognitive Science* 2007; 31: 733–764.

6. J. Austin, The Meditative Approach to Awaken Selfless Insight-Wisdom, in *Meditation: Neuroscientific Approaches and Philosophical Implications*, ed. S. Schmidt and H. Walach (Berlin: Springer, 2014), 23–55. This essay amplifies topics considered in the present book.

Part V: Epigraph

C. Bernard, *An Introduction to the Study of Experimental Medicine* (New York: Macmillan, 1927).

Chapter 14 New Research Horizons

1. B. Joeng and H. Gak, *The Mirror of Zen: The Classic Guide to Buddhist Practice by Zen Master So Sahn* (Boston: Shambhala, 2006), 9. The present author's preference is to translate this phrase as "just this," following the way it is usually translated from the Pali (see chapter 1).

2. H. Benoit, *Let Go: Theory and Practice of Detachment According to Zen*, trans. A. Low (New York: Samuel Weiser, 1973), 203.

3. Cognition converges during concentrative meditation. It tends to diverge during receptive meditation. Our eyes converge automatically when we focus on an object close to our body. They begin to diverge as soon as we look out into the distant horizon. "Out there," in a conjugate gaze toward infinity, their axes become essentially parallel. These reflexive adjustments originate among circuits in the upper brain stem. However, networks at higher levels undergo comparable shifts when they generate more complex mental functions. Again, we use the same terms, *convergence* and *divergence*, when speaking of these psychological shifts. Some of these concepts take on ego- and allo-implications (see chapter 11) as well as having implications for creative problem solving.

4. J. Williamson, A. Al Wafai, V. Drago et al., The Influence of Meditation on Creativity, poster presented at the 29th Annual Conference of the International Neuropsychological Society, February 2–5, 2011.

5. T. Dotan Ben-Soussan, J. Glicksohn, A. Goldstein et al., Into the Square and Out of the Box: The Effects of Quadrato Motor Training on Creativity and Alpha Coherence, *PLoS One* 2013; 8(1): e55023, doi: 10.1371/journal.pone.0055023. One control group performed predictable motor steps; the other vocalized the direction of the steps that they had been commanded to take. As one example, an alternate uses task asks subjects to imagine different ways that a "brick" might be used.

6. L. Colzato, A. Ozturk, and B. Hommel. Meditate to Create: The Impact of Focused-Attention and Open-Monitoring Training on Convergent and Divergent Thinking, *Frontiers in Psychology* 2012; 3: 116. The data suggested that short episodes of focused meditation did *not* sustain convergent thinking toward a single solution, but that receptive meditation did support divergent thinking. Positive words served to reinforce the receptive form of meditation. Examples of such verbal affirmations included "I am open," "I let go," "I accept myself as I am." Meditators who prefer a less egocentric formulation could use "opening," "letting go," "accepting."

7. K. Subramaniam, J. Kounios, T. Parrish, and M. Jung-Beeman, A Brain Mechanism for Facilitation of Insight by Positive Affect, *Journal of Cognitive Neuroscience* 2009; 21(3): 415–432.

8. H. Takeuchi, Y. Taki, H. Hashizume et al., The Association between Resting Functional Connectivity and Creativity, *Cerebral Cortex* 2012; 22(12): 2921–2929. This network, often called a default network, has a high metabolic rate. It is not, in fact, "resting" during the conditions under which it is being measured. [SI: 70–76].

9. A. Abraham, K. Pieritz, K. Thybusch et al., Creativity and the Brain: Uncovering the Neural Signature of Conceptual Expansion, *Neuropsychologia* 2012; 50(8): 1906–1917. This process was regarded as distinct from the mechanisms involved in general divergent thinking, working memory, or cognitive load.

10. M. Ellamil, C. Dobson, M. Beeman, and K. Christoff, Evaluative and Generative Modes of Thought during the Creative Process, *Neuroimage* 2012; 59(2): 1783–1794.

11. M. Harré, T. Bossomaier, and A. Snyder, The Perceptual Cues That Reshape Expert Reasoning, *Scientific Reports* 2012 (Jul 11), doi: 10.1038/srep00502 [Epub ahead of print]. The literature seems to be accepting that an ideal expert will take some 10,000 hours of experience to learn a skill.

12. B. Lee, J. Park, W. Jung et al., White Matter Neuroplastic Changes in Long-Term Trained Players of the Game of "Baduk" (GO), *Neuroimage* 2010; 52(1): 9–19. Decreased FA values were seen in the premotor and right precuneus regions.

13. M. Bilalic, L. Turella, G. Campitelli, et al., Expertise Modulates the Neural Basis of Context Dependent Recognition of Objects and Their Relations, *Human Brain Mapping* 2012; 33(11): 278–240. Flexible responses to random novel chess positions recruited the collateral sulci in the inferior temporal regions and the retrosplenial cortex on both sides. This report suggests the kinds of object recognition and topographical memory resources that subjects can draw on for navigation during novel visual tasks.

14. C. Price, A Review and Synthesis of the First 20 Years of PET and fMRI Studies of Heard Speech, Spoken Language and Reading, *Neuroimage* 2012; 62(2): 816–847. Figure 4 in that article illustrates in color how totally the left lateral temporal lobe is invested in language functions of one kind or another. Clearly, the left hemisphere's language capacities are responsible for countless contributions to civilization. But this chapter asks: what about some of its overactive emotional attachments to fixed expectations, ill-timed prejudgments, and word-thought distractions? Can't these cause cognitive dissonance that interferes with the sequences involved in human creativity, insight, and the states of

insight-wisdom? While one or two words might help point toward the inexpressible, it is traditional for Zen masters to "never stop cursing words and letters." [ZBR: 358–361].

15. G. Pobric, E. Jeffries, and R. Lambon, Category-Specific versus Category-General Semantic Impairment Induced by Transcranial Magnetic Stimulation, *Current Biology* 2010; 20(10): 964–968. In contrast, the left inferior *parietal* lobe impairment induced by TMS is specific for human-made objects. It cannot be assumed that the indirect effects of magnetic or direct current stimulation remain localized to one electrode region.

16. S. Han, Y. Jiang, and L. Mao, Right Hemisphere Dominance in Perceiving Coherence of Visual Events, *Neuroscience Letters* 2006; 398: 18–21.

17. T. Asari, S. Konishi, K. Jimura, et al., Amygdalar Modulation of Frontotemporal Connectivity during the Inkblot Test, *Psychiatry Research* 2010; 182(2): 103–110. A separate database from the authors' cultural control group served to establish which verbal responses could be classified as "unique" (such a word was never spoken by any of the 217 controls). In contrast, responses classified as "frequent" occurred more often than 2 percent of the time in controls. "Infrequent" responses occurred only 0–2 percent of the time. The subjects' conventional responses correlated with activations in their prefrontal (Brodmann area 10) and bilateral occipitotemporal (BA 37/19) regions. This study used specialized parametric connectivity calculations to analyze the data.

18. N. Cohn, M. Paczynski, R. Jackendoff, et al., (Pea)nuts and Bolts of Visual Narrative: Structure and Meaning in Sequential Image Comprehension, *Cognitive Psychology* 2012; 65(1): 1–38. The pattern-predictive waveform was an N300/N400 negative wave complex.

19. R. Chi and A. Snyder, Facilitate Insight by Non-invasive Brain Stimulation, *PLoS One* 2011; 6(2): e16655, doi: 10.1371/journal.pone.0016655. Sixty subjects were studied during direct current flows that lasted for up to 17 minutes. When the positive electrode depolarizes the resting potential of underlying nerve cells, it tends to make the cells more excitable; the negative electrode hyperpolarizes and tends to make the cells less excitable.

20. Modulation is the operative word at the present time. Modulation indicates that the low amperage direct current flow acts only to facilitate or to inhibit basic neural functions. These are *already* ongoing or are on the verge of being discharged. These electrophysi-

ologically induced changes modify the existing membrane potentials of nerve cells and perhaps influence their glia (support cells) as well. The resulting changes affect the release and effectiveness of neurotransmitters (e.g., glutamate, GABA, acetylcholine) and neuromodulators (e.g., biogenic amines) both locally and at distant synapses. Where does the maximum intensity of current flow occur? "Not underneath large electrode pads but in regions between the two electrodes." See A. Antal, M. Bikson, A. Datta et al., Imaging Artifacts Induced by Electrical Stimulation during Conventional fMRI of the Brain, *Neuroimage* 2012 (Oct 23), doi: 10.1016/j.neuroimage.2012.10.026 [Epub ahead of print].

21. The following studies represent a small sample of the promising research that has opened up in this tDCS field:.

(1) M. Meinzer, D. Antonenko, R. Lindenbert et al., Electrical Brain Stimulation Improves Cognitive Performance by Modulating Functional Connectivity and Task-Specific Activation, *Journal of Neuroscience* 2012; 32(58): 1859–1866.

(2) J. Medina, J. Beauvais, A. Datta, et al., Transcranial Direct Current Stimulation Accelerates Allocentric Target Detection, *Brain Stimulation* 2013; 6: 433–439. Right anodal/left cathodal tDCS, delivered to the posterior parietal cortex, facilitated the detection of targets allocentrically.

(3) L. Bardi, R. Kanai, D. Mapelli, and V. Walsh, Direct Current Stimulation (TDCS) Reveals Posterior Parietal Asymmetry in Local/Global and Salience-Based Selection, *Cortex* 2012; doi: 10.10106/j.cortex.2012.04.016.

(4) C. Stagg, J. Best, M. Stephenson et al., Polarity-Sensitive Modulation of Cortical Neurotransmitters by Transcranial Stimulation, *Journal of Neuroscience* 2009; 29: 5202–5206. Magnetic resonance spectroscopy shows that the anodal facilitation by tDCS correlates with a local decrease in GABA. Cathodal inhibition correlates with a local decrease in glutamate.

(5) D. Keeser, T. Meindl, J. Bor et al., Prefrontal Transcranial Direct Current Stimulation Changes Connectivity of Resting-State Networks during fMRI, *Journal of Neuroscience* 2011; 31: 15284–15293. The authors used a higher amperage current for left dorsolateral prefrontal tDCS (2 milliamperes for 20 minutes). This did not change the resting state activity patterns of the anterior cingulate (BA 24/32) or the subgenual gyrus (BA 25). It did increase the estimates of connectivity within the default and frontoparietal attention networks.

(6) V. Clark, B. Coffman, A. Mayer et al., TDCS Guided Using fMRI Significantly Accelerates Learning to Identify Concealed Objects, *Neuroimage* 2012; 59(1): 117–128. When fMRI-identified locations over the right inferior frontal or parietal cortex were facilitated by tDCS for up to 30 minutes, normal subjects could almost double their capacity to identify visual threats (e.g., bombs, snipers) that were concealed in natural scenes. Indices of arousal need to be measured in the future (see chapter 11, note 1).

22. The issues involved in the mechanisms of creativity, insightful problem solving, and the effects of tDCS are vastly more complex than can be condensed here. For starters, see J. Austin, *Chase, Chance, and Creativity: The Lucky Art of Novelty* (Cambridge, MA: MIT Press, 2003), 136–143, 159–168, 173–185; A. Vartanian, A. Bristol, and J. Kaufman, *Neuroscience of Creativity* (Cambridge, MA: MIT Press, 2013); and L. Jacobson, M. Koslowsky, and M. Lavidor, tDCS Polarity Effects in Motor and Cognitive Domains: A Meta-analytical Review, *Experimental Brain Research* 2012; 216: 1–10.

23. R. Chi and A. Snyder, Brain Stimulation Enables the Solution of an Inherently Difficult Problem, *Neuroscience Letters* 2012; 515(2): 121–124. Subjects might need to shed two prejudgments that date back to their childhood. One is the rule-based habit of running in a straight line between the bases in baseball. The other is the rule for playing tic-tac-toe inside the square enclosure formed by four lines and eight lanes. This nine-dot task has different rules. We are required to connect all nine dots, using four consecutive straight-line strokes, without lifting the pen from the paper or retracing a line. However, no rules in this task prohibit us from moving or thinking or engaging in subconscious processing "outside the box."

24. R. Polania, W. Paulus, and M. Nitsche, Modulating Corticostriatal and Thalamocortical Functional Connectivity with Transcranial Direct Current Stimulation, *Human Brain Mapping* 2012; 33: 2499–2508. These researchers acquired fMRI images before and after they applied tDCS to the scalp over their subjects' frontopolar and motor cortex regions. The fMRI data suggested that enhanced anodal coupling had occurred between the cortex and thalamus, and between the cortex and caudate nucleus.

25. For example, tDCS does change the EEG. See T. Zaehle, P. Sandmann, J. Thorne, et al., Transcranial Direct Stimulation of the Left Dorsal Prefrontal Cortex Modulates Working Memory Perfor-

mance, *BMC Neuroscience* 2011 (Jan); 12: 2. In this study, when anodal tDCS was applied to this left dorsolateral prefrontal cortex it enhanced working memory performance for letters and enhanced the underlying theta and alpha EEG activity. [MS: 135–138] Could the thalamus be involved in such changes? The lateral nucleus of the inferior pulvinar has been shown to connect with the cortex higher up in the ventral allocentric processing stream. [SI: 90, 285] These (and other) major interactions link all of the overlying cortex with nuclei of the thalamus. Therefore, thalamocortical interactions could be relevant to the potential mechanisms of tDCS effectiveness. Moreover, the reticular nucleus of the thalamus is poised at the interface between thalamus and cortex. Its synaptic contacts could easily shift, up or down, some phase relationships of the synchronized oscillations along the lower thalamotemporal pathway. How could such shifts, in phase and out of phase, reshape the integration of frontotemporal lobe functions? This question needs to be studied first in animal models using shielded intracranial recording electrodes. The following review provides an excellent discussion of how such network synchronizations shape normal brain functions: F. Varela, J. Lachaux, E. Rodriguez, and J. Martinerie, The Brainweb: Phase Synchronization and Large-Scale Integration, *Nature Reviews Neuroscience* 2001; 229–239. High-frequency gamma oscillations (60–250Hz) correlate with cortical activation and with increased blood-oxygen-level -dependent (BOLD) fMRI signals. [ZBR: 44–48] Single nerve cells are also more likely to fire when their firing threshold is reduced by cross-frequency couplings. These couplings occur between low-frequency oscillations in the theta range and high-frequency gamma oscillations. See R. Knight, Neural Oscillations and Prefrontal Cortex, in *Principles of Frontal Lobe Function*, 2d ed., ed. D. Stuss and R. Knight (New York: Oxford University Press, 2013), 751–764.

26. J. Austin, *Chase, Chance, and Creativity: The Lucky Art of Novelty* (Cambridge, MA: MIT Press, 2003), 185–189.

27. E. Luders, K. Clark, K. Narr, and A. Toga, Enhanced Brain Connectivity in Long-Term Meditation Practitioners, *Neuroimage* 2011; 57(4): 1308–1316. It is worth emphasizing that each large myelinated tract is also a heterogeneous bundle of axons. Some conduct impulses in one direction, others conduct impulses in the opposite direction. Moreover, these axons are expressing diverse excitatory *and* inhibitory functions at their terminal end-

ings. After only two hours of training on a spatial navigation task, both humans and rats showed DTI changes interpretable as evidence of neuroplasticity. See Y. Sagi, I. Tavor, S. Hofstetter, et al., Learning in the Fast Lane: New Insights into Neuroplasticity, *Neuron* 2012; 73(6): 1195–1203. However, it is safe to say that we still do not understand the precise ultrastructural correlates of the DTI and structural MRI changes in gray or white matter. See: D. Kang, H. Jo, W. Jung, et al., The Effects of Meditation on Brain Structure: Cortical Thickness Mapping and Diffusion Tensor Imaging. *Social, Cognitive, and Affective Neuroscience*, 2012, doi: 10.1093/scan/nss056; N. Fayed, D. Lopz, E. Andres, et al., Brain Changes in Long-term Zen Meditators Using Proton Magnetic Resonance Spectroscopy and Diffusion Tensor Imaging: A Controlled Study, *Public Library of Science One*. March 2013; 8(3):e58476. Doi: 10.1371; K. Kantarci, M. Senjem, R. Avula, et al., Diffusion Tensor Imaging and Cognitive Function in Older Adults With No Dementia, *Neurology* 2012; July 5; 77(1): 26–34 doi: 10.1212/WNL. obcobo13e31822313dc.

28. H. Slagter, R. Davidson, and A. Lutz, Mental Training as a Tool in the Neuroscientific Study of Brain and Cognitive Plasticity, *Frontiers in Human Neuroscience* 2011 (Feb 10); 10: 5–17, doi: 10.3389/fnhum.2011.00017.

29. O. Klimecki, S. Leiberg, M. Ricard, and T. Singer, Differential Pattern of Functional Brain Plasticity After Compassion and Empathy Training, *Social, Cognitive and Affective Neuroscience* 2013 (May 9); [Epub ahead of print].

30. These summary pages have the title "A Sequence of Topics to Help Clarify the Mechanisms of Selfless Insight-Wisdom."

31. E. Luders, F. Kurth, A. Toga, et al., Meditation Effects Within the Hippocampal Complex Revealed by Voxel-based Morphometry and Cytoarchitectonic Probabilistic Mapping, *Frontiers of Psychology* 2013 (July 9); 4:398, doi: 10.3389/fpsyg.2013.00398. eCollection 2013.

32. J. Austin, *Chase, Chance, and Creativity: The Lucky Art of Novelty*, 201.

33. Racehorses have been required to pass a saliva test for many years. Human athletes are now stripped of their awards after drugs are detected that could have given their performance an exceptional boost. One can foresee that attempts will be made to apply the principles underlying tDCS to enhance the effectiveness of meditative training. How will the basic mechanisms and neuroimaging

correlates of the concentrative and receptive styles of meditation be changed when tDCS is aimed precisely at the most relevant targets in the two hemispheres? Only the most careful sham-controlled behavioral and neuroimaging research can answer this question. Cultural prohibitions that had prevailed at the racetrack will again surface. In the past, authentic Zen Buddhist precepts expressed a conservative posture: "meditation, not medication." Given the accelerating pace of electronic technology, how soon might such a caveat be amended toward phrases like "meditation, not electricity"?

Chapter 15 Resources of Enduring Happiness; Opening to "Just This"

1. M. Ricard, *Happiness: A Guide to Developing Life's Most Important Skill* (Boston: Little, Brown, 2003), 123, 266.
2. J. Masefield, The Ending (Poems from "The Wanderer,"), in *The Collected Poems of John Masefield* (London: Heinemann, 1923), 923, available at dspace.wbpublibnet.gov.in:8080/jspui/bitstream/ 10689/1483/23/Chapter%2020_928%20-%20969p.pdf.
3. Y.-Y. Tang, M. Rothbart, and M. Posner, Neural Correlates of Establishing, Sustaining, and Switching Brain States, *Trends in Cognitive Sciences* 2012; 16: 330–337.
4. M. Dambrun, M. Ricard, G. Després et al., Measuring Happiness: From Fluctuating Happiness to Authentic-Durable Happiness, *Frontiers in Psychology* 2012 (Feb 7); 3: 16, doi: 10.3389/fpsyg .2012.00016.
5. cf. Udana 2.1, Muccalinda Sutta: About Muccalinda, trans. T. Bhikku, available at Access to Insight, accesstoinsight.org/ tipitaka/.
6. J. Kluger, The Happiness of Pursuit, *Time,* July 8–15, 2013, 25–45. This five-part article includes two surveys. One is the 2012 World Happiness Report, ranking the United States (at only #23), far behind Iceland (#1) and New Zealand (#2). The other is *Time*'s 2013 telephone survey of 801 Americans, 18 and older, revealing that 38 percent of the respondents were using prayer or meditation to improve their mood.
7. J. Austin, *Chase, Chance, and Creativity: The Lucky Art of Novelty* (Cambridge, MA: MIT Press, 2003), 129–136.
8. J. Austin, *Chase, Chance, and Creativity: The Lucky Art of Novelty,* 59–96.
9. J. Panksepp and L. Biven, *The Archaeology of Mind: Neuroevolutionary Origins of Human Emotions* (New York: Norton, 2012). The lucid discussion is supported by 46 pages of references.

10. Thich Nhat Hanh, *Peace Is Every Step* (New York: Bantam, 1992), 57. His experiences during the Vietnam War exemplify engaged Buddhism.

11. Thich Nhat Hanh, *Fear: Essential Wisdom for Getting Through the Storm* (New York: HarperCollins, 2012), 4–5, 7. You and your underpants know when you've been *really* scared, acutely.

12. J. Ford, *If You're Lucky, Your Heart Will Break: Field Notes from a Zen Life* (Boston: Wisdom, 2012), 163–172. The heartbreak referred to will break *open* our former hard-heartedness. This liberation from our prior selfish personality constraints helps release our native virtues of compassion (see chapter 5).

13. K. MacLean, M. Johnson, and R. Griffiths, Mystical Experiences Occasioned by the Hallucinogen Psilocybin Lead to Increases in the Personality Domain of Openness, *Journal of Psychopharmacology* 2011; 25(11): 1453–1461. The six descriptors come from the NEO personality inventory. The first group of 35 subjects also received methylphenidate on separate occasions.

14. R. Carhart-Harris, D. Erritzoe, T. Williams et al., Neural Correlates of the Psychedelic State as Determined by fMRI Studies with Psilocybin, *Proceedings of the National Academy of Sciences* 2012; 109(6): 2138–2143. This report describes the results in the first minutes following the rapid *intravenous* injection of 2000 micrograms of psilocybin into 30 hallucinogen-experienced volunteers. Their average age was in the early 30s. An acute, major drop of cerebral blood flow occurred (12% in the thalamus and posterior cingulate cortex), together with reduced fMRI signals in multiple cortical and subcortical regions. Notably, these *de*activated sites included the thalamus as well as the medial prefrontal cortex, the posterior cingulate cortex, and the angular gyrus. Each cortical region is a major component of the default network. Preclinical experiments indicate that the stimulation of serotonin 2A receptors goes on to enhance GABA inhibitory transmission. Clinical evidence further correlates these same 5-HT2A receptors with many of the subjective effects of related psychedelics and with tendencies toward spiritual ideation. [ZBR: 78] The findings in this psilocybin study are relevant to the plausible model of thalamocortical physiology developed in chapters 3, 6, and 11. Its subjects' first-person reports confirm that this intravenous dose of psilocybin immediately captured their full attention. This could readily trigger a reciprocal, *de*activating response from de-

fault regions. This brisk endogenous reactivity is consistent with the inhibitory capacities of the reticular nucleus and its allies. The lines of evidence discussed also raise the possibility that psilocybin could enhance the basic mechanisms that increase GABA-ergic inhibitory transmission. Similar GABA-induced inhibitions of thalamocortical oscillations are a key sequence in the proposal to understand how Self-referential functions dissolve during the state of kensho. [SI: 88 (figure 6), 103–121].

15. A. Bjørnebekk, A. Fjell, K. Walhovd, et al., Neuronal Correlates of the Five Factor Model (FFM) of Human Personality, *Neuroimage* 2013; 65(1): 194–208. This was a cross-sectional study.

16. Y. Taki, B. Thyreau, S. Kinomura et al., A Longitudinal Study of the Relationship between Personality Traits and the Annual Rate of Volume Changes in Regional Gray Matter in Healthy Adults, *Human Brain Mapping* 2012 (Jul 17), doi: 10.1002/hbm.22145 [Epub ahead of print]. Gross structural changes seek ultrastructural explanations.

17. J. LeDoux, Rethinking the Emotional Brain, *Neuron* 2012; 73: 653–676.

18. D. Denton, M. McKinley, M. Farrell, and G. Egan, The Role of Primordial Emotions in the Evolutionary Origin of Consciousness, *Consciousness and Cognition* 2009; 18: 500–514. This review also cites our intense normal desires to be free from pain, to seek relief from the anguish caused by an overdistended bladder or bowel, to sleep after having been sleep-deprived, etc. These kinds of emotions are associated with opposing changes in multiple regions. For example, severe thirst was found to activate 13 fMRI sites and to deactivate nine other sites. The two opposing sets of network sites are consistent both with (1) the elementary sensory stimuli that had registered, (2) with the anguished emotions and resistance then aroused, and (3) with the subjects' immediate motivational intention to seek relief.

19. Besides zero fear (fearlessness), other bare existential comprehensions arise during this awakened state. They include zero time (eternity), zero Self (selflessness), zero words (silence), and a sense of all-inclusiveness (oneness).

20. J. Feinstein, C. Buzza, R. Hurlemann et al., Fear and Panic in Humans with Bilateral Amygdala Damage, *Nature Neuroscience* 2013; 16: 270–272. This rare genetically determined disorder is called Urbach-Wiethe disease. Other candidate sites that generate fear

include our hypothalamus and the brain stem activating regions. [ZB: 189–196, 157–164].

21. J. Buhle, H. Kober, K. Oschsner et al., Common Representation of Pain and Negative Emotion in the Midbrain Periaqueductal Gray, *Social Cognitive and Affective Neuroscience* 2013; 8(6): 609–616.

22. D. Grupe, D. Oathes, and J. Nitschke, Dissecting the Anticipation of Aversion Reveals Dissociable Neural Networks, *Cerebral Cortex* 2013; 23(8): 1874–1883.

23. J. Kinnison, S. Padmala, J. Choi, and L. Pessoa, Network Analysis Reveals Increased Integration during Emotional and Motivational Processing, *Journal of Neuroscience* 2012; 32: 8361–8372.

In Closing

1. D. Suzuki, *Studies in the Lankavatara Sutra* (London, Routledge and Kegan Paul, 130), 297.

2. A. Switzer, *D. T. Suzuki: A Biography* (London: Buddhist Society, 1985).

3. J. Austin, *Chase, Chance, and Creativity: The Lucky Art of Novelty* (Cambridge, MA: MIT Press, 2003), 139–141.

4. R. Wright. Why We Fight—and Can We Stop? *The Atlantic*, 2013, 321 (11):102–118. The author suggests a wide role for meditation in nourishing the seeds of enlightenment among the world's hostile tribes.

Appendix A

1. W. Wordsworth, The Tables Turned, in *The Complete Poetical Works* (London: Macmillan, 1888).

2. This was B.C.E., before the chainsaw era.

3. U. App, Linji's Evergreens, *Japanese Journal of Religious Studies* 1994; 21(4): 425–436.

4. G. Jun, *Essential Chan Buddhism: The Character and Spirit of Chinese Zen* (Rhinebeck, NY: Monkfish, 2013), 23.

5. D. Suzuki, *Zen and Japanese Culture* (Princeton, NJ: Princeton University Press, 1959). The Japanese edition was published in 1938.

6. Personal communication from Albert Stunkard, M.D., May 2000. Cryptomeria trees are also known as Japanese cedar trees. Some of these stately pyramidal trees can grow up to 200 feet in height. The aroma of their crushed foliage resembles that of an orange peel.

7. Engaku-ji ("monastery of complete enlightenment") was founded in Kamakura in 1282.

8. B. Park, Y. Tsunetsugu, T. Kasetani, et al., The Physiological Effects of Shinrin-yoku (Taking in the Forest Atmosphere or Forest Bathing): Evidence from Field Experiments in 24 Forests across Japan, *Environmental Health and Preventive Medicine* 2010; 15(1): 18–26.

9. Y. Miyazaki, J. Lee, B. Park, et al., Preventative Medical Effects of Nature Therapy, *Nihon Eiseigaku Zasshi* 2011; 66(4): 651–656.

10. Q. Li and T. Kawada, Effect of Forest Environments on Human Brain Natural Killer (NK) Activity, *International Journal of Immunopathology and Pharmacology* 2011; 24(1 suppl): 39S–4S. This investigation suggested that the increase in anticancer killer cell activity could last for a month. Further study is required to clarify how this increase could be related to the actual release of phytoncides (oil molecules released from pine forest needles) to decreased stress hormones or to other mechanisms.

11. R. W. Emerson, Nature, in *Essays: Second Series* (1844); *Emerson's Essays,* ed. I. Edman (New York: Crowell, 1926), 382.

12. M. Berman, E. Kross, K. Krpan et al., Interacting with Nature Improves Cognition and Affect for Individuals with Depression, *Journal of Affective Disorders* 2012; 140(3): 300–305. The improvements in memory span were measured by improved scores on the backward digit span test. These improvements did not appear to be correlated with the improvements in mood. The participants did not consider that the thought content of their ruminations was different during the two separate walks.

13. P. Aspinall, P. Mavros, R. Coyne, and J. Roe, The Urban Brain: Analyzing Outdoor Physical Activity with Mobile EEG, *British Journal of Sports Medicine* 2013 (Mar 6), doi: 10.1136/bjsports-2012 -091877 [Epub ahead of print].

Appendix B

1. Source unknown; often attributed to James Thurber.

2. A. Sokolov, M. Erb, W. Grodd, and M. Pavlova, Structural Loop between the Cerebellum and the Superior Temporal Sulcus: Evidence from Diffusion Tensor Imaging, *Cerebral Cortex* 2012 (Nov 20), doi: 10.1093/cercor/bhs346 [Epub ahead of print].

3. J. Chikazoe, K. Jimura, T. Asari et al., Functional Dissociation in Right Inferior Frontal Cortex during Performance of Go/No-go Task, *Cerebral Cortex* 2009; 19(1): 146–152.

4. K. Kim and M. Johnson, Extended Self: Medial Prefrontal Activity during Transient Association of Self and Objects, *Social Cognitive and Affective Neuroscience* 2012; 7(2): 199–207.

5. S. Harris, S. Sheth, and M. Cohen, Functional Neuroimaging of Belief, Disbelief, and Uncertainty, *Annals of Neurology* 2008; 63: 141–147. The subjects were reacting to visual statements. The statements represented the following seven different categories of facts: autobiographical, ethical, factual, geographical, mathematical, religious, or semantic. They pressed a button to specify whether they found a statement to be true, false, or undecidable. Whereas belief was correlated with increased signals in the *head* of the caudate (L>R), disbelief correlated with increased activity in both the *head and tail* of the caudate (R>L). These observations confirm that we can activate this part of the dorsal striatum asymmetrically at a time when our personal belief systems lead us to either accept or reject events in the outside world. [SI: 133–139] (See also chapter 10, note 13.).

6. J. Ford, *If You're Lucky, Your Heart Will Break: Field Notes from a Zen Life* (Boston: Wisdom, 2012), 44–45.

7. We today cannot be certain which cultural interpretations were placed on the original words for "just this" when they were uttered in other languages in distant lands. But some interpretations may have corresponded with the ineffable experience of advanced states of "suchness." During such rare moments of awakening, when all things are comprehended directly—as *they* really are—their original nature is realized both in the fullness of allocentric processing and in the emptiness of Self. The Zen teaching is that the insight-wisdom of *prajna* unveils this moment of objective vision. [ZB: 549–553, ZBR: 361–364, 416–417].

Appendix C

1. ZB: 281–286; ZBR: 187–193; SI: 266–267; MS: 107–108. When dynamic causal modeling (DCM) is applied to neuroimaging data, it suggests the potential presence of cause-and-effect relationships and directions of communication that could link successive brain regions.

2. A readable antidote for the current overemphasis on neuroimaging, even though its pages do not discuss meditation, is S. Satel and S. Lilienfeld, *Brainwashed: The Seductive Appeal of Mindless Neuroscience* (New York: Basic Books, 2013).

3. Z. Li, A. Moore, C. Tyner, and X. Hu. Asymmetric Connectivity Reduction and its Relationship to "HAROLD" in Aging Brain. *Brain Research* 2009; Oct. 27; 1295: 149–158. doi: 10.1016/j.brzinres .2009.08.004. Epub 2009 Aug 8.

Appendix D

1. S. Morinaga, *The Ceasing of Notions: An Early Zen Text from the Dunhuang Caves, with Selected Comments* (Boston: Wisdom, 2012), 93. Ven. Myokyo-ni and M. Bromley produced this readable English translation of a Tang Dynasty treatise. Soko Morinaga-Roshi practiced in the traditional, Kyoto style of Rinzai Zen for almost five decades. [SI: 12–13] The epigraph is one of many sage commentaries in *The Ceasing of Notions*. For example, Morinaga points to a "great and decisive difference" (69–72). This difference separates hesitant novices, stuck in their clinging attachments, from advanced practitioners, free to move instantly, flexibly, and appropriately in response to each changing circumstance. [ZB: 668–677].

2. The Blind Man and the Elephant (Udana 6.4), in *In the Buddha's Words: An Anthology of Discourses from the Pali Canon,* ed. B. Bodhi (Boston: Wisdom, 2005), 214–215.

3. R. Spreng, J. Sepulcre, G. Turner, et al., Intrinsic Architecture Underlying the Relations among the Default, Dorsal, Attention, and Frontoparietal Control Networks of the Human Brain, *Journal of Cognitive Neuroscience* 2013; 25(1): 74–86.

4. K. Kim and M. Johnson, Extended Self: Medial Prefrontal Activity during Transient Association of Self and Objects, *Social Cognitive and Affective Neuroscience* 2012; 7(2): 199–207. Four other attributes describe the higher-level, more abstract psychological activities of the Self. They include its capacities to (1) recognize one's own personal appearance, (2) be aware of one's own actions, (3) know one's own personality traits and abilities, and (4) process thoughts about one's own hopes and duties.

5. B. Demiray and S. Bluck, The Relation of the Conceptual Self to Recent and Distant Autobiographical Memories, *Memory* 2011; 19: 975–992. Six higher-level psychological characteristics of the Self are cited in this article. They include (1) Self-acceptance, (2) positive relations with others, (3) autonomy, (4) environmental mastery, (5) purpose in life, and (6) personal growth, development, and realization of one's potential.

6. J. Austin. Zen and the Brain: Mutually Illuminating Topics. *Frontiers in Psychology* 2013; article 784, pp. 1–9, October doi: 10.3389/fpsychg.2013.00784.

Index

dorsal system (*see* Dorsal attention system)
focal, 25
functional MRI in, 78–79, 219n5
in hearing, 54, 55, 56
involuntary, xiv, xix, 201n3 (*see also* Ventral attention system)
in outdoor settings, 188
and prosocial attitude, 230n39
in receptive meditation, 26
reciprocal interactions in, 29, 32, 199
in remindfulness, 77
and Self-centeredness, 29
sharpening skills in, 16
subconscious process in, xix
upward and outward, 56–57
ventral system (*see* Ventral attention system)
visual, 16, 56
voluntary, xix, 201n3 (*see also* Dorsal attention system)
Attentive processing, 191
Auditory cortex
association, 55, 56
primary, 55, 56
Aurora
borealis, 128, 129
meditatorum, 128, 129–130, 137, 192
Autobiographical functions, 17, 27f, 32, 133, 193, 200, 227n18
Automatic involuntary processes, xix—xx, 29
in hearing, 55
in unexpected stimulus, 28–29
Avalokiteshvara, 41
Aversive stimuli
brain response to, 180
retreat behavior in, 180–181
Avian Zen, xiv, 52–64

Awakening
auditory triggers of, 29, 41, 52, 53–54, 56, 59, 184, 209n17
awareness in, 82
deep, 93–94
impression of reality in, 29, 93, 94
initial state of (*see* Kensho)
loss of word-thoughts and concepts in, 30
non-duality in, 94
sense of Self in, 85, 221–222n11
silence in, 30, 207n9
in upward gaze, xix, 36, 181
Awareness, 191
already there but not conscious of itself, 22, 206n2
awakening, 82
bare, 26, 76, 191
bilateral, 28
cognition, 82
ever-present, 84
global, 25, 26, 28
hierarchical depth in, 91
in "just this" experience, 194
long-term transformations of, 83–89
maturation of, 21, 91–92, 185
of mind-wandering during meditation, 79, 80
other-referential, 184, 206n2
present-moment, mindfulness in, 75–89
ripening of, 20, 21
in sleep, 84, 85
subconscious background qualities in, 89–96
tacit, 82
thought-free, functional MRI in, 81–83
verbal, 82
Axmacher, N., 117

and dorsal attention system, 13, 15f, 31, 100f–101f, 102

in egocentric processing, 100f–101f, 116

emotion processing pathways in, 118–119

functional anatomy of, 13–18, 14f–15f, 27f, 205n6

functional MRI of (*see* Magnetic resonance imaging, functional)

in hearing, 55–56

in kensho, 93–94

language areas in (*see* Language areas in brain)

morning and evening variations in, 78, 219n4

in near-death experience, 216–218n8

in near space and far space tasks, 116

neuroplasticity of, 91 (*see also* Neuroplasticity)

in pain anticipation and experience, 80–81, 219n6

paradoxical facilitation of function, 73

and psychic aspects of Self, 17–18, 23, 27f, 32

in real and make-believe events, 95

reciprocal interactions in (*see* Reciprocal interactions of brain areas)

and retinal origins of color sequences during meditation, 136–137

salience networks in, 79

and somatic aspects of self, 13–17, 23

stroke damage of, 74, 214–215nn5–6

transcranial direct current stimulation of, 164–166, 238–241nn19–25

and ventral attention system, 15f, 26, 31, 100f–101f, 138, 215–216n7, 225–226n1

Brain stem, 14f

Braun, A., 88

Breathing, attention to, 25, 78–79

word labeling of in-breaths and out-breaths in, 194, 212n10

Broca, Pierre Paul, 31

Brodmann areas, 27f–28f, 55

Brooks, David, 66

Brown, D., 87

Buddha

Bahiya requesting advice from, 6–9, 156, 178, 203–204nn6–8

death of, 41, 47

inspired utterances of, 6

on letting go, 10, 206n4

Malunkya requesting advice from, 3–6, 178, 203n6, 204n9

meditating under trees, 45, 186

on places to meditate, 46

on sleeping at ease, 44

teaching with simsapa leaves, 42

touching earth as symbolic gesture, 37

wordless gesture with single flower, 41–42, 209n18

Buhle, J., 180

Calmness, 19, 20

Cancer, immune function against, 188, 247n10

Caudate nucleus, 207n9, 216n7

Emerson, Ralph Waldo, xviii, 20, 188

Emotions, 172–174
cortical processing pathways in, 118
fear, 173–174 (*see also* Fear)
happiness, 170–182 (*see also* Happiness)
limbic system in, 24, 27f, 118–119
negative, 118–119, 173, 178
primordial, 179, 245n18
revisualizing and reprocessing with elevated gaze, 99–123
subcortical gates in thalamus affecting, 118–119
terms for, 173

Emptiness (Sunyata) meditation, 81–82

Empty-full qualities in selflessness, 11

"Energies of Men" (James), 69

Engaku-ji, 187, 246n7

Engler, J., 87

Enlightenment, 85, 87

Erb, M., 81–82, 138

Etcoff, N., 73

Eternity, 190

Evening hours
brain metabolism in, compared to morning hours, 78, 219n4
meditation in, 90, 91

Event-related potential studies, 114–115, 163–164

Excitatory role of limbic nuclei, 24

Experts, problem-solving by, 159, 160–161
in chess, 161, 237n13

Eye movement desensitization and reprocessing (EMDR), 120

Facial expressions
brain damage affecting interpretation of, 74
detection in peripheral visual fields, 113, 226–227n10

Fear, 173–174, 179–181, 245–246nn19–20
amygdala in, 117, 179–180
lability of memories of, 114
loss of, in kensho, 179, 245n19
primal, 179–181
retreat behavior in, 180–181
revisualization of memory of, with upward gaze, 104–106, 123
visual mental imagery in, 113

Fetters, 5, 203n5

Fight or flight response, 180

Five fetters, 5, 203n5

Flexibility, ideational, 157

Flowers
lotus, 40–41, 45, 48, 146
wordless gesture of Buddha with single flower, 41–42, 209n18

Fluency, ideational, 157

Ford, James, 174

Forest bathing, 187–188

Forest setting as sanctuary, xx, 186–189

Forest Therapy, 187–188

Forman, Robert, 84–87

Foxton, Suzanne, 121–122, 229n35

Foyan Quingyuan, 73, 74, 89, 185

Fractional anisotropy, 160–161

Freud, Sigmund, 12, 17

Freund, A., 92

Frontal cortex, 101f, 226n1

Frontal eye field, 13, 15f, 100f–101f, 116